Gabriel F. Hornung
Esther against Joseph's Backdrop

Beihefte zur Zeitschrift für die alttestamentliche Wissenschaft

Edited by
John Barton, Reinhard G. Kratz, Nathan MacDonald,
Sara Milstein, and Markus Witte

Volume 553

Gabriel F. Hornung

Esther against Joseph's Backdrop

The Theology and History of an Intertextual
Relationship

DE GRUYTER

ISBN 978-3-11-121413-9
e-ISBN (PDF) 978-3-11-121611-9
e-ISBN (EPUB) 978-3-11-121683-6
ISSN 0934-2575

Library of Congress Control Number: 2023951727

Bibliographic information published by the Deutsche Nationalbibliothek
The Deutsche Nationalbibliothek lists this publication in the Deutsche Nationalbibliografie;
detailed bibliographic data are available on the internet at http://dnb.dnb.de.

© 2024 Walter de Gruyter GmbH, Berlin/Boston
Typesetting: Meta Systems Publishing & Printservices GmbH, Wustermark
Printing and binding: CPI books GmbH, Leck

www.degruyter.com

MIX
Papier | Fördert
gute Waldnutzung
FSC
www.fsc.org   FSC® C083411

Acknowledgements

Since this book developed out of a course I took and subsequent dissertation I wrote in graduate school, I would like to begin by thanking my former advisor, Professor Jon D. Levenson, for the steadfast guidance he provided me and the kindness he has continued to show me. Since he taught me to maintain a sense of humor while exploring the intricacies of theology and exactness of history, so much of this study, which centers around two biblical stories Professor Levenson has interpreted throughout his career, is indebted to him.

In addition to Professor Levenson, a number of other faculty members helped me along my long and winding academic road. When I was in college, Professors Larry Lyke and Elli Findly first kindled my interest in the study of religion. In my MA program, Professors Joel Baden and John J. Collins introduced me to the rigors and intrigues of scholarship, and, during my doctoral work, Professors Peter Machinist, D. Andrew Teeter, and Bernd Schipper all played pivotal roles in teaching me both the details and larger contours of biblical criticism.

Over the years, I have enjoyed the good fortune of encountering unusually kind, smart, and thoughtful colleagues, classmates, and students. At Trinity, a place I now call home for a second time, my departmental colleagues have offered me professional camaraderie and real friendship. To Professors Leslie Desmangles, Elli Findly (who had to deal with me as both student and colleague!), Ron Kiener, Mark Silk, Tamsin Jones, Tim Landry, Mareike Koertner, Susanne Kerekes, and Ben Steiner, I extend my sincere gratitude for the intellectual support and fun McCook atmosphere.

While in graduate school, I studied alongside a remarkable group of classmates. My thanks, in particular, to Maria Metzler, Jonathan Kline, and Joanna Greenlee-Kline for discussing aspects of this project with me and the long-lasting friendships such conversations helped to generate; I would also like to thank my former classmate and friend, Eric Jarrard, for reading parts of this manuscript and commenting so helpfully on it. As a faculty member, my good luck has continued, as I have enjoyed getting to know and working alongside a number of excellent students. Though listing them all here would be impossible, I would like to single out one, Philip Jaeggi-Wong, who helped me prepare the chart in Part Two of this study and so skillfully edited the entire piece. But to all of my students, I express my sincere thanks for sharing your authentic creativities and energizing me through moments of fatigue.

To my family, whose love and laughter saw me through it all: I remember stressing over graduate school admissions essays at my parents' dining room table, seeking shelter with them in a Cambridge restaurant from the freezing cold rain that my May graduation day somehow brought, and testing their Job-like patience

https://doi.org/10.1515/9783111216119-202

as I agonized over the ups and downs of job searches while stretched, physically and metaphorically, across their living room floor. I recall trying to explain to my sister, who after college got a series of real jobs in real cities, what graduate school in religious studies was all about. Over countless dinners, my uncle offered his impeccable judicious counsel after listening to me fret over the endless intricacies of academic politics, and it was in the warm hospitality of his beautiful West Hartford apartment that I began writing these Acknowledgements. With Max, I talked about life, school, and everything in between while listening to Coltrane on my old couch, and, with Ev, whose infectious laugh always reminded me how small work stress is in comparison to real life, I ate yet another snack with legs crossed on the indoor blue beach stoop. Thank you to all of you, and to my grandmother in Chicago and three departed grandparents, for the wisdom and calmness you taught me, all the years of tennis and swimming at the beach you gave me, and the European connections you showed me.

That this project, which explores how a threatened diaspora created a theology of divine absence, finds publication at a Berlin house while I happen to be working in Connecticut feels particularly poignant to me. As my maternal grandparents made Connecticut our home for generations to come, my paternal grandmother had to flee Berlin right when the Nazis stormed in. This same city of intoxicating possibility and unspeakable pain is also where my close friend and confidant, Steffen Jenner, passed away in 2022 after opening his doors to an American graduate student chasing glimpses of his family's broken past. Though Professor Markus Witte of the Theology Faculty at the Humboldt University in Berlin knew only bits and pieces of these larger storylines, I thank him for first encouraging me to submit to the BZAW series and welcoming me to his storied department all those summers I spent on Steffen and Thea's couch.

Finally, to my wife, whose magical presence in my life has done more than anything else to bring this book and far more to completion. As she has opened up avenues as elegant as they were utterly unknown to me – from the California sunshine to birthdays in Mumbai, from loving in-laws to the embrace of a brother-, sister-in-law, and nephew, and aunts, uncles and cousins around the world – I dedicate this book to her with gratitude and love.

Contents

1 Introduction: Currents in Scroll and Intertextual Scholarship

As intertextual studies have become more prominent in recent years, a number of well-known inner-biblical associations have been reevaluated to reflect the growing understanding of the biblical authors' allusive techniques and purposes. Despite such work ranging across both Testaments,[1] one particular relationship – the connections between MT Esther and the Joseph story in Genesis 37–50 – has largely evaded this intensified focus. Designed to address this gap, the present study renews attention to the textual links between the Scroll and Joseph to demonstrate how previous attempts to analyze this relationship have fallen short of appreciating the full breadth and aim of the association. While this work further refines the general guidelines for identifying deliberate inner-biblical allusions and then interpreting them, it also points toward a specific way through a long-standing exegetical impasse. For as debate concerning the theological worth of the Megillah has continued to simmer, attention to Esther's sustained interaction with Joseph helps to illustrate the specific religious stance the Scroll takes.

Such considerations reflect the general direction this work follows. Instead of uncovering a brand new avenue of investigation, it rather applies theoretical advances in the intertextual field to a known test case in order to respond to entrenched issues in Scroll scholarship. As a result, this study revolves around three interrelated poles. The first, which is the focus of Part One, pivots on the depth and reach of Esther's links to Joseph.[2] As linguistic, thematic, and narrative parallels tie the two stories together, Chapter Two introduces two extended exam-

---

1 For the ways in which intertextual study has altered pentateuchal scholarship, see, for example, Bernard M. Levinson, *Deuteronomy and the Hermeneutics of Legal Innovation* (New York: Oxford University Press, 1997). In the prophetic context, Michael Lyons, *From Law to Prophecy* (New York: T&T Clark, 2009), has renewed attention to Ezekiel's well-known usage of earlier legal texts to offer a fresh understanding of Ezekiel's purpose, and Marc Zvi Brettler's reflections on the Psalms, "Identifying Torah Sources in the Historical Psalms," in *Subtle Citation, Allusion, and Translation in the Hebrew Bible*, ed. Ziony Zevit (Bristol, CT: Equinox Publishing, 2017): 73–90, show how this mode of inquiry has also influenced work on the poetic biblical sections. In the world of New Testament studies, Richard B. Hays, *Echoes of Scripture in the Letters of Paul* (New Haven: Yale University Press, 1989), still represents a classic effort to approach Paul's usage of earlier Hebrew Bible texts with modern intertextual approaches.

2 A brief note on terminology: as Part Two of this study makes clear, the present work is focused mainly on the connections between MT Esther and Joseph. As a result, when the terms Esther, Scroll, or Megillah are used without specific identifiers, they refer to MT Esther and the authors behind this particular version. Of course, this does not count for those moments when the character Esther is being addressed, a difference that context always clarifies.

https://doi.org/10.1515/9783111216119-001

ples of contact between Esther and Joseph that begin demonstrating the outlines of this particularly close relationship. Though Scroll scholarship has long appreciated aspects of these similarities, Chapter Two also shows how commentators interested in these connections have tended to isolate the individual components of Esther's relationship with Joseph and thus overlook the full import that the intertwined nature of the links suggests. Chapter Three then turns to the ways in which scholarship has approached Esther's other intertextual relationships, and a noticeable pattern emerges: if interpretations of Esther's relationship with Joseph have tended to be more narrow, then understandings of Esther's other inner-biblical allusions have frequently been too broad. After exploring this point, the third chapter brings Part One of the present study to its conclusion by examining one more example of Esther's interaction with Joseph in an effort to concretize the differences between the present intertextual approach and previous efforts to read the Scroll allusively.

The second major point of emphasis, which comes to the fore in Part Two, reflects the historical basis of the present analysis. Though previous efforts to examine Esther's biblical allusions have often endeavored to demonstrate authorial intent, such works have not adequately contended with the complex compositional history of the Scroll. While this persistent oversight has caused intertextual approaches to the Megillah to rely on problematic, and often unexamined, notions of unified authorship, Chapters Four and Five engage directly with Esther's Greek witnesses to offer a crucial corrective. Instead of assuming that the same pen, and therefore the same aim, stands behind each and every external reference, attention to Esther's ancient versions demonstrates how the allusive purpose of the Scroll developed alongside its literary history. As this analysis shows, an early Esther core, reflected in large parts of the Greek Alpha Text, contains some philological and structural connections to Joseph, while the later MT version of Esther, which likely came about through one major redaction, expands the inchoate relationship found in this earlier core to make it a central component of the canonical book.

With these textual and historical points established, Part Three engages the third and final issue – the exegetical implications this relationship has for interpreting the Hebrew book of Esther. Accordingly, Chapter Six demonstrates how attending to Esther's connections to Joseph offers fresh insight into the debated theological worth of the Scroll. By highlighting how yet another unusually favored Israelite rises in a foreign court to deliver herself and her people against all odds, this intertextual approach details how God's absence in the Scroll combines with the links to Joseph to articulate a powerful theology of divine absence. Since God remains out of sight, Esther develops its relationship with Joseph to indicate how the providential patterns of the past continue into the present even when the divine presence remains obscured.[3] While this analysis serves as a focal point for the entire study, Chapter Seven engages one last textual point – the place the book of Daniel holds in Joseph and Esther's intertextual chain, and the ways in which Esther's relationship to Joseph distinguishes itself from the admitted points of contact found in Daniel's court narratives.

After these major arguments have been pursued, the Conclusion brings this work to an end with two final theoretical reflections. In the first instance, a series of procedural refinements is offered to the blooming study of inner-biblical allusion; in the second, the study of divine presence and absence is shown to have afforded surprisingly little focus to Esther – the one biblical book that never mentions God directly.[4] Pointing to this problematic trend, this work thus closes by insisting that the perspective developed by the Scroll be included in this important conversation. Before turning to the details of such threads, however, a review of Scroll scholarship, along with an analysis of key intertextual guidelines and historical parameters, is necessary to situate these broader ideas in their proper contexts.

1.1 The History of Religious and Unreligious Interpretations

Since this study is in large measure designed to show how the relationship with Joseph expresses a heretofore unappreciated aspect of Esther's theological stance – a point that comes to the fore in Chapter Six – this Introduction begins with an evaluation of the scholarly uncertainty concerning the presence of religious reflection in the Scroll. Despite complexities from several angles, three general interpretive patterns can be observed. While some critics have seen God's absence as evidence of the nationalistic interest and therefore unreligious nature of the story, others have argued that Esther's creative literary techniques reference God, Israel, and even the Torah to bring the book into line with more dominant modes of biblical thinking. As these two positions represent the more extreme poles of Scroll

---

3 This analytic line, which is explored in particular detail in Chapter Six, is indebted to a key distinction developed by Brittany N. Melton, *Where is God in the Megilloth?* (Leiden: Brill, 2018). For as Melton notes, questions of divine privation conflate two fundamental issues: while absence can represent an existential lack, so can it also signal the state of being away (6). By situating the events of the Megillah against a previous precedent, Esther's sustained connections to Joseph suggest the second of Melton's two options. Instead of questioning divine existence, the Scroll is rather shown to operate in a present that is devoid of a heavenly presence but retains the patterns God has initiated in the past.
4 While Song of Songs is sometimes also thought to refrain from addressing God directly, this analysis tends to see שלהבתיה (Song 8:6) as a reference to the Ancient Israelite God.

scholarship, an intermediate alternative, which sees the divine silence purposefully calling upon the faith of Esther's characters and readers, has also developed.

For those skeptical of the religious value of the Megillah, some combination of the following ideas has tended to predominate: that Esther's divine silence suggests a secular component, and that the distinctive literary style of the book,[5] coupled with the disquieting violence that marks the celebratory festival it establishes, puts it at odds with much of the rest of the Hebrew Bible. As these arguments have questioned Esther's canonical and artistic integrity, the following survey of four key positions outlines the broad parameters and specific divergences of this unreligious interpretive side.

Though this exegetical standpoint is frequently traced back to ancient skepticism concerning Esther's canonicity,[6] Lewis Bayles Paton's 1908 commentary provides an instructive starting point.[7] Suggesting that Esther's author, though himself a believer, purposefully left God out due to the unruliness of Purim, Paton sees the resulting "non-religious" book reflecting an "intense[ly] national spirit" (63). In light of such worldly concerns, Paton doubts Esther's scriptural position. "Morally, Est. falls far below the general level of the OT., and even of the Apocrypha. The verdict of Luther is not too severe: 'I am so hostile to this book that I wish it did not exist, for it Judaizes too much, and has too much heathen naughtiness'" (96). No longer interested in his believing author, Paton concludes along these harsher lines. "The book is so conspicuously lacking in religion that it should never have been included in the Canon of the OT., but should have been left with Judith and Tobit among the apocryphal writings" (97).[8]

While Carey Moore reaches divergent positions in his commentary, certain similarities to Paton's analysis are found. Moore starts with Esther's earthly focus.

---

5 In her commentary, Sidnie White Crawford points to precisely this interpretive pattern. "The book of Esther," she notes, "has received rather low marks for its prose style" (*The Book of Esther* [Nashville: Abingdon Press, 1990], 858).

6 For a helpful overview of the most important ancient debates, see, for example, Carey A. Moore, *Esther* (Garden City: Doubleday, 1971), XX1–XXXIV.

7 Lewis Bayles Paton, *A Critical and Exegetical Commentary on the Book of Esther* (New York: C. Scribner's Sons, 1908).

8 Paton's disparaging tone, which has unfortunately on occasion been a characteristic of this non-religious side, continues. "There is not one noble character in this book. Xerxes is a sensual despot. Esther, for the chance of winning wealth and power, takes her place in the herd of maidens who become concubines of the King. She wins her victories not by skill or by character, but by her beauty ... Mordecai sacrifices his cousin to advance his interests (2:8), advises her to conceal her religion (2:10, 20), displays wanton insolence in his refusal to bow to Haman (3:2–5), and helps Esther in carrying out her schemes of vengeance (8:9*sq.*). All this the author narrates with interest and approval. He gloats over the wealth and the triumph of his heroes and is oblivious to their moral shortcomings" (96).

> In the MT's present state many, if not most, of the distinctive religious features of biblical Judaism are missing. The most conspicuous of these is, of course, Yahweh himself. The king of Persia is mentioned 190 times in 167 verses, but God is not mentioned once. Neither Law nor Covenant, two key concepts running throughout the entire Old Testament, is so much as alluded to, let alone acknowledged. (XXXII)[9]

With religious issues thus sidelined, Moore then casts doubt onto Esther's literary merit. If Paton wonders about the moral stature of the book, Moore expresses reservations about the caliber of its narrator. "His [Esther's narrator] major characters are so superficially drawn that it is difficult to identify very long or intensively with either the book's villains or heroes" (LIII). Moore's dim view of the matter continues.

> In the Hebrew version it is more asserted than illustrated that Mordecai was wise and good; while beautiful and courageous, Esther nonetheless seems to be almost two-dimensional, lacking in depth. Despite the insistence of ii 20 that Esther concealed her identity as a Jew because Mordecai had so instructed her, the impression remains that Esther's Jewishness was more a fact of birth than of religious conviction. (LIV)

Though Moore's work does include more positive notes, as it does, for example, recognize Esther's storytelling ability and effective usage of irony (LV–LVI), Heinrich Ewald's remarks return to some of the broad aspects of the interpretive patterns here traced.[10] For according to Ewald, Esther stands at the tail end of an Ancient Israelite historiographical tradition that, at the time the Scroll was being written, was regrettably starting to lose the creative spirit with which it had once been so infused.

> In its [Esther's] mode of treating an historical subject, also, it closes the cycle of old Hebrew history, and is already subject to the influence of an utterly different mode of regarding and treating history. We have indeed already seen how historical writing gradually burst its old bounds and took an artist's license to reanimate its subject-matter by means of a new thought. But the animating thought which then converted old fading traditions into pleasing new stories, sprang at all events from the living well of the old religion, and might therefore in favourable cases conjure up figures both beautiful and truly Hebrew. But the Book of Esther shows, for the first time, that even this well is beginning to dry up and be lost to the historian. Its story, though rendered attractive through art, highly cultivated of

---

9 Labeling Paton's theory for God's absence "tempting" (XXXIII), Moore ultimately sides with the explanation Shemaryahu Talmon lays out in his essay, "'Wisdom' in the Book of Esther," *VT* 13 (1963): 419–55. Since Esther ought to be seen as historicized wisdom, the absence of religious markers is most reflective of its genre (XXXIII–IV).

10 Heinrich Ewald, *The History of Israel*, vol. 1, trans. and ed. Russell Martineau (London: Longmans, Green, 1883).

its kind, knows nothing of high and pure truths, but allows low calculations of expediency, the force of blind faith, and the caprice of passion, to reign supreme. We fall here as if from heaven to earth; and looking among the new forms surrounding us, we seem to behold the Jews, or indeed the small men of the present day in general, acting just as they do now. Moreover, through the entire narrative the author, as if by design, avoids the name of God; either because the story was addressed to minds unwilling to be reminded of higher names and things, or rather that he himself remains to the end true to the same low view of things in which the general plan and spirit of this festal story took its rise. (196–97)

While Paton, Ewald, and, to some extent, Moore question Esther's religious significance and, therefore, canonical status due to its supposedly fallen concerns, Bernhard Anderson's essay suggests that theological import can be found in the Scroll.[11] For Anderson, Esther's religious significance comes out of its fundamental interest in election. "Esther raises the profoundest question, viz., the meaning of the election of Israel. Since this is the premise of both the Old and the New Testaments, the Jewish problem in the final analysis is a question which is posed by God's unique revelation in those historical events of which the Bible claims to be the record and the witness" (36).

Despite this important difference, however, other aspects of Anderson's work display overlaps to the three positions previously surveyed. Anderson, for example, also perceives Esther as less than other biblical works.[12] In yet a further echo, Anderson links this negative assessment to the worldly focus that he feels Esther's divine silence implies. "One gains the first impression that the author had an indifferent, if not cynical, attitude toward the Jewish religion. Not least of all, the book is inspired by a fierce nationalism and an unblushing vindictiveness which stand in glaring contradiction to the Sermon on the Mount" (32). Despite his theological pursuit, Anderson thus ultimately concludes with Ewald. "As we turn to it [Esther] from other books of the Bible, 'we fall, as it were, from heaven to earth'" (32).

As these divergent but still related positions make up the non-religious side of Esther scholarship, critics committed to the theological value of the Scroll refute the notion that God's absence indicates Esther's religious, canonical, and literary inadequacy. While Wilhelm Vischer's book offers a bold but historically unsupported christological take,[13] Avraham Cohen, Werner Dommershausen, and

---

11 Bernhard W. Anderson, "The Place of the Book of Esther in the Christian Bible," *JR* 30:1 (1950): 32–43.

12 "Like Saul among the prophets," Anderson writes, "the Book of Esther seems strangely out of place in the Christian Bible. This is not merely because the book, in comparison to the frequented oases of inspired Scripture, is an uninviting wilderness ... Most offensive, however, is the discordant note which the book strikes in the ears of those accustomed to hearing the Christian gospel" (32).

13 Wilhelm Vischer, *Esther* (Munich: Chr. Kaiser, 1937).

Michael Fox's positions present more constructive signposts for this other, more religiously interested, interpretive side. In this vein, Cohen's essay marks one edge of the spectrum.[14] Suggesting that the פור of Esther ought to be viewed as "chance-fate" (89), Cohen seeks to rebut some of the charges laid out above by arguing that this *pur* represents "God operat[ing] behind the overt events in Esther" (89). Cohen explains:

> This interpretation proceeds from the only accurate reading which *Esther* allows, viz., that God acts behind the veil of causality and chance, on behalf of the people of Israel. It is specifically to accentuate this point that the name of God is not mentioned in the Megillah, while all the events are "cast" to give the appearance of chance-occurrences, or, *purim*. For the author of Esther, this position is at once a statement of history and of everyday reality. (89)[15]

Cohen also responds to the negative valuations of Esther's canonical status and style. In addition to noting how the "dramatic account ... has uplifted and delighted Jewish hearts" (87), he suggests that an allusion to Exodus makes Esther at home in its canonical context. "Purim, preceding Passover by exactly one month, came to parallel and affirm Passover's meaning of Divine providence towards the Jewish people" (91).

As Cohen finds God's veiled activity in Esther's silence,[16] Dommershausen, in his commentary, stakes out an intermediate position.[17] After beginning with an affirmation of Esther's literary prowess (11–16), Dommershausen turns to Esther 4 to suggest that even though God is not present, the characters' belief is.

---

14 Avraham D. Cohen, "'Hu Ha-goral': The Religious Significance of Esther," *Judaism* 23 (1974): 87–94.

15 To appreciate the sustained influence Cohen's work has had, consider, for example, Isaac Kalimi's work, which follows key aspects of Cohen's interpretive line.. "The absence of God's name," Kalimi writes, "from the book of Esther does not mean that the author has no interest in theological issues. On the contrary, his message is intended for Jews in general, and for those in the Diaspora in particular, that God is devoted to Israel. Every generation has its 'Haman,' but God is always there to keep his promise and help his people, directly (like the redemption from Egypt, by taking them *out* of the land) or indirectly while acting silently 'behind the curtain' (like the redemption *in* the framework of the Persian Empire, without any 'new exodus'). The author trusts, seemingly, that God's covenant with Israel is everlasting" ("The Place of the Book of Esther in Judaism and Jewish Theology," *TZ* 59:3 [2003]: 193–204; here: 202).

16 This general approach, one that detects God's hand orchestrating behind the scenes, is found in a number of other works, as well. Consider, for example, James A. Loader, *Das Buch Ester* (Göttingen: Vandenhoeck & Ruprecht, 1992), and David Firth, *The Message of Esther* (Dowers Grove, IL: IVP Academic, 2010).

17 Werner Dommershausen, *Die Estherrolle* (Stuttgart: Verlag Katholisches Bibelwerk, 1968).

> Mordekai hat den festen Glauben, daß *sein Volk unter dem Schutz der Vorsehung* steht und deshalb nicht untergehen wird. Es ist der Glaube an den getreuen Gott, der einst gesprochen: "So gewiß die Himmel droben nicht zu ermessen und die Grundfesten der Erde drunten nicht zu ergründen sind, so gewiß will ich die Geschlechter Israels nicht verwerfen um all ihrer Taten willen" (Jer 31:37). Mordekai weiß um Jahwes wunderbare Rettungstaten in der Geschichte seines Volkes, und er ist überzeugt, Esthers außerordentliche Erhebung zur Königin ist der Anfang einer neuen Rettung. (75)

In some distinction to Dommershausen's notion of Mordecai's unarticulated faith,[18] Fox's more recent work presents a third variation that also echoes aspects of the previous positions surveyed.[19] Suggesting that Esther's theological significance is found in its indeterminacy, Fox argues that the religious purpose of the Megillah is to challenge its readers to remain both active and faithful in the face of earthly uncertainty.

> [Esther's] carefully crafted indeterminacy is best explained as an attempt to convey uncertainty about God's role in history ... the author conveys his belief that there can be no definitive knowledge of the workings of God's hand in history. Not even a wonderful deliverance can prove that God was directing events; nor could threat and disaster prove his absence. The story's indeterminacy conveys the message that the Jews should not lose faith if they, too, are uncertain about where God is in a crisis ... The willingness to face history with an openness to the possibility of providence – even when history seems to weigh against its likelihood, as it did in the dark days after the issuance of Haman's decree – this is a stance of profound faith. (247)

While the difference to Dommershausen is important – if Dommershausen speaks of the characters' faith, Fox here addresses the belief of Esther's later readers – the general parameters of the scholarly effort to read Esther in a religious light come into focus. As the commentators on this more theological side uphold the literary worth and canonical placement of the Scroll, so do they also tend to combine an insistence on God's hidden but still active hand with some concern for the faith of Esther's characters or later readers.

---

18 Demonstrating the fluidity of those positions associated with a theologically significant Esther, Dommershausen, toward the end of his commentary, approaches a perspective similar to that which Cohen outlines. "Die *theologische Aussage* der Estherrolle ist deshalb nicht leicht zu erkennen, weil sie in ein uns fremdes Gewand gehüllt ist. Doch gerade hinter dieser Verhüllung verbirgt sich der Glaube des Autors an *Gottes Heiligkeit*, seine Ehrfurcht vor dem Sakrosankten, das nur zu leicht der Profanierung anheimfällt. Dem Frommen der Spätzeit tritt Gott nicht mehr anthropomorph gegenüber, er wirkt zwar durch Menschen, bleibt aber selbst transzendent, unsichtbar. Das Auge des Glaubenden jedoch schaut sein geheimnisvolles Walten gerade in den vielen '*Zufälligkeiten*' der Esthergeschichte und in dem 'wundervollen' Ablauf der Ereignisse" (157).
19 Michael V. Fox, *Character and Ideology in the Book of Esther* (Columbia, SC: University of South Carolina Press, 1991).

While Fox's indeterminacy has gained some traction,[20] Arndt Meinhold's and Beate Ego's works represent key complexities that traverse across some of the interpretive grooves here noted. By suggesting that the Megillah maintains theological significance despite its worldly focus, Meinhold incorporates aspects of both non-religious and theological veins of thought.[21] On precisely this point, he notes a comparison to Joseph: since the threat in Egypt is natural but the danger in Esther politically motivated, then a sharpening of the diaspora problem must be perceived in the Scroll. Meinhold continues along these lines: since the way out of the predicament in Esther depends on human action and not divine intervention, as is, at least in part, the case in Joseph, then Esther's accent must ultimately lie in this earthly realm.

With this earthly focus established, Meinhold then turns to the theological in Esther 4. Though מִמָּקוֹם אַחֵר does not name the divine directly, it does, he argues, suggest that God would act in the event that all else fails.

> Wenn unsere Deutung von Esth. 4,13 f. richtig ist, dass den Juden – nach Ausfall ihrer eigenen Möglichkeiten, die sie nutzen müssten – von einem anderen Ort, mimmāqōm 'aḥēr, also von Jahwe her (trots fehlender Gottesbezeichnung), Rettung und Erleichterung kommen würden, dann heisst das, dass der Verfasser von Esth. Jahwe die Funktion des Beobachters der Existenz der Juden und sein Trachten darauf einräumt. Jahwe erhält eine Beobachterrolle zuerkannt bis zum Augenblick der menschlichen Unmöglichkeit, selbst einen immanenten Ausweg zu finden. Erst dann, wenn alle Versuche, allein zurechtzukommen, nicht stattgefunden haben oder gescheitert sind, greift er von aussen ein. (324)

For Meinhold, the theological deliberations are thus doubled. On the one hand, the divine in Esther is left as an observer waiting for humans to use their own initiative; on the other, however, since the author of Esther leaves the Jews to fend for themselves as any other people would, the theological weight of Esther also testifies to the mystery of God's inscrutable decision to elect Israel (331).

While Beate Ego takes a tack different from Meinhold,[22] her work does frequently follow Peter Nagel's essay, which, in a fashion similar to Fox, emphasizes

---

20 Consider, for example, Linda Day's insightful work, *Esther* (Nashville: Abingdon Press, 2005). While she also suggests that theological indeterminacy is the point of the book, she refrains from suggesting that such issues are intended to engender faith in Esther's later readers. "The absence of God in the book of Esther is not, in actuality, its problem, but its benefit. Not to be explained away, the book's theological ambiguity is indeed the point. The book of Esther is a story of uncertainties. Is God involved, or is it chance that is running the show? It is impossible to know for sure" (18).

21 Arndt Meinhold, "Theologische Erwägungen zum Buch Esther," *TZ* 34:6 (1978): 321–33.

22 Beate Ego, *Ester* (Göttingen; Bristol, CT: Vandenhoeck & Ruprecht, 2017).

Esther's "theology of possibilities."[23] Into this thought realm, however, Ego injects a key dimension. Suggesting that the reversals in the Scroll reflect a version of the deed-consequence-nexus, Ego argues that the correlation between an event and its result establish, in subtle but undeniable fashion, God's agency in Esther.

> Wie in der narrativen Analyse gezeigt werden konnte, spielt für die Estererzählung zudem die sog. *reversal structure* eine bedeutende Rolle. Der Erzähler, der das Spiegelprinzip zum integralen Bestandteil seiner Geschichte macht, bringt damit seine Überzeugung zum Ausdruck, dass das innerweltliche Geschehen durch einen funktionierenden Tun-Ergehen-Zusammenhang bestimmt wird, der letztlich in Gottes Handeln gründet. (54)

For particular Scroll scenes, Ego's focus on a functioning judicial nexus offers illumination. Consider, for example, her comment concerning Haman's fate upon his own petard. "In freier Abwandlung des Wortes: 'Wer anderen eine Grube gräbt ...' soll es bald heißen: 'Wer anderen einen Holzpfahl baut ...'" (297). Of course, the insight stems beyond the clever phrasing. Since the wisdom tradition so often considers precisely this worldly organization evincing the divine administration,[24] then its presence in Esther, Ego's work hints, must also gesture in such a direction.

As this rehearsal indicates the range in which Esther's religiosity, or lack thereof, has tended to be understood, the general plan of the present study begins to take shape. Though this work supports those efforts that find theological purpose in the Scroll, its attention to Esther's sustained parallels to Joseph generates three points of interpretive variance that illustrate the importance of approaching this intertextual relationship anew. In the first instance, if several scholars find God's shrouded but still active hand in the Shushan twists and the Jews' ultimate fate, then this approach underscores how Esther invokes Joseph to articulate a theological posture that hinges on the complexities and challenges of divine retreat.[25] The second point of divergence responds to those positions that see the characters of the Megillah exhibiting faith in an absent God. In contradistinction to such a find, this intertextual reading demonstrates how MT Esther purposefully leaves God and any of the characters' thoughts about heavenly involvement to

---

23 Peter Nagel, "LXX Esther: 'More' God 'Less' Theology," *Journal for Semitics* 17:1 (2008): 129–55; here: 150.

24 See, for example, Klaus Koch's seminal article, "Gibt es ein Vergeltungsdogma im Alten Testament?" *ZTK* 52:1 (1955): 1–42; Yael Shemesh, "Measure for Measure in the David Stories," *SJOT* 17:1 (2003): 89–109; and Yehonatan Yaakobs, *Midah Ke-neged Midah Ba-sipur Ha-Miḳrai* (Alon Shevut: Hotsa'at Tevunot, Mikhlelet Yaʿaḳov Hertsog Le-yad Yeshivat Har-ʿEtsyon, 2005) [Hebrew].

25 For some reflections on the importance of decipherable divine action for determining God's immediate presence, see, for example, Ingolf U. Dalferth, *Becoming Present: An Inquiry into the Christian Sense of the Presence of God* (Leuven: Peeters, 2006), 28–31, 48–52, in particular.

the side. For as a key later section demonstrates (§ 6.3), while the earlier Esther core from which MT likely descended speaks both directly of God and some of the characters' reactions to divine involvement, MT Esther consistently refrains from wading into such waters, making interpretations that depend on such gaps less probable.

These alterations lead to a final and related exegetical revision. While Fox, and those who have followed his line, see Esther expressing the importance of belief to later communities of Jews, this analysis repeatedly points out how attention to the compositional development of the Scroll displays an anachronism in such a position. Since the Greek witnesses confirm that Esther was written at multiple different stages by people who never realized their work would become authoritative scripture, reading the Scroll for its instruction to future generations admits of a mindset beyond that which Esther's authors could have reasonably attained.[26] As this work thus differentiates itself from these previous tendencies, it keeps its focus on Esther's deliberate connections to Genesis to offer an exegetical alternative. Instead of bringing God's presence in by leaving it out, or seeking to engender a faith that is never actually expressed, Esther repeatedly invokes the Joseph story to suggest that the details of its unique present be understood in light of paralleled events from the past.

1.2 Movements in Modern Esther Criticism

The import of these refinements comes into even sharper focus through a more thorough review of the diverse directions that current Esther criticism has taken. For despite some key interpretive advances in the last thirty years, fundamental disagreements, and often along lines similar to the religious/non-religious debate laid out above, have maintained. In this vein, consider Timothy Beal's work on Esther, which reads the Megillah as witness to the significance of modern theory.[27] After discussing the problematic location he inhabits as a modern Protestant reader of a biblical book Martin Luther sought to discredit, Beal sets out to chart

---

26 Interestingly, Fox himself stresses this very point. "Not only," he writes, "could the author [of Esther] not have known that there would be a Bible, but the lack of reference to God probably shows that he did not intend his book to be regarded as sacred scripture" (*Character and Ideology*, 238). While the present argument ultimately reaches a different conclusion concerning God's absence in Esther, the point at issue here is the subtle but telling pull between Fox's two positions. If Esther's authors could not have known that their work was to become canonical, then the book ought not to be seen as designed to teach later groups of believing Bible readers.

27 Timothy K. Beal, *The Book of Hiding: Gender, Ethnicity, Annihilation, and Esther* (London: Routledge, 1997).

a new course by determining that the Megillah reflects on the challenge of finding fixed identities in hybrid contexts. Noting how Haman's lowered stance in Esther 6 is reminiscent of Mordecai's in Esther 4, Beal couples continental thought with feminist critique to offer a novel theory: since Zeresh's repetition of לפני in Esth 6:13 brings Levinas' face-to-face encounter to bear, her prediction of Mordecai's victory in the same verse expresses an ironic refraction of a latent anti-Jewishness. Through appeals to the Spanish inquisition and leaflets protesting Elie Wiesel, Beal cautions against taking Zeresh's pro-Jewish declaration at face value.

> The text cannot possibly present this view in an unambiguously serious manner, as a clear affirmation of the special power of "Jewish seed." Indeed, there is the first irony: Mordecai has no seed (or at least has not planted any). Mordecai himself, moreover, has certainly not thus far appeared to be rising in power and prestige. On the contrary, he has been busy digging himself deeper and deeper into trouble, and this new turn for the better, along with Haman's humiliating turn for the worse, has happened largely by accident. Moreover, Jewish identity itself – particularly Mordecai's identify as Jew – has remained fundamentally ambiguous and largely invisible up to this point in the story. It is something that must be revealed to be known. It would be wrong, then, to take this superstitious view about special Jewish power as a straightforward affirmation, any more than one would affirm Haman's construal of the "Jewish problem" in Esther 3, precisely because it relies on assumptions about Jewish identity that are being called into question at every turn. (83)

Though this creative attempt admirably acknowledges and seeks to work through some of the damaging presuppositions modern criticism has brought to the Esther book, a poignant irony arises to cast doubt onto the specifics of Beal's interpretive venture. For despite his stated effort to use modern theory to "unhome" (3) himself from the Protestant tradition that schooled him, his fresh interpretive stance comes quite close to reformulating key aspects of past exegetical frames. Much as Ewald views Esther as a fallen text that cannot cope with loftier concerns, so does Beal's emphasis on earthly identity give the impression of a book only interested in worldly affairs. While Beal's work does not view this negatively, which may very well be the critical difference between his conclusion and those that once marked his own religious tradition, this noticeable slant suggests Beal may not be that far removed from the intellectual context he actively seeks to outpace.

While Kenneth Craig also explores how modern theoretical developments can help to make sense of Esther's text, his work turns to Bakhtin to suggest that the Scroll represents "an early example of the literary carnivalesque."[28] Accordingly, Craig's specific conclusions mark a contrast to Beal's: if Beal sees an irony in

---

28 Kenneth M. Craig, *Reading Esther: A Case for the Literary Carnivalesque* (Louisville, KY: Westminster John Knox Press, 1995), 24.

Zeresh's words, Craig views Esth 6:13 as evidence of predetermined history. "According to those who now speak," Craig writes, as he also links Esther 6 back to Esther 4,

> it is not because Mordecai has power by himself to overcome Haman, but because he is part of an inevitable movement ... This quoted speech of Mordecai [Esth 4:14] and of Haman's wife and associates in 6:13 suggests that history is, according to the author, guided. The Jewish people will endure in a world even when events are channeled against them. It is as though Gentiles know in advance, as many readers no doubt would, that Amalek cannot destroy Israel (cf. Exod 17:14–16 and 1 Sam 15). Their words in 6:13 suggest that history is not only foreshadowed, but ethnically predetermined. (124)

Though Craig's sensitive reading of the Megillah offers many fresh insights, his analysis here is reminiscent of Cohen's. If Cohen finds divine guidance behind the events of Esther 3, then Craig reads a fixed fate in Esther 6. The problem with such an approach, however, is articulated by the Scroll itself. Since Haman's real threat causes Esther and Mordecai to make a series of difficult choices in live time – the queen's decision to risk her life on her people's behalf (Esth 4:16), for example – the security of predestination does not adequately account for the buildup of tense drama that the Megillah so skillfully narrates.

In an effort to change the thematic focus of this conversation, Francisco-Javier Ruiz-Ortiz tries to unlock Esther's deeper purpose by turning to the significance the Megillah places on violence.[29] As a result of this specified aim, his analysis of key theological concerns remains somewhat underdeveloped. Consider, for example, his statement about Esther's religious import amidst his impressive insight into Esther's doubled literary structure.

> The double plot means also a duality in the kinds of plot. In general we could describe plot A as a plot of revelation, whereas plot B is a plot of resolution. However, this division is not so straightforward. The revelation contributes to the resolution of the conflicts while as quarrels appear, the characters are obliged to reveal both their identity and some of the decisive information for the final resolution of the struggles. In general, the plot of resolution conceals the action of God in the reversals and coincidences even though deliverance is only possible through human agents and their qualities, such as Mordecai's loyalty to his people and Esther's shrewdness. Thus the combination of this tandem uncovers what needs to be known with the resulting salvation of the Jews. Notwithstanding this characteristic, the final result in the book of Esther is the product of both human and divine actions expressed in a plot which is at the same time revelatory but which also implies resolution. (100)

While Ruiz-Ortiz's point concerning Esther's interconnections spanning across distinct plot elements is well-taken and underscored in Part Two of this work, his

---

29 Francisco-Javier Ruiz-Ortiz, *The Dynamics of Violence and Revenge in the Hebrew Book of Esther* (Leiden: Brill, 2017).

claim for divine action slips on the lack of specific evidence brought. For as is explored in greater detail below (§ 6.3), the Hebrew Megillah never once references God, and the Greek evidence indicates it more likely than not that the absence of God in MT Esther reflects a deliberate choice made by those responsible for the Hebrew version of the book.

As these considerations complicate Ruiz-Ortiz's effort to explain Esther's complex resolution through divine activity, Thomas Wetzel's recent monograph also focuses on Esther's controversial violence – but it does so to forward an even bolder proposal.[30] God is found, Wetzel argues, not in the suggestive turns of the Megillah, as Ruiz-Ortiz might see it, but rather in the body of the Jewish people themselves. Once again, the issue turns on Esth 6:13: if Beal sees these words carrying the latent but still ignoble mark of the anti-Semitic, and Craig finds them expressing Jewish determinism, then Wetzel detects the elusive trace of the divine. Not only, Wetzel contends, does the term מזרע, "from the seed," connote "one who ... has been consecrated ... to accomplish some work relative to the preservation or restoration of Israel" (73), but so also does the ultimate Jewish victory that Esther narrates show important parallels to both myths of divine combat and divinely inspired bans (חרם).

First, consider his point concerning the violence in Esther and other biblical proscriptions. While Haman's decision to cast lots and eradicate all the Jews creates some initial resonances (131–32), much of Wetzel's case for seeing a formal ban in the Megillah hinges on Esther's intertextual link to Saul. If Saul misunderstands God's command in 1 Samuel 15 as a ban of divine portion as opposed to one of eradication (153),[31] then Esther's conclusion rectifies this mistake to provide a more targeted purpose for the Scroll conflict. "The picture created by this

---

30 Thomas Wetzel, *Violence and Divine Victory in the Book of Esther* (Tübingen: Mohr Siebeck, 2022). Helge Bezold, *Ester – eine Gewaltgeschichte* (Berlin: De Gruyter, 2023) represents yet another current work that focuses on the importance of violence for understanding the book of Esther. While Wetzel finds the theological in the violent, Bezold brings focus to the social and political. Reading Hebrew Esther as a product of the Hasmonean period, Bezold suggests that the Megillah represents ancient Jewish reflections on the place and necessity of armed resistance against larger world powers.

31 Wetzel's analysis, which is influenced by Susan Niditch, *War in the Hebrew Bible: A Study in the Ethics of Violence* (New York: Oxford University Press, 1993), distinguishes between a *ḥērem* of God's portion and a *ḥērem* of divine justice. While bans of God's portion, which see gods participating in human battle, require that "the divine warrior then receives a portion of the spoils proportionate to the degree of his or her involvement in the battle" (142), the ban of "divine justice sought to please God by eradicating from the divine presence something that God finds abominable" (142). In this way, a key nuance of Wetzel's take on Esther is underscored. Since Saul misunderstands the *ḥērem* of justice that God has intended for a ban of portion, Mordecai's effort to remove the abominable Amalekite people is thus an effort to right this previous wrong.

rich set of allusions [which connect Saul to Mordecai, and Haman to the enemy Amalekites] establishes the Jewish battle in the Esther story as a form of *ḥērem* as divine justice, an assault upon an irreformable and irredeemable force of disorder intentionally opposed to the divine order of creation" (165).

This line of thinking leads to the second major pole of Wetzel's argument. Since creation, in Wetzel's view, is usually marked not by something peacefully coming out of nothing but rather God's ordering of a world that is inherently chaotic,[32] Esther's divinely inspired conflict takes on an additional layer of significance. Given that the Persian empire, which, during the time narrated by the book of Esther, includes Jerusalem and its Temple, only finds order after the Jews win, the battle playing out in the Shushan streets echoes the creative act by providing organization to an otherwise unruly reality (165). Thus, by arguing that Esther and Mordecai's violent victory completes that which God previously requested of Saul while also maintaining the conditions for God's created world, Wetzel sums up his interpretive aim.

> In MT Esther, *Agagite* points mysteriously toward Amalek, and the references to Kish and Shimei point in a similar dark manner toward the ancient narrative of King Saul. But other signs are present. The references to Mordecai and his people as "the Jews" become in this narrative a sign pointing to Israel, and Israel's survival becomes the most obvious – and yet most difficult to discern – sign of them all: Israel survives only because there exists a divine warrior who fights through them. Indeed, the final chapter of MT Esther suggests that the Jewish communities of the Persian Empire flourish in the wake of the great military victory. Violence and the endurance of Israel are proof in the world of MT Esther that the God of Israel is alive and active in creation. (167)

Though Wetzel's approach provides a stirring read of the Scroll, his thought-provoking take relies on a set of textual connections that are not corroborated with specific philological links. The most obvious is his case for Esther as a ban. As he repeatedly notes, the problem may be simpler than the solution he develops. Since the Hebrew word חרם is never found in Esther, the effort to turn the Scroll into this specific form of battle pushes against the actual evidence. Connecting Esther to myths of creation slips on an equally straightforward objection. Though Wetzel's

---

32 For Wetzel, though Genesis 1 represents a peaceful account of creation, most every other account in the Hebrew Bible and Ancient Near East offers more complex challenges. "The creation account in Genesis 1 is not typical of the biblical tradition; the Hebrew Bible portrays the divine acts of creation in numerous other ways, many of them filled with disorder, challenges to the creator's authority, and even violence. The creation account that immediately follows Genesis 1 and is found in Genesis 2–3 serves as just one such example" (99). For the scholarly history of and some nuances to this particular line of argument, see, for example, Jon D. Levenson, *Creation and the Persistence of Evil: The Jewish Drama of Divine Omnipotence* (San Francisco: Harper & Row, 1988).

points concerning the nature of the creative act and the counterintuitive importance of Jewish victory for Persian order compel, no specific philological links between the host of creation stories Wetzel surveys and the text of MT Esther seem to be present.

As this intertextual analysis thus refrains from seeing God's direct presence in the Jewish people's victory, the ways in which current Scroll scholarship has come to reformulate key aspects of previous debates clarify. For despite these new approaches and sophisticated theoretical advances providing any number of exegetical breakthroughs, a familiar basic pivot has remained. Either God's presence is imported into the Scroll, or the one biblical book that does not directly mention God is viewed through earthly lenses.

1.3 Intertextual Methodology and Relative Chronologies

Before turning to the specific textual, interpretive, and historical aims that the present study aims to pursue, some crucial methodological considerations for this historically-sensitive intertextual analysis are necessary. Though no blanket formula for determining intentional allusions has been determined, scholarship has developed a number of helpful criteria for navigating such tricky waters. In a well-taken 2008 article, for example, Jeffrey Leonard articulates eight.[33] While some of his categories admit of overlap, his overarching position guides much of this study. Shared language (1), he notes, is the single most important factor; not only is this feature more indicative than non-shared language (2), but so also do rare or distinctive phrases (3) increase the likelihood of an intentional allusion.

Leonard's emphasis on linguistic considerations continues. Much as shared phrases suggest a connection stronger than individual terms (4), so does the accumulation of shared language (5) present a case more compelling than any individual example. His final three considerations explore the interaction of language with form and content: shared language found in similar contexts is stronger than shared language all on its own (6), and examples of shared language need not be accompanied by similar ideologies (7) or literary forms (8).

Since these principles have been broadly accepted in biblical criticism,[34] the present work adheres to the spirit of Leonard's criteria by building its case for

---

33 Jeffrey M. Leonard, "Identifying Inner-Biblical Allusions: Psalm 78 as a Test Case," *JBL* 127:2 (2008): 241–65.
34 For different ways in which these foundational guidelines have been implemented, see, for example, William A. Tooman, *Gog of Magog: Reuse of Scripture and Compositional Technique in Ezekiel 38–39* (Tübingen: Mohr Siebeck, 2011); Jonathan Kline, *Allusive Soundplay in the Hebrew Bible* (Atlanta: SBL Press, 2016); and D. Andrew Teeter, "Jeremiah, Joseph, and the Dynamics of

deliberate allusions with shared phrases that are both philologically distinct and found in paralleled contexts. In so doing, it also notes how most other studies of Esther's intertextuality have strayed from these baseline principles. Though several works have sought to determine the intentionality with which Esther's authors invoked Exodus, the David story, and other prophetic books, Part One explores how these previous argumentations too frequently rely on language that is not sufficiently distinct and found in contexts that admit of too much dissimilarity.

A brief analysis of Harald Martin Wahl's intertextual approach to Esther offers an early illustration of this very concern.[35] For at least on its surface, Wahl's work follows a template similar to the course pursued here: Esther's religiosity, Wahl repeatedly asserts, can be found through its inner-biblical allusions. While he marshals a host of claims to support such a reading,[36] two specific moves illustrate the crux of his intertextual agenda. The first reminds of Cohen's analysis. Since פור in other Hebrew Bible cases approaches the unknowable will of the divine, so should its mysterious presence in Esther be understood (*Das Buch Esther*, 196–97).

The second turns to the remarkable sequence of events in Esther 3–4 and argues that the conflict Mordecai ignites is as divinely inspired as the solution Esther finds. Despite numerous biblical characters prostrating themselves without problem or recrimination, Wahl views this Scroll instance illustrating an undeniable religiosity.[37] "Der tiefere Grund der Weigerung ist, daß für Mordechai diese Geste allein seinem Gott vorbehalten bliebt" (*Das Buch Esther*, 90).

Analogy: On the Relationship between Jeremiah 37–44 and the Joseph Story," *HeBAI* 10:4 (2021): 443–87.

35 While Wahl's commentary is particularly important, *Das Buch Esther: Übersetzung und Kommentar* (Berlin: de Gruyter, 2009), two articles are also significant: "'Glaube ohne Gott?' Zur Rede vom Gott Israels im hebräischen Buch Esther," *BZ* 45:1 (2001): 37–54, and "'Jahwe, wo bist du?' Gott, Glaube und Gemeinde in Esther," *JSJ* 31:1 (2000): 1–22.

36 In addition to its allusive nature, Esther's religious praxis, motifs, and terms and topics fill out Wahl's argument for the religiosity of the Scroll. Taken together, Wahl asserts, these considerations bring the Israelite God onto the Shushan page. "Wir konstatieren: Bei näherer Betrachtung begegnet Jahwe im hebräischen Buch Esther auf Schritt und Tritt. Der Gott Israels ist nicht eine ferne, numinose Macht, die nur im Hintergrund wirkt. Der Glaube an ihn und sein heilvolles Wirken in der Geschichte trägt das Buch. Die Rede von Jahwe ist jedoch nur mit dem Vorwissen der biblischen Tradition eindeutig zu dechiffrieren: Jahwe ist in der religiösen Praxis das Gegenüber. Auf ihn weisen für den zeitgenössischen Leser der persischen Diaspora zahlreiche Anspielungen und Motive im ganzen Buch hin, sein Wirken ist in Begriffen und Topoi deutlich konturiert" (*Das Buch Esther*, 43).

37 It has long been known, however, that Mordecai's Jewish identity does not in and of itself explain his peculiar refusal. Levenson puts it best: "That a Jew may bow down to another man is clear from the Bible itself, where this happens repeatedly (e.g., Gen 23:7; 27:29; I Kings 1:31)" (*Esther: A Commentary* [Louisville: Westminster John Knox, 1997], 67). As Levenson, and others (see, for example, Moore, *Esther*, 36–37), go on to note, this may reach back to Haman's heritage. "Some

For Wahl, as long as such an ambiguous act remains only for God, then the far more overt penitence rites of Esth 4:1–3 become direct appeal.

> Die Buße ist ein spontan ausgedrückter oder auch kollektiv vollzogener (oder angeordneter) Selbstminderungsritus, der sich immer an Jahwe richtet (Joel 1,13–15; 2,12–13). In ihm entsprechen sich äußere Gesten und innere Umkehr (Tob 12,8–12). Von Hiob einmal abgesehen, setzt die Buße das Wissen um die Verfehlung voraus, die dann zur bewußten rituellen Selbstminderung führt. Der Buße geht insofern die Einsicht der Schuld voran, der dann wirkliche Reue folgt. Die Buße ist begangene Umkehr. Mit dieser Hinwendung zu Gott drückt der Büßende gleichzeitig die Bitte um Errettung aus der Not und Verschonung vor dem drohenden Übel aus (Gen 37,34; Ps 30,12; 36,24; Jer 31,13; Esra 8,21–23; Dan 9,3). (*Das Buch Esther*, 116)

Despite the list of verses Wahl included as parallels, his argumentation does not seek to prove authorial intent; rather, his work hinges on how these Megillah verses would have been received. "Ein Bußritus, der ohne das geglaubte Gegenüber Gott vollzogen wird, ist für einen Juden undenkbar. Was sollte diese Buße nützen?" (*Das Buch Esther*, 112).[38] As scholarship has long appreciated, however, the deliberate design of Leonard's authorial criteria is not the same as Wahl's focus on reception, and, as an examination of the verses Wahl identifies highlights, the textual nexus he here singles out does not rise to the level of purposeful allusion and thus falls short of determining that Esther was intended to mean that which he – and his original audience – hears.

On first glance, the verses Wahl compares do seem to suggest a genetic relationship. In most of them, some combination of the following Hebrew roots and words are found: צ.ו.מ ,שַׂק, ס.פ.ד, א.ב.ל, ע.ר.ק, ק.ע.ז. A closer look, however,

---

scholars," Levenson continues, "have seen the issue as one of ethnicity. Agag's nation, the Amalekites, had long been conceived as the archetypal enemy of Mordecai's nation, the Israelites or Jews (e.g., Exod. 17:8–16; Deut. 25:17–19). In light of the savagery of the Amalekite assault upon Israel in the wilderness and the perduring imperative upon Israel to annihilate Amalek, for Mordecai to do homage to Haman would, so the theory goes, have been a gross betrayal of his nation's honor. This theory seems possible," Levenson concludes, "but is without corroboration" (67).

38 This exact same emphasis on Esther's reception, as opposed to the specific textual designs that often indicate authorial intent, is also found in Wahl's essay on the matter, "Jahwe, wo bist du." After noting how the phrase תלה על העץ (Esth 2:21–23; 7:10; 9:7–10) is found throughout the Pentateuch, Wahl then argues that the parallels with Joseph are particularly expressed. "Thematisch sind die Stellen mit denen aus Esther vergleichbar: Joseph und der Hofbäcker, dessen Name nicht gennant wird, sind wegen todeswürdiger Verbrechen angeklagt. Beiden droht die Todesstrafe durch Aufhängen am Holz. Der unschuldige Joseph entkommt dem Urteil, am schuldigen Bäcker wird es vollstreckt. Mit den an den schuldigen Feinden der Juden vollzogenen Exekutionen wird das Gesetz der Tora beachtet (Gen 40:19, 22; 41:13). Das Buch Esther, so hört der Zeitgenosse, erfüllt die Forderungen der Tora und respektiert so den Willen Jahwes. Nebenher klingt der Gedanke an, daß Jahwes Weisung überall gültig ist und der König Israels gerecht richtet" (6).

gestures to some initial complications; not only are all of these words and roots frequently spread across the Hebrew Bible, but so also do the contexts in which these verses come show significant variation. While some come in prophetic oracles of return (Jer 31:13), others are found in God's redemptive response to poetic laments (Ps 30:12); if some serve as introduction to a divinely inspired vision (Dan 9:3), others include no mention of God at all (Gen 37:34).

As these contextual divergences give pause to the lexical similarities noted, they also indicate how these linguistic features are likely reflective of a shared lament form. As a result, a key supplement to Leonard's criteria comes into focus: philological similarities that reflect shared stock phrasings cannot be used to prove deliberate borrowing. Precisely this point has been helpfully emphasized by Benjamin Sommer's work on Second Isaiah's intertextual character.[39]

> All students of allusion must distinguish between two types of textual similarity: cases in which one writer relies on another and cases in which two writers use similar language coincidentally. Several texts may use the same vocabulary not because a later author depends on an earlier one but because they utilize a common tradition, or because they are discussing a topic that naturally suggests certain vocabulary. This problem becomes acute in a highly traditional literature such as the Bible. Stock prophetic, legal, or poetic vocabulary or the common use of some familiar trope or type-scene may lead two texts to look similar whether or not one author knew the other ... A central methodological principle follows from this: we cannot view an older text as a source for a passage in Deutero-Isaiah if both utilize stock vocabulary, exemplify a literary form such as a lament, or treat a subject that calls for certain words. (32)

The rejoinder to Wahl, and the ways in which the present study differentiates itself from his work, thus sharpen. Since his work here does not firmly support a claim for deliberate allusion, a distinction must be drawn between how an ancient audience might have heard the Scroll and what Esther's authors intended to communicate.[40]

---

39 Benjamin Sommer, *A Prophet Reads Scripture: Allusion in Isaiah 40–66* (Stanford: Stanford University Press, 1998).

40 The anecdote Ziony Zevit uses to open his edited volume on intertextual concerns in biblical studies (*Subtle Citation*) speaks precisely to this issue. Invoking Emily Dickinson's usage of Matt 6:28, Zevit frets over a version of a problem countless modern-day Bible professors have encountered. "What happens," he wonders, "to her allusion when a twenty-first century reader unfamiliar with the biblical passage thinks instead about *The Lilies of the Field*, a 1962 novel by Edmund Barret, or, more likely, the highly-regarded, 1963 film adaptation of the book? Dickinson's allusion falls flat; in fact, it becomes nonsensical. No meaning is shoehorned into anything anywhere" (2). Zevit's example, though more extreme than the current concern, gestures to the same idea standing behind this critique – that any given reader hears an allusion, either at a moment close to the time of textual production or some point thereafter, does not determine that the perceived relationship was intended by the author.

In contradistinction to Wahl's argumentation, the present approach focuses on authorial intent by adhering to Leonard's stricter methodological guidelines; in addition, it also frequently interacts with two further considerations raised by Sommer.[41] The first concerns the different levels of significance that allusions may carry. Referencing Ziva Ben-Porat's influential work, Sommer identifies four distinct interpretive stages that deliberate references can attain: "noticing the marker, identifying the source, bringing the marked sign to bear on the interpretation of the sign which includes the marker, and also noting additional aspects of the source text which affect the reading of the alluding text generally" (15).[42] While this study traces how a series of linguistic and thematic overlaps to Joseph suggest that Esther's authors intended for all aspects of the source text to be conjured – level four in Sommer and Ben-Porat's parlance – it once again notes how previous attempts to read the Scroll allusively have failed to consider this crucial scaffolding. For as Ben-Porat's and Sommer's works show, not every allusion carries the same exegetical value, and, despite a number of claims to the contrary, some occasional linguistic and contextual similarities do not provide an adequate basis for intertextual interpretations that see the entire meaning of the alluding text coming out only through its external references.

In addition to emphasizing this key methodological concept, the analysis followed here also consistently responds to the categories Sommer identifies that explain the purposes of inner-biblical allusions. While Sommer notes how biblical authors invoked other texts to explain the meaning of an earlier text, revise or polemicize against previous positions, or bolster their own new ones (22–31), attention to Esther's connections with Joseph offers a helpful refinement. As the Scroll positions its Persian story against an Egyptian background, the repeated allusions to Joseph present a suggestive context in which Esther is best understood: events continue to contrast with those intended, good-looking Israelites continue to beat all odds to rise in foreign courts, and the divinely initiated patterns of the past

---

41 Sommer, *A Prophet Reads Scripture*. Sommer's work raises yet a third issue that is worth mentioning here – intertextual terminology. (For a complete and up-to-date discussion of this concern, see Eric X. Jarrard, "'Remember This Day on Which You Came Out of Egypt': The Exodus Motif in Biblical Memory" [ThD diss., Harvard University, 2020].) Though Sommer makes a compelling case for distinguishing between intertextuality and influence (6–10), this study follows a different convention: in all instances, the term intertextuality here refers to the historical idea of author-oriented intertextuality. Moreover, while Sommer presents a hierarchical understanding of references – allusion, influence, echo, and exegesis – the present work uses these terms (save exegesis, which the present study does not employ to refer to inner-biblical allusions) interchangeably to describe references to the Joseph story that Esther's authors intended.

42 As noted, Sommer's work extends out of two Ben-Porat publications, "Intertextuality," *Ha-Sifrut* 34 (1985): 170–78 [Hebrew], and "The Poetics of Literary Allusion," *PTL: A Journal for Descriptive Poetics and Theory of Literature* 1 (1976): 105–28.

continue even when God remains absent. In this way, then, the previous Genesis text not only bolsters Esther's present position, but it also serves as a basis out of which the specific contours of the Scroll story develop.

Though representing some divergence from Sommer's classification, this approach finds support in Michael Lyons' monograph on Ezekiel, which notes how Ezekiel uses the Holiness Code as instruction for the past, present, and future.[43] After detailing countless examples in which Ezekiel depends on, refers to, and even alters the Holiness Code, Lyons sums up the purpose behind this extensive intertextual activity. "Ezekiel is doing more than just borrowing words from H. By the manner in which he uses these locutions in his argument, he is demonstrating that he views these legal regulations of H as normative standards for behavior" (129). Though Esther, apart from its Purim section, refrains from this kind of didacticism, its interaction with Joseph admits of a similar dynamic. If Ezekiel argues that abiding by certain laws of a past code can bring about redeemed life in the present, then the Scroll suggests that even when God remains absent, the divinely initiated patterns of the past bring about another unexpected foreign deliverance in the current moment (§ 6.2).

With these basic methodological parameters sketched, one final preliminary matter – issues of dating – must be addressed. First the more straightforward Megillah case: since Ahasuerus is generally understood as Xerxes, who sat on the Persian throne from 486–465 BCE, Esther's *terminus post quem* has long stood at the latter end of this reign. While some push the *terminus anti quem* into the first century BCE,[44] Moore argues that a contrast to the book of Daniel suggests the second century BCE as the latest credible date. If the visions in Daniel 7–12 reflect the "negative attitudes and situation of the early Maccabean Period" (LIX–LX), Esther's generally innocuous stance toward a Gentile king indicates that the book was likely written before the Seleucid persecution of 167–165 BCE. Though some recent works have questioned this point and advocated a Maccabean provenance for at least certain Scroll passages,[45] the present work suggests that since the Per-

---

43 Lyons, *From Law to Prophecy.*

44 Hans Bardtke, *Das Buch Esther* (Gütersloh: Gütersloher Verlagshaus Gerd Mohn, 1963), 253, invokes 2 Maccabees to push the latest date all the way to 50 BCE, and Elias Bickerman, *Four Strange Books of the Bible: Jonah, Daniel, Koheleth, Esther* (New York: Schocken Books, 1967), 207, turns to the colophon in LXX Esther to suggest 78/77 BCE. For a fuller articulation of Bickerman's argument concerning the date of the colophon, see his essay, "The Colophon of the Greek Book of Esther," *JBL* 63:4 (1944): 339–62.

45 Two recent commentaries make significant cases suggesting that the Hellenistic and Maccabean periods are precisely the environment in which Esther is best understood. In both instances, the arguments have turned to context. Jean-Daniel Macchi argues that since the earliest version of the Esther story shows "an intimate knowledge of literature in Greek about Persia, the work was probably produced in a milieu strongly influenced by Greek culture" (*Esther*, trans. Carmen Palmer

sian court and its humorous depiction play such important roles in Esther, it makes most sense for the earlier Esther traditions to have taken initial shape when the Persian empire still existed.[46] As a result, this analysis suggests the following general historical parameters: a basic core, which spans roughly from MT Esth 1–8:1,[47] was written in the second half of the Persian period, while the final chapters and some key expansions found throughout the book were composed and then included in the Hebrew Megillah in the late Persian or early Hellenistic era.

As a result of Esther's late dating, a chronology relative to Genesis has stayed reliable, even as prominent European voices have begun arguing for a later and later Joseph. Consider, for example, Bernd Schipper's innovative recent work.[48] Noting how Joseph's Egyptian background has traditionally been seen as support

---

[Stuttgart: W. Kohlhammer, 2018], 44). Macchi goes on to suggest that this early core, which "provides the impression that it is possible for Jews to live harmoniously within an empire whose system in general, and the emperor in particular, are not malevolent" (45), then underwent a redaction that "paint[s] a much harsher and ironic picture of the empire, which becomes profoundly dysfunctional" (46–47). Since this much more negative picture clashes with the earlier depiction and, according to Macchi, "assume[s] a radical rupture in confidence regarding imperial institutions" (47), it likely reflects the context of the Maccabean crisis. In her commentary, Ego follows a similar line (56–69). Emphasizing Esther's potential concern for limited religious expression and the tension surrounding proskynesis, Ego suggests that these factors, which fit most clearly in the Hellenistic context, pull the completion of the base Esther narrative into the Greek period. Consequently, her work goes on to argue that the final chapters, which admit of open clash between the Jews and those around them, likely reflect the Maccabean context. In this vein, Bezold (*Ester*) also follows this trend and argues that the Hebrew Megillah is a product of the Hasmonean period, since, in his view, Esther's accent on Jewish violence likely reflects the upheaval and tension of this age; the two Greek versions, he argues, are even later, as he dates them into the Roman and even Christian era. Since the present analysis is most concerned with Esther's relative dating to Joseph, it remains open to such efforts that endeavor to date Esther later and later; it does, however, continue to suggest that the emphasis on the Persian court makes it most likely that Esther's initial compositional activities occurred either during or closely after the actual Persian reign. For a thorough attempt to pick through the challenge of adjudicating between a Persian or Hellenistic background, see Jill Middlemas, "Dating Esther: Historicity and the Provenance of Masoretic Esther," in *On Dating Biblical Texts to the Persian Period: Discerning Criteria and Establishing Epochs* eds. Richard J. Bautch and Mark Lackowski (Tübingen: Mohr Siebeck, 2019). While fully realizing that no definitive answer may be reached, Middlemas also suggests that Esther's base narrative (Esth 1–9:19, in her mind) likely reflects the later Persian period, while the end of Esther 9 and all of Esther 10 were likely composed in a Hellenistic context.

46 For similar perspectives, see, for example, Moore, *Esther* LIX–LX; Adele Berlin, *Esther=[Ester]: The Traditional Hebrew Text with the New JPS Translation* (Philadelphia: Jewish Publication Society, 2001), xliii; Levenson, *Esther*, 26; and Crawford, *Esther*, 855–56.

47 In Part Two of this study, text critical and redactional issues are explored, and an analysis of Esther's two ancient Greek witnesses suggests that much of MT Esth 8:2–10:3, along with a set of expansions throughout the earlier Hebrew chapters, likely stem from a secondary redaction.

48 Bernd Schipper, "The Egyptian Background of the Joseph Story," *HeBAI* 8:1 (2019): 6–23.

for an early dating, Schipper suggests that an Egyptian fragment preserved in Berlin requires a reevaluation. Since this papyrus (pBerlin 23071) bears similarities to Joseph but dates to the Persian period, Schipper argues that Joseph's Egyptian connections actually indicate that the story was written in Egypt in either the fifth or fourth century BCE.

Though approaching the matter differently, Thomas Römer reaches a similar conclusion.[49] Emphasizing internal pentateuchal evidence, Römer points to a potential problem with pre-exilic datings of Joseph. Since the Joseph verses traditionally ascribed to P do "not offer a coherent narrative" (197), arguments for a pre-exilic Joseph being incorporated into P create an inconsistency. Given that the priestly redactors are often thought to have acted differently with the Abraham and Jacob material they inherited, Römer proposes a re-creation of P that knows nothing of Jacob's second-youngest son.[50] As this model allows him to view all specific references to Joseph as non-P additions, he concludes that Joseph must have been "an independent Diaspora novella composed during the Persian period" that was then "inserted at the end of Genesis *after* the integration of the P-texts" (201).

While this study is not designed to evaluate among different proposals for explaining Joseph's complicated compositional history, its relationship with Esther sheds some light onto the debate. Since the first Esther traditions were most probably written in the latter part of the Persian period, the present analysis suggests a slight narrowing of Joseph's *terminus ante quem*. While Schipper and Römer's criteria allow for Joseph to have been composed as late as the fourth century BCE, Esther's usage of the Genesis story suggests that Joseph was likely written somewhat earlier and thus already in circulation by the middle part of the Persian period. As Konrad Schmid has also recently forwarded a similar end date for Joseph's composition,[51] a point central to the current study

---

49 Thomas Römer, "The Joseph Story in the Book of Genesis: Pre-P or Post-P?" in *The Post-Priestly Pentateuch: New Perspectives on its Redactional Development and Theological Profiles*, eds. Federico Giuntoli and Konrad Schmid (Tübingen: Mohr Siebeck, 2015): 185–201.

50 For the details of Römer's textual analysis, see "The Joseph Story," 196–200.

51 Following a line similar to both Schipper and Römer, Konrad Schmid, "Die Josephsgeschichte im Pentateuch," in *Abschied vom Jahwisten: Die Komposition des Hexateuch in der jüngsten Diskussion*, eds. Jan Christian Gertz, Konrad Schmid, and Markus Witte (Berlin: de Gruyter, 2002): 83–117, has proposed a minor but important variation. While Schipper turns to Egyptian considerations, Schmid, like Römer, considers internal factors; unlike Römer, however, Schmid argues that a pre-priestly Joseph played an important role in the priestly effort to bring Genesis and Moses texts together and, therefore, must have been composed no later than the early Persian period. Thus, while Schipper and Römer suggest that Joseph's compositional window extends all the way into the fourth century BCE, Schmid proposes that the diaspora nature of the story suggests a date between 722 BCE and the early Persian period.

is underscored: even if later dates for Joseph are accepted, a relative dating with Esther can still be upheld.[52]

---

52 Any number of other proposals have dated Joseph to pre-exilic contexts. Since these positions would clearly pose no issue for the relative dating on which this study relies, these suggestions are not reviewed in detail. For the specifics of such arguments, see, for example, Claus Westermann, *Genesis 37–50: A Commentary*, trans. John J. Scullion (Minneapolis: Fortress, 1986); David M. Carr, *Reading the Fractures of Genesis: Historical and Literary Approaches* (Louisville: Westminster John Knox Press, 1996), 277; and, more recently, Erhard Blum and Kristin Weingart, "The Joseph Story: Diaspora Novella or North-Israelite Narrative?" *ZAW* 129:4 (2017): 501–21.

Part One: **The Allusive Megillah and the Scholarly Attempts to Understand It**

2 Textual Connections and Scholarly Histories

2.1 The Import of Self-control and the Unusual Language Used to Express It

To begin this study, Part One concentrates on two intertwined points. As a series of textual examples indicate the breadth and depth of Esther's connection to Joseph, an examination of past scholarship shows how the full exegetical reach of the relationship has not yet been entirely appreciated. While exploring these ideas spans across this chapter and the next, attention to the import of self-control, in addition to the unusual Hebrew root, א.פ.ק, used to articulate it, kick-starts these initial aims.[53]

Expressed in Genesis through Joseph's shifting receptions of his brothers' three descents to Egypt, this theme of internal discipline initially comes to the surface as the brothers approach the vizier for the first time. When they bow down before him just as Joseph's dreams predicted (Gen 37:5–11, 42:6), the move-ment of the plot indicates the painful irony the vizier is confronting – for it was his brothers' negative reaction to the very same dreams they have unwittingly just fulfilled that landed him at the bottom of a pit in the first place (Gen 37:5–11, 18–24).

However, despite any vindicating impulse he might be experiencing, Joseph maintains a steeled exterior that keeps his own identity hidden from his brotherly visitors. As he recognizes them but they not him (Gen 42:7), he neither gloats nor ends the painful familial schism; rather, by keeping his reaction entirely in check, he begins the difficult process of probing whether his brothers have matured beyond the violent jealousies of their past. Though his coldness may seem retribu-tive, it comes to play a key role in the ultimate reunification. For by detaining yet another brother and requiring that the youngest be brought down on any future trip (Gen 42:18–20), Joseph is setting his brothers up to confront for a second time a situation similar to what they previously did to him so that he can observe how they will react.

---

53 This root, always in the *hithpael* stem with the general meaning "to restrain or control one-self," is found only seven times in the entire Hebrew Bible: the three instances discussed in this chapter – Gen 43:31, 45:1 and Esth 5:10 – in addition to 1 Sam 13:12, and Is 42:14, 63:15, and 64:11. Though working well before Leonard developed his criteria, Ludwig A. Rosenthal, who was the first to explore many of Esther's connections to Joseph in the modern scholarly context, noted how this unusual language can be used as evidence for a deliberate relationship ("Die Josephs-geschichte, mit den Büchern Ester und Daniel verglichen," *ZAW* 15:1 [1895]: 278–84, here: 280).

https://doi.org/10.1515/9783111216119-002

If this opening trip is marked by the test that Joseph's complete self-control allows him to enact, then the brothers' second descent to the vizier hinges on Joseph's struggle to maintain that same cold exterior. When Benjamin then comes, and Joseph's own design brings him face-to-face with his only full brother, the force of the occasion begins to overwhelm the vizier's carefully constructed cover. Two key verses and one unusual root, א.פ.ק, mark the significance of the action. "With that [Joseph's seeing and speaking to Benjamin], Joseph hurried out, for he was overcome with feeling toward his brother and was on the verge of tears; he went into a room and wept there. Then he washed his face, reappeared, and – now in control of himself (ויתאפק) – gave the order, 'Serve the meal'" (Gen 43:30–31). That Joseph must leave the room in his moment of emotional upheaval underscores the present point. Much as his investigation of his brothers' deeper intent is a precondition for familial reunification, so does his ability to test his brothers hinge on his own self-control, and, since his probe has not yet determined what it was designed to reveal about his brothers, Joseph must remove himself from their presence when his emotions briefly break through his all-important facade.

While the root (א.פ.ק) expressing Joseph's uncanny ability to catch himself at exactly the right moment is rarely found in the Hebrew Bible, it does come at an instance of equal importance in the Megillah. There, after Esther has finally been convinced to approach Ahasuerus on behalf of her now endangered people (Esth 4:16), she finds an unexpectedly gracious king. "What troubles you, Queen Esther?" asks the king in response to her uninvited and unlawful approach. "And what is your request? Even to half the kingdom, it shall be granted you" (Esth 5:3). When Esther responds in curious fashion, choosing not to address the problem of her people's threatened safety that she has come to solve (Esth 5:4), the previous fear she felt (Esth 4:11, 16) makes her reaction all the stranger. Though she seems to be in perfect position to speak up for the Jews and then walk away unscathed, she asks for a series of banquets that only elongates her involvement in the complicated process of deposing Haman and fighting against his edict.

At least initially, this plot delay does not seem to bode well for Esther's cause. Directly after the first exclusive banquet, Haman, on his way home from the party, merry and drunk with his own impressively high status, encounters an intolerably insolent Mordecai for what is now a second time. "That day Haman went out happy and lighthearted. But when Haman saw Mordecai in the palace gate, and Mordecai did not rise or even stir on his account, Haman was filled with rage at him" (Esth 5:9). However, instead of lashing out with the foolish impulsivity he has come to be known for (Esth 3:5–6; 5:13–14; 6:6–9), the Persian prime minister inverts expectation by finding the sort of self-control that has hitherto been associated with Joseph. "Nevertheless, Haman controlled himself (ויתאפק המן) and went home" (Esth 5:10).

As the seldom-used root sounds an echo to Joseph, it also recalls how an earlier expression of the same insult initially engenders the major conflicts of the Scroll. In Esther 3, after Haman has mysteriously been promoted to prime minister for seemingly no reason at all (Esth 3:1), he insists that everyone must bow down to him (Esth 3:2). When Mordecai curiously refuses (Esth 3:2),[54] and Haman catches wind of the civil disobedience (Esth 3:4–5), the prime minister reacts without any hint of the control he shows in Esther 5. Rather, in an echo of the king's opening decision to turn a marital slight into harsh state policy (Esth 1:16–22), Haman also makes Mordecai's insult a nationwide campaign. "He [Haman] disdained to lay hands on Mordecai alone; having been told who Mordecai's people were, Haman plotted to do away with all the Jews, Mordecai's people, throughout the kingdom of Ahasuerus" (Esth 3:6).

Though this earlier action makes Haman's later ability to catch himself (ויתאפק המן, Esth 5:10) all the more unlikely, it nicely sets up the prime minister's utter inability to maintain the self-discipline he somehow managed to find. Upon returning home after catching his immediate rage, Haman sets about losing the very self-control he just exhibited. After bragging to his wife and friends about the wealth he has and high status he enjoys, Haman then unleashes the anger he momentarily suppressed. "Yet all this means nothing to me," he rants, "every time I see that Jew Mordecai sitting in the palace gate" (Esth 5:13). Seeking to soothe a prime minister now spiraling very much out of control, Haman's supporters propose a plan that ironically plays right into Mordecai's hands. "Let a stake be put up," they recommend to the jilted Haman, "fifty cubits high, and in the morning ask the king to have Mordecai impaled on it" (Esth 5:14).

While Haman gleefully agrees to such an overblown solution,[55] the king, who has just heard how Mordecai had saved his life (Esth 2:21–23, 6:2), has other ideas

---

54 This crucial action in Esther 3 also contains a notable linguistic link to Joseph. When the courtiers cannot understand Mordecai's stubborn stance, they ask why he continually insists on transgressing the king's command (Esth 3:3). Though Mordecai never answers, the narrator does: "When they spoke to him day after day and he would not listen to them (ויהי באמרם אליו יום ויום ולא שמע אליהם), they told Haman, in order to see whether Mordecai's resolve would prevail; for he had explained to them that he was a Jew" (Esth 3:4). While such a response gestures to the well-known Amalekite conflict, it also resonates with the Joseph story, where suggestively similar action is expressed in strikingly similar language. For in Egypt, when Potiphar's wife repeatedly demands that Joseph lie with her, the Israelite steadfastly refuses. "And much as she coaxed Joseph day after day, he did not yield to her request," ויהי כדברה אל יוסף יום יום ולא שמע אליה (Gen 39:10). If Mordecai's stubbornness places himself and his people in grave danger, then so does Joseph's uprightness here throw him into a foreign jail. Thus, much as the language of self-control helps to concretize the larger narrative connections presently under discussion, so is this smaller narrative interplay also anchored by this nearly identical phrasing.

55 Such action completes the aforementioned parallel to Ahasuerus' response to Vashti's earlier refusal. In Esther 1, when the king agrees with his advisors, an untenable law is passed: all women

in mind. When the prime minister then seeks royal approval for his murderous scheme and foolishly prepares to reward himself along the way (Esth 6:6–9), the king's response flips the script. "'Quick, then!' said the king to Haman. 'Get the garb and the horse, as you have said, and do this to Mordecai the Jew, who sits in the king's gate'" (Esth 6:10). As Mordecai is then triumphantly paraded through the Shushan streets by the very man seeking to kill him (Esth 6:10–11), the import of self-control in both stories emerges. If Joseph's ability to maintain control of his emotions allows him to implement the test of his brothers, a test that ultimately determines whether a lasting reunification is possible, then Haman's fleeting show of self-discipline flips back against him to portend his coming and decisive downfall.

A final, and most important, usage of א.פ.ק solidifies these linguistic, thematic, and narrative connections. For back in Egypt, as the brothers' third trip to the vizier forces them to address the concocted but incriminating evidence found in their bags (Gen 44:11–13), Judah offers to sacrifice himself so that the falsely implicated Benjamin can return home (Gen 44:32–34). Since such selfless dedication to father and family is the exact opposite of how the brothers previously acted with Joseph (Gen 37:18–24), and therefore precisely the characteristic the vizier's elongated test has been straining to uncover, the brothers' newfound commitment to protect a son of Jacob's favored wife shatters the powerful barrier Joseph has up to now been so careful to protect.

> Joseph could no longer control himself (ולא יכל יוסף להתאפק) before all his attendants, and he cried out, "Have everyone withdraw from me!" So there was no one else about when Joseph made himself known to his brothers. His sobs were so loud that the Egyptians could hear, and so the news reached Pharaoh's palace. Joseph said to his brothers, "I am Joseph. Is my father still well?" But his brothers could not answer him, so dumbfounded were they on account of him. (Gen 45:1–3)

As the seldom-used root once again marks the momentousness of the occasion, the deeper layers of the connection between the two stories are made manifest. Much as Haman's one-time display of self-control (ויתאפק המן, Esth 5:10) does not hang Mordecai but rather fells the prime minister and improbably lifts the Jews, so does Joseph's unexpected loss of discipline (ולא יכל יוסף להתאפק, Gen 45:1) not detain Benjamin but rather end the brothers' prolonged agony by bringing about a stunning familial reunification. Indicative of a purposeful inter-

---

are supposed to obey their husbands in all circumstances (Esth 1:19–22). Much as this law is repeatedly flouted throughout the Megillah (Esth 5:14, 8:7–8), so too does Haman here follow his supporters' outlandish suggestion even though it ultimately flips against him. Thus, as the king comes to take his cues from Queen Esther, then so does Haman hang on the stake his wife encouraged him to erect for Mordecai (Esth 7:10).

twining of plot elements, these philological links detail how an identically phrased theme and the unexpected consequences of its swerves drive the major action in both Joseph and Esther's stories.

2.2 The Scholarly History of Esther's Relationship with Joseph

While this first example gestures toward the ways in which the linguistic, thematic, and narrative aspects of Esther and Joseph's similarities complement each other, scholarship on the issue has tended to view Esther's relationship with Joseph in more singular terms. In 1895, Ludwig Rosenthal's philological analysis initiated modern interest in the topic by identifying a number of linguistic similarities found across Joseph, Esther, and Daniel.[56] Rosenthal observes, for example, how the opening banquet in Esther, עשה משתה לכל שריו ועבדיו (Esth 1:3), reminds of the language used for the Pharaoh's birthday party, ויעש משתה לכל עבדיו (Gen 40:20), and how much as the king and his ministers are pleased in Esth 1:21, וייטב הדבר בעיני המלך והשרים, so are the Pharaoh and his advisors in Gen 41:37, וייטב הדבר בעיני פרעה ובעיני כל עבדיו (278). Moreover, if Joseph recommends that the Pharaoh appoint overseers in Egypt so that the grain can be gathered to stave off the famine, ויפקד פקדים על הארץ ... ויקבצו את כל אכל השנים הטבת הבאת האלה (Gen 41:34–35), then so is Ahasuerus similarly advised to appoint officers over the land of Persia so that beautiful maidens can be gathered to begin the search for a new queen: ויפקד המלך פקידים בכל מדינות מלכותו ויקבצו את כל נערה בתולה טובת מראה (Esth 2:3; Rosenthal, 279).

Such connections, Rosenthal points out, also extend to the book of Daniel.[57] Comparable to the language for the images of the cows in Pharaoh's dream, יפות מראה ובריאת בשר (Gen 41:2), is the expression for the handsome appearances of Daniel and his companions: מראיהם טוב ובריאי בשר (Dan 1:15; Rosenthal, 279–80). These types of correspondence are also found between Esther and Daniel:

---

56 Rosenthal, "Die Josephsgeschichte."
57 That Rosenthal first turns to the book of Daniel midway through his already brief article indicates the emphasis he places on Joseph and Esther's particularly tight connection. "Da mir Daniel nur als drittes Glied in der Kette des Vergleichs dienen kann, so komme ich erst hier dazu, die oben noch nicht erwähnten Wahrnehmungen – sie hätten sich ohne Verwirrung dort nicht anbringen lassen – nun anzuführen" (281). While this work follows Rosenthal's lead by consistently stressing Joseph and Esther's unique relationship, it also, in Chapter Seven, seeks to refine Rosenthal's position concerning Daniel. Since important structural differences found in Daniel prevent the admittedly present similarities of language and theme from sounding as loudly in or exerting such influence over the plot developments of Daniel's court narratives, Daniel's relationships to both Joseph and Esther are ultimately best understood not as the third link in this chain but rather as a different strand of comparison altogether.

much as the Shushan hero is introduced as a descendant of those whom Nebuchadnezzar exiled (Esth 2:6), so does Daniel 1 bring its protagonists into the story (Dan 1:6) in the wake of the exact same event (Dan 1:1–2; Rosenthal, 282).[58]

While Rosenthal keeps his focus on linguistic features, his 19th-century philology hampers him from adequately making sense of the many connections he identifies. Assuming that classical Hebrew was on the wane when these later biblical books were written,[59] Rosenthal suggests that these correspondences reflect linguistic necessity. "Hier hätten wir also einen Beleg dafür vor uns," he concludes, "dass man für die Darstellung späterer Verhältnisse, weil die Sprache nicht mehr lebendig war, die Erzählungen der alten Bücher der Bibel zum Vorbild genommen hat" (284).

Writing some 60 years later, Moshe Gan crucially expands Rosenthal's philological focus to emphasize how Joseph and Esther share significant literary motifs, as well.[60] Pointing out how the protagonists' rises in each story stand as the culmination of a series of upward and downward movements, Gan shows how both tales pivot at banquets attended by invited guests who do not know their hosts' true motivations (147). As the brothers attend Joseph's banquet (Gen 43:25–34), they enter the vizier's house without even knowing who is hosting them, and, when excitedly coming to the first banquet the queen requests (Esth 5:5–8), Haman arrives completely unaware of Esther's intention to finger him as the guilty author of the terrible edict.

Having recognized the parallels in these two banquets, Gan then demonstrates overlap in their aftermaths. In the Joseph story, the brothers leave the vizier's dinner surprisingly happy and relieved only to be surprised yet again. Overtaken by Joseph's accusing servant, they are then forced back to Egypt despite their innocence (Gen 44:6–13). As this deep fall swings to engender the brothers' final and steepest rise – upon their return to Egypt, Joseph loses that steely self-control (ולא יכל יוסף להתאפק, Gen 45:1) and thus begins the most improbable process of familial reunification – the echo to the Megillah comes. For in Shushan, after attending the first banquet Esther has thrown, a happy and drunk Haman is on his way home when he sees Mordecai refusing even to stir (Esth 5:9). When this causes the prime minister to check himself publicly (ויתאפק המן, Esth 5:10) before raging privately (Esth 5:11–13), his own supporters then ironically seal his fate by recom-

---

58 As Rosenthal notes, Dan 5:13 is also to be seen in this context (282).

59 For a more up-to-date treatment of the history and development of classical Hebrew, see, for example, Joseph Naveh and Jonas C. Greenfield, "Hebrew and Aramaic in the Persian Period," in *The Cambridge History of Judaism*, vol. 1, eds. W. D. Davies and Louis Finkelstein (Cambridge: Cambridge University Press, 1984): 115–29.

60 Moshe Gan, "Megillat 'Esther Be'aspaqlariyat Qorot Yoseph Be'misrayim," *Tarbiz* 31 (1961): 144–49 [Hebrew].

mending that he erect a stake on which to impale Mordecai (Esth 5:14). That Mordecai is promptly honored (Esth 6:10–11) and Haman eventually impaled on his own
petard (Esth 7:9–10) highlights the reach of Gan's insight: the banquets in both
stories, thrown for motivations that remain unknown to their attendees, generate
the rising and falling actions that move key elements of both plots forward.

Despite the clear advance Gan's work represents, he concludes on a somewhat inconclusive note. "It is clear," he writes, "that the author of the Megillah
was influenced, consciously or unconsciously so, by the story of Joseph in Genesis,
and that he built his story with the inspiration of the story there, Genesis 39–41
in particular."[61] While Gan's hesitation concerning the intent of these overlaps
prevents him from exploring the interpretive implications of the very links he
illustrates, Shemaryahu Talmon, writing just two years after Gan, perceives the
relationship in a different but ultimately still singular frame: if Rosenthal fore-
grounds the philological and Gan the repetition of motifs, then Talmon suggests
that Esther's connections to Joseph are explained by the wisdom elements in both
stories.[62] Relying on Gerhard von Rad's take on Joseph,[63] Talmon concludes that
Esther, much like its counterpart in Genesis, represents a historicized wisdom-
tale. "Their [Esther and Joseph's] similarities therefore are to be accounted for
not only by their probable interdependence but also by their dependence upon
one common literary tradition" (454–55).

Such an interpretive scheme causes Talmon to appreciate intriguing links
between Mordecai, Haman, and Joseph, on the one hand, and the court-scribe
template, on the other. The role of each character "bring[s] him into contact with
foreign cultures," and requires that his loyalty remain to his earthly master and
his focus stay on the "proper execution of his functions at court" (434). While this
point is well-taken and may likely explain certain features that Mordecai, Haman,
and Joseph all share, Talmon's work falters when it asserts that Esther's characters display the kind of one-dimensional natures that express the values found
in the more usual instances of wisdom literature. Suggesting, for example, that
the Esther-Mordecai axis represents categorical good, while the Haman-Zeresh
pole indicates the dangers of evil, Talmon sees the Scroll characters operating as
flatter illustrations of these pre-determined ideals.

> The typological factor is further underlined by the lack of depth in the portrayal of the heroes
> which becomes even more obvious in the bare delineation of the minor figures, e.g. Ahasue-
> rus' courtiers, Esther's maids or Haman's sons. In contrast to the biblical historical narrative,

---

61 מתברר כי מחבר המגילה הושפע ביודעין או שלא ביודעין מסיפור הדברים בספר בראשית,
מ״א – ל״ט בפרקים בעיקר שם הסיפור בהשראת סיפורו את ובנה (144).
62 Talmon, "'Wisdom' in the Book of Esther."
63 Gerhard von Rad, "Josephsgeschichte und ältere Chokma," *VTSup* 1 (1953): 120–27.

> as best seen in the David-stories, the heroes of the Esther-narrative do not undergo any meaningful development. The situations change – the dramatis personae remain static in character. (440)

Ironically, however, Talmon's own argumentation comes to indicate the problematic aspect of his point. For even if static personal characters are hallmarks of a certain sort of biblical and Ancient Near Eastern wisdom, the dizzying ups and downs of the Megillah make such straightforward traits difficult to find in the most important Shushan characters.[64] In fact, gesturing in this direction himself, Talmon observes: "Their [Esther and Mordecai's] virtues become apparent in the subjection of their private interests to the requirements of the communal weal, whereas Haman was prepared to sacrifice a nation in order to satisfy his personal hatred of one man" (448). But by correctly noting the nuances of Esther and Mordecai's goodness, Talmon begins to undercut his overarching position. For as long as the two protagonists' wisdom is expressed through their dedication to a good that can come at the expense of their own personal wishes, then Esther's crucial character development, which represents a dynamic that pushes against any static understanding of her character, must be appreciated.

The most salient example of this decisive movement comes in Esther 4. When Mordecai first asks Esther to approach the king, the good of her people is the furthest thing from her mind (Esth 4:8–11), and it is exactly this selfish impulse that Mordecai must work to cut through. That Mordecai appeals to her own safety (Esth 4:13–14) in his effort to convince her to act on behalf of her people emphasizes the point: since Esther is not initially inclined to use her position of influence for a good greater than her own, she must fundamentally change if she is going to become a wise and courageous queen.

As opposed to the definitive moral lessons of staid characters, this dramatic plot articulates Esther's unique circumstance. Once a young woman characterized by benevolent obedience (Esth 2:10, 15), Esther must transform herself into an active ruler capable of delivering herself and her people from imminent danger. Without denying the presence and importance of certain wisdom features in the Scroll, these reflections suggest that much as the Megillah is not entirely encapsu-

---

64 Picking up on these threads, Day suggests that even if Haman is the epitome of evil and Ahasuerus the hapless king, the heroic nature of the Jewish characters is more complex. After noting how Mordecai remains an "enigma" (*Esther*, 6), she indicates the significance of the queen's transformation. "Esther, as is often noted, is the only character who approaches a rounded personality. More than one-dimensional, she is also the only character to change throughout the course of the story. First seen as a passive young girl, Esther matures into a shrewd and courageous individual who determines the future of an entire population" (6). Thus, even if Talmon is right about the minor characters, a differentiation between them and the more developed protagonists must be appreciated.

lated by a wisdom designation, neither can its connections to Joseph be fully appreciated through this one analytic lens.

Pointing to a related issue, Arndt Meinhold notes the problems that come with Talmon's uncritical acceptance of von Rad's thesis concerning Joseph, as Joseph's intricacies, Meinhold argues, also expand beyond this one genre designation and thus complicate any comparison that hinges on it.[65] Given this well-placed concern, it is curious to note how Meinhold's program is dedicated to a similar sort of interpretation. For much as Talmon before him, Meinhold also sets out to prove that the similarities between the two stories are best explained by a shared literary genre. While Talmon's work emphasizes the ideals of wisdom literature, Meinhold focuses on twelve plot stages that, in his mind, comprise the *Diasporanovelle*.[66]

After both tales begin with a *Vorgeschichte* (I, 311; II, 76), a smaller *Aufstiegs-bericht* introduces the origins of each protagonist's favor and success (I, 315–16; II, 78–79). In this section, Meinhold also notes how the difficulties for the protagonists in both stories start to add up. After Potiphar's wife slanders Joseph (Gen 39:14–18), an intensifying famine brings the threat of starvation (Gen 41:54, 42:1), and, after Haman devises his murderous plan (Esth 3:8–9), the king unwittingly authorizes it as the unchangeable law of the empire (Esth 3:10–11).[67]

Faced with such overwhelming challenges, the main characters must then work to fight off these terrible possibilities. If the cupbearer's faulty memory para-

---

65 Arndt Meinhold, "Die Gattung der Josephsgeschichte und des Estherbuches: Diasporanovelle," Part II, *ZAW* 88:1 (1976): 72–93; for the specifics of Meinhold's critique of von Rad, see 74–75.

66 While "Die Gattung," Part II describes how Esther fits into the *Diasporanovelle*, then "Die Gattung der Josephsgeschichte und des Estherbuches: Diasporanovelle," Part I, *ZAW* 87 (1975): 306–24 explores how Joseph also represents this designation. Noting the deep influence Meinhold's work has exerted, especially in German-speaking scholarship, Blum and Weingart's recent article, "The Joseph Story," develops an incisive critique. While they raise a number of crucial considerations, two intertwined points stand out in the present context. First, much as the Egyptians' benefit is not the point of the story, neither does the text actually insist on the uniqueness of the Israelite God, as Meinhold would have it (511–12). Second, with this diaspora accent present in the text but not as controlling for the meaning, they note how other texts from the Ancient Near East – Egypt, in particular – also take place in foreign lands but were certainly not written in a diaspora setting. In other words, just because the story takes place outside the land does not mean it was written only for an exilic audience. As Blum and Weingart put it: "Its own [Joseph's] claim seems rather to be that survival was in this case only possible in Egypt due to divine providence (Gen 45:5 ff.; 50:20 f.). Generalizing and applying such an understanding to the Diaspora, however, would completely twist the meaning of the exile from an act of judgement to an act of salvation history" (513). While appreciating the force of these points, the present analysis still recognizes how Meinhold's work draws out significant parallels between Joseph and Esther's literary structures.

67 Naming such actions "Die Standhaftigkeit trägt der Hauptperson Schwierigkeiten und Gefahren ein," Meinhold draws a parallel from Gen 39:13–20a to Esth 3:4b, 5–15 (I, 315; and, II, 81–82).

doxically brings Joseph before the Pharaoh at precisely the right moment (Gen 41:9–14), then Mordecai's uncouth reaction (Esth 4:1–2) convinces Esther to move past her own danger and intercede with the king (Esth 4:7–16; Meinhold I, 316 and II, 82).[68] When these paralleled developments then raise Joseph, Esther, and Mordecai in their respective foreign courts, Meinhold perceives a direct comparison developing. If Joseph represents an effort to bring the universal and particular into theological unity,[69] then Esther reflects a contrastive mindset. "Sie [the Esther novella] hat eher polemischen Charakter, der sich gegen ein Diasporaverständnis richtet, das sich in einer von Jahwe gewirkten aktiven Zuwendung dem Fremdvolk gegenüber entfaltet, wie es in der Josephsgeschichte gestaltet ist" (II, 92).

Despite the clear structural advances Meinhold's work brings, such an analysis also admits of the problems that one-dimensional approaches to Esther's relationship with Joseph tend to create. Much as Talmon and von Rad's stricter wisdom designation does not adequately reckon with Esther and Joseph's multiple literary facets, then so does Meinhold's notion of a particular Esther responding to a universal Joseph betray the rigidity of his formal approach. For by examining each stage of Esther and Joseph's plots on their own, Meinhold's program overlooks an important irony embedded in the interaction of Joseph's different constituent parts. Since the Egyptians are only able to stay alive because of Joseph's prescient food-storing plan, they must then enslave themselves to a program initiated by a previously enslaved Israelite (Gen 47:18–26). Thus, if von Rad overstates Joseph's links to the wisdom tradition – as Meinhold in part shows – then Meinhold himself overstates any controlling concern the story shows for a universal good. This critique once again takes on a familiar shape. Instead of denying certain universalistic impulses in Joseph, it emphasizes how Joseph's admittedly present universalism cuts in multiple, and at times even conflicting, directions to limit the reach and accuracy of any genre designation that relies on only one aspect of it.

While Rosenthal, Gan, Talmon, and Meinhold's analyses seek, albeit in different ways, to explain much of Esther's relationship to Joseph through individual

---

68 "Eigene Aktivität der Hauptperson, um die Schwierigkeiten und Gefahren abzuwehren," according to Meinhold (I, 316; and, II, 82).

69 "Die *Theologie der Josephsgeschichte*," Meinhold explains, "ist geprägt von dem Versuch ihres Verfassers, die universalistischen und die partikularistischen Tendenzen der Geschichte theozentrisch zu einigen ... Da das Volk Josephs nach Gen 41:57 lediglich unter כל הארץ subsumiert ist, liegt hier aller Nachdruck auf einem theologisch begründeten Universalismus. Das Fremdland mit seinen weltlichen Problemen ist akzeptiert, ja mehr noch: das positive Engagement für das Fremdland ist von Gott gewollt und gewirkt, legitimiert. Die freundliche Haltung gegenüber dem Fremdland durchzieht nicht nur die Kap. 39–41, sondern ist für die gesamte Josephsgeschichte bezeichnend" (I, 320).

factors, Sandra Beth Berg's 1979 work represents an early movement toward a more integrative approach.[70] Consider, for example, her take on the similarities and differences between Joseph's dramatic jailbreak and Mordecai's unexpected defeat of Haman.

> The two eunuchs in the Joseph story play a significant role, while they are of minor importance in Esther. In Genesis, Joseph's ability to interpret the eunuchs' dreams anticipates Joseph's subsequent explanation of Pharaoh's dreams. Joseph's success at dream interpretations demonstrates that he ironically lives up to the contemptuous nickname given by his brothers, "lord of dreams." The account of the two eunuchs in the Joseph narrative functions as an integral part of a dream motif which pervades the story.

> By contrast, Esth 2:21–23 plays a less significant role in the tale. The primary function of this notice is to allow Haman to honor Mordecai in Esther 6. This reward in turn presages the change in fortune of the Jewish people. Following the brief notice of their conspiracy, the eunuchs inconspicuously drop out of the story; they are executed two verses after their introduction into the account. Joseph's successful interpretation of dreams leads directly to his promotion at court. Mordecai, however, remains "at the king's gate" following his discovery of the eunuchs' plot against Ahasuerus. He is elevated to a position of power at court only after Esther informs Ahasuerus of Mordecai's relationship to her. (126–27)

Continuing to note how overarching similarities can lead to telling discrepancies of detail, Berg perceives a key difference in Esther and Joseph's ultimate stances. Though Joseph invokes God sparingly, the story still makes it clear that God is the actual reason behind Joseph's elevation (177); Esther, in contradistinction, never once mentions God and, in so doing, accentuates a two-pronged theology. On the one hand, Berg argues, the Scroll asserts "the role of human responsibility in shaping history"; on the other, it "indicate[s] the hiddenness of God's control of history" (179). Thus, if Fox feels that Esther's divine silence creates a theology of indeterminacy, Berg sees the two aspects she identifies combining to create a religious conditionality.

> The events at Susa indicate that Yahweh continues to act, in some sense, in history for the benefit of His chosen people. In the Book of Esther, however, the assurance that history will prove beneficial to the people of Israel is not total; it is conditional. Only when each individual Jew is willing to assume responsibility for the fate of his/her people is Israel's place in history assured. Each Jew thereby shares with God the responsibility for the successful outcome of events, and plays his/her role in the *Heilsgeschichte*. (183)

While Berg's attention to the ways in which Esther and Joseph both correspond to and diverge from each other marks yet another step forward in the scholarly understanding of the intertextual relationship, her emphasis on later Jewish re-

---

70 Sandra Beth Berg, *The Book of Esther: Motifs, Themes, and Structure* (Missoula, MT: Scholars Press, 1979).

sponses and insistence on finding God's activity where the divine is not follow key aspects of previous scholarship (§ 1.1). In some distinction to these more hewn interpretive paths, the following subsection brings a second textual example that continues to articulate the distinct approach followed here. As opposed to linguistic necessity, genre similarity, or comparisons of a direct sort, this next discussion once again indicates how Esther's consistent invoking of Joseph's language, themes, and narrative developments presents the Egyptian parallels as a suggestive backdrop for the Shushan events.

2.3 The Shared Syntax of Judah and Esther's Decisive Speeches

To demonstrate this point, consider Jacob's paternal conflict, on the one hand, and Esther's royal problem, on the other. After Jacob's sons jealously toss their younger brother into a waterless pit, it all starts falling apart. First comes the famine (Gen 41:53–54) and then the loss of Simeon to an unusually harsh vizier (Gen 42:19, 24). That the brothers must also bring Benjamin back with them if they ever are to return to Egypt (Gen 42:20) doubles the difficulty: not only must they now return to their father with yet another brother missing, but so must they also try to convince Jacob to release Benjamin – exactly what he has been trying to prevent (Gen 42:4) – into their increasingly unreliable hands. When Reuben then endeavors to break the deadlock by foolishly wagering his two sons' lives (Gen 42:37), Jacob's reluctance to send his youngest (Gen 42:4) seems all the more justified.

As the famine then intensifies (Gen 43:1), and Jacob is forced to ask his sons to procure more food (Gen 43:2), Judah begins the first of his two decisive speeches by outlining the impossibility of his father's stance. Since the vizier demanded that either the youngest brother join them or the rest of the brothers be met with death, Jacob, Judah reminds, cannot have both: the remaining sons can either go procure food, or Benjamin and the rest can stay home at the risk of starvation for all (Gen 43:3–5). After Jacob continues to hesitate (Gen 43:6–7), Judah makes his final plea. "Send the boy in my care," he urges his father, "and let us be on our way, that we may live and not die – you and we and our children!" (Gen 43:8).

When Jacob resignedly assents – "If it must be so" (Gen 43:11) – a key shift emerges. Even if Jacob sends Benjamin reluctantly, his selfless decision to risk Benjamin for the sake of his whole family brings an initial and unexpected twist of good fortune to a family wracked with difficulty. Upon the brothers' second arrival in Egypt, their invitation to dine with the vizier (Gen 43:16) coincides with yet another surprisingly positive twist – Simeon's prompt return (Gen 43:23). But just as quickly as their father's change of heart switched momentum in their favor, so does the ricochet of their own jealousy boomerang back against them. After leaving with everything for which they dared to hope – the precious grain, the brother who was held, and the one they have been at pains to protect – the vizier then entraps them for theft and makes Benjamin appear the guiltiest party (Gen 44:1–2).

As the brothers rush back to the vizier (Gen 44:13), the reversals at the core of Joseph's previously initiated test crystalize. If Joseph was kidnapped from the land of the Hebrews (Gen 37:28) and did nothing to deserve being thrown into that dungeon (Gen 40:15), then so are the brothers now wrongfully accused and unfairly forced to return to face bondage in Egypt; moreover, just as Joseph had no recourse whatsoever to getting himself out of wrongful incarceration and had to wait helplessly for the cupbearer to remember him, so must the brothers, with all of the evidence stacked against them, now hope for the impossible clemency of the vizier.

As the seeming intractability of this situation in Genesis 44 reminds of the dilemma Jacob faced in Genesis 43, Judah once again steps forward with his growing oratory prowess. Since he is unable to accept the outcome that appears sealed, his words demonstrate the selfless maturation that Joseph's test has been designed to detect. If the brothers once held Joseph's elevated familial status against him, now Judah shows his unshakeable newfound determination to protect his father's other favored son – even at the cost of his own freedom.

> Your servant my father said to us, "As you know, my wife bore me two sons. But one is gone from me, and I said: Alas, he was torn by a beast! And I have not seen him since. If you take this one from me, too, and he meets with disaster, you will send my white head down to Sheol in sorrow." Now, if I come to your servant my father and the boy is not with us – since his own life is so bound up with his – when he sees that the boy is not with us, he will die, and your servants will send the white head of your servant our father down to Sheol in grief. Now your servant has pledged himself for the boy to my father, saying, "If I do not bring him back to you, I shall stand guilty before my father forever." Therefore, please let your servant remain as a slave to my lord instead of the boy, and let the boy go back with his brothers. For how can I go back to my father unless the boy is with me? Let me not be witness to the woe that would overtake my father! (Gen 44:27–34)

While this sacrifice for Benjamin balances against the violent jealousy the brothers previously perpetrated against Joseph, the unusual syntax of Judah's final words – כי איך אעלה אל אבי והנער איננו אתי פן אראה ברע אשר ימצא את אבי (Gen 44:34) – finds direct echo in a speech Esther gives toward the end of the Megillah. After learning of Haman's horrendous decree, Mordecai sees his position tighten in familiar fashion. If Jacob's sons have to find some way to convince their father to release Benjamin so that they can escape famine and death, then so must Mordecai, in Esther 4, rouse a recalcitrant queen into action or else face the bloody consequences of the prime minister's sealed decree.

Much as Judah decides to face his obstinate father and coax him to send his beloved Benjamin so that the youngest can appear before a dangerous foreign ruler for his family's sake (Gen 43:3–10), so must Mordecai plead for Esther to put her personal concern aside and approach the Persian king on her helpless people's behalf (Esth 4:7–14). While the foolishness of Reuben's first attempt only hardens Jacob's stubborn resistance (Gen 42:37–38), then so is Mordecai's first pass batted away by the queen's growing concern for herself. By reminding him of a law he should already know, she too begins with a demurral. "All the king's courtiers and the people of the king's provinces know that if any person, man or woman, enters the king's presence in the inner court without having been summoned, there is but one law for him – that he be put to death. Only if the king extends the golden scepter to him may he live. Now I have not been summoned to visit the king for the last thirty days" (Esth 4:11).

Just as Judah pushes past his father's first refusal (Gen 42:38) and eventually succeeds in convincing him (Gen 43:11–14), so does Mordecai remain undeterred in the face of Esther's initial objection. "Do not imagine," he rejoins in famous fashion, "that you, of all the Jews, will escape with your life by being in the king's palace. On the contrary, if you keep silent in this crisis, relief and deliverance will come to the Jews from another quarter, while you and your father's house will perish. And who knows, perhaps you have attained to royal position for just such a crisis" (Esth 4:13–14).

When Esther then agrees (Esth 4:14–16), the parallels to Joseph continue. Much as Jacob's assent puts Benjamin's life in the unpredictable vizier's control, so does Esther now find her wellbeing perilously dependent on the whims of her impetuous husband; if the brothers' fortunes unexpectedly turn in their favor after Judah makes his second impassioned plea (Gen 45:1 f.), so is the queen's decision to approach Ahasuerus unlawfully met not with life-threatening danger but rather overwhelming graciousness. "'What troubles you, Queen Esther?' the king asked her. 'And what is your request? Even to half the kingdom, it shall be granted you'" (Esth 5:3). After the queen uses her favor to set up a series of banquets for deposing Haman (Esth 5:6–8; 7:1–10), she then turns to address the former prime minister's still valid edict. "If it pleases the king," she entreats the Persian ruler,

> and if I have won his favor, and if the thing seems right before the king, and I have his approval, let an order be written to revoke the letters devised by Haman son of Hammedatha the Agagite, which he wrote giving orders to destroy the Jews who are in all the provinces of the king. For how can I bear to see the disaster which will befall my people! And how can I bear to see the destruction of my kindred! (Esth 8:5–6)

Since the similarities between Esther's last plea and Judah's final words come out most strongly in Hebrew, they are worth comparing directly.

Gen 44:34: כי איך אעלה אל אבי והנער איננו אתי פן אראה ברע אשר ימצא את אבי

Esth 8:6: כי איככה אוכל וראיתי ברעה אשר ימצא את עמי ואיככה אוכל וראיתי באבדן
מולדתי

After the two verses begin with a form of the adverb אֵיך, an imperfect verbal form follows; then comes a conjugated form of the root ר.א.ה, imperfect in Genesis and converted perfect in Esther, followed by a relative אשר clause with a conjugated form of the verbal root מ.צ.א: from Judah, פן אראה ברע אשר ימצא את אבי, and from Esther, וראיתי ברעה אשר ימצא את עמי. Moreover, despite the lexical difference between the two objects of מ.צ.א, "my father" for Judah and "my people" for Esther, both terms are semantically quite similar, as Esther's people, עמי, are the very sons and daughters of Jacob, who is, of course, Judah's father, אבי.

While Rosenthal's work simply notes these philological correspondences,[71] this analysis highlights how the aftermaths of the two unusually effective speeches also intertwine. Though the unchangeability of Persian law ties Ahasuerus' maladroit hands, he still manages to maneuver a way for Esther and Mordecai to author a counter-decree calling for Jewish self-defense. "You may further write with regard to the Jews as you see fit. [Write it] in the king's name and seal it with the king's signet, for an edict that has been written in the king's name and sealed with the king's signet may not be revoked" (Esth 8:8). Thus, in both Genesis and the Scroll, this distinct syntax sows the seeds for resolutions: as Judah's words in Egypt demonstrate to Joseph that the brothers' dedication to Benjamin makes the family ready for reunification, so does Ahasuerus' response to Esther's plea allow for the Jews to fight off the still present and dangerous residue of Haman's murderous intent.

That so much of this movement hangs on the distinctive syntax highlights how the different aspects of the relationship combine. In the Scroll, just as in Joseph, swings of fortune are articulated with identical roots (א.פ.ק) and similar syntaxes (כי איך), as the actions in both stories pivot on main characters' abilities to control their own emotions and speak convincingly to foreign rulers in moments of serious danger. While previous scholarship has tended to isolate these features and then seek to make sense of them individually, the present approach underscores the import of seeing these linguistic, thematic, and narrative connections in holistic fashion. For when that is done, the fourth rung of Ben-Porat and Sommer's allusive ladder is approached, as the parallels to the entire Joseph story begin to be recalled throughout the telling of the whole Megillah.

---

71 "In ganz gleichem Satzbau," Rosenthal writes in his usual laconic style, "spricht Ester in ähnlicher Lage" ("Die Josephsgeschichte," 281).

3 Other Intertextual Relationships and Esther and Joseph's Good Looks

3.1 Approaches to Esther's Other Intertextual Connections

With the basic parameters of Esther's connections to Joseph established and the general ways the relationship has been understood sketched, attention now turns to the scholarly efforts to explore Esther's other intertextual associations. If the connections between the Scroll and Joseph have usually been seen in narrower terms, then this chapter indicates how scholarship on Esther's intertextual links with other biblical texts has tended in the opposite direction. By straying from the methodological rigor outlined by Leonard, Sommer, and Ben-Porat, commentators interested in Esther's links to the exodus, Saul cycle, and David story have afforded these other relationships an overly expansive exegetical significance. After noting some of the problems this interpretive pattern has generated, a third example of Esther's specific interaction with Joseph brings Part One to a close by demonstrating how the present approach distinguishes itself from these past works.

3.1.1 Gerleman and the Exodus

Gillis Gerleman's innovative 1970 study illustrates some of these very concerns.[72] Suggesting that a series of internal lacks found throughout the Megillah necessitates recourse to an outside text, Gerleman proposes a broad-ranging intertextuality that sees Esther only making sense once its references to Exodus are heard. Since, for example, there is no reason for Mordecai and Esther to share the protagonist's role, Gerleman suggests that the doubled characters must be alluding to Moses and Aaron (14); in similar fashion, as Esther's unusual familial background plays no substantive role in the Megillah, Gerleman claims that this feature must be an allusion to Moses as an adopted son (15); finally, since Esther keeps her Jewishness hidden for no explicit reason, this action, according to Gerleman, can only be explained by Moses' secret identity in Pharaoh's court (16).

While such an approach finds a Scroll littered with gaps for which the Megillah itself does not account, a fairer read of Esther's internal integrity gestures to key problems in Gerleman's scheme. Consider how this dynamic plays out in Gerleman's take on the repeated banquets Esther requests. Insisting that creating the space for the telling twist in Esther 6 is not sufficient reason for this elongated

72 Gillis Gerleman, *Esther* (Neukirchen-Vluyn: Neukirchener Verlag Des Erziehungsvereins, 1973).

https://doi.org/10.1515/9783111216119-003

action, Gerleman once again suggests that this apparently purposeless narrative feature can only be understood on analogy to Exodus: much as the Pharaoh's ultimate decision is consistently postponed, so does Esther push off her decisive moment with the Persian king (19–20).

For Gerleman, this sustained narrative dependency results in a direct exegetical comparison. If the Israelites are threatened with the hard labor of slavery in Egypt, then the Jews of Persia are confronted with something far worse – complete annihilation. Thus, since deliverance in Exodus relies on God's intervention, Esther's more dramatic rescue has purposefully removed all religious tones to present a sarcastic critique of the earlier tale.

> Die literarisch-strukturelle Affinität des Estherbuches zur Exoduserzählung aktualisiert aufs neue eine merkwürdige Tatsache: das durchaus weltliche Gepräge des Buches. Gewöhnlich hat man das so erklären wollen, der Erzähler habe wegen des profanen Märchen- und Sagenstoffes alle theologischen Gesichtspunkte fernhalten wollen. Wie wir gesehen haben, ist der verwendete Stoff gart nicht profan, sondern im Gegenteil einer hochsakralen heilge-schichtlichen Überlieferung entnommen. Es handelt sich nicht um einen heidnischen, mit einer theologischen Geschichtsschau schwerlich zu vereinbarenden Erzählstoff, sondern um eine bewußte und konsequente Entsakralisierung und Enttheologisierung einer zentralen heilgeschichtlichen Tradition. Daß die Exodusgeschichte dem Esthererzähler als Literatur vorgelegen hat, darüber kann kein Zweifel bestehen. Was auffällt, ist die seltsame Art, wie dieser geistige Besitz von ihm gepflegt wird: anlehnend, überbietend, kritisch. (23)

Even though the field has viewed these conclusions with general skepticism,[73] the present approach develops two fresh critiques to situate the analytical lines the present study follows. The first returns to Leonard's linguistic criteria. Since Gerleman trains his focus on ideological intent, he gives less attention to specific verbal parallels; as a result, his philological evidence is often wanting. Take, for example, his effort to connect Esther to Exodus through the repetition of אִישׁ and מָקוֹם. Arguing that Esth 9:4 alludes to Ex 11:3, Gerleman points out that a character's name is followed by the word "man" only six other times in the Hebrew Bible (17). While this qualification does indicate the infrequency of this

---

73 While Carey Moore's review (*JBL* 94:2 [1975]: 293–96) notes Gerleman's important contributions, it expresses general hesitation. "While I willingly concede that there may be some influence (conscious or unconscious) of the Exodus story on the Book of Esther, that influence is not, I think, controlling or overriding" (295). In German scholarship, Meinhold articulates a similar sentiment: "Wenn er [Gerleman] meint, es handle sich beim Erzählstoff des Estherbuches 'um eine bewußte und konsequente Entsakralisierung und Enttheologisierung einer zentralen heils-geschichtlichen Tradition,' dann entsprich diese Qualifizierung nicht dem tiefen strukturellen wie theologischen Unterschied zwischen Exoduserzählung und Esth, daß nämlich in Ex ein Aus-zugsgeschehen aus dem Fremdland geschildert (und im Passahfest zu feiern) ist, in Esth dagegen ein Verbleiben und Überleben der jüdischen Diaspora im Fremdland gedeutet und bewältigt wird (und mit dem Purimfest gefeiert werden kann)" ("Die Gattung," II, 74).

particular combination, the commonness with which the word אִישׁ is used and the generic nature of such a phrase throw doubt onto the worth of the philological case.

Precisely this problem extends to his analysis of Esth 4:14 and Ex 3:5, as well. In addition to both verses containing מָקוֹם, Gerleman sees connections between their contexts. "Es macht die Übereinstimmung besonders eindrücklich, daß die betreffenden Szenen einander architektonisch genau entsprechen. Hier wie dort handelt es sich um die Gelegenheit, wo der künftige Retter den Auftrag erhält, zur Hilfe Israels einzuschreiten" (19). The rejoinder, however, is equally doubled: if a word as common as מָקוֹם does not fulfill the spirit of Leonard's linguistic criteria, then both scenes narrating an opportunity for helpful intervention falls short of demonstrating architectonic correspondence. While these two examples are anchored in at least some linguistic link, certain specific correspondences Gerleman notes have no philological basis whatsoever. Pointing to an intriguing similarity between Moses' hesitation to speak with Pharaoh and Esther's initial preference not to appear before Ahasuerus, Gerleman argues that this particular Scroll scene in Esther 4 invokes the elongated Exodus action (18). In all the verses he notes, however (Esth 4:11 ff.; and, Ex 3:11; 4:10, 13; 6:12, 30), no philological connection is explored; as a result, these resonances, however suggestive they may be, remain unsubstantiated.

Though important in their own right, these methodological concerns become all the weightier when the individual points to which they are objecting are shown to exert an outsized influence over the ultimate exegetical conclusions Gerleman reaches. Since his looser intertextual controls allow him to see an Esther filled with references to Exodus, he claims that such allusions form the fundamental purpose of the book. "Die Geschichte von Esther und Purim," Gerleman writes, "ist von Anfang an als ein Gegenstück zur Erzählung von Exodus und Passah angelegt und gestaltet worden" (13).

The details, however, paint a different picture. Even if Esther's demurral echoes Moses' hesitation, and הָאִישׁ מָרְדֳּכַי הוֹלֵךְ וְגָדוֹל (Esth 9:4) recalls הָאִישׁ מֹשֶׁה גָּדוֹל מְאֹד (Ex 11:3), the identification of the source text, the second level of Ben-Porat and Sommer's allusive ladder, might very well be achieved. However, the absence of philological specificity combines with the contextual divergences noted to prevent all of the Exodus details from being consistently conjured throughout the rest of the Megillah. As these disjunctions suggest that any correspondences Esther develops with Exodus do not reach Sommer and Ben-Porat's fourth level, the second major objection to Gerleman's work is shown to extend out of the first. Since a good number of the individual allusions he posits are not entirely convincing cases, then the ranging exegetical conclusions he draws are shown to stretch beyond the textual evidence his work provides.

3.1.2 Expansive Intertextuality in Grossman's Hidden Reading

In many ways, Jonathan Grossman's work on Esther represents a sharp turn from Gerleman.[74] If Gerleman sees Esther's allusions to one other biblical text suggesting a critical posture toward dominant aspects of the Ancient Israelite religious tradition, then Grossman detects a series of references pulling the Scroll unmistakably toward the more prominent biblical themes of land, law, and temple. In other regards, however, these opposed conclusions betray an underlying similarity; for as this analysis of Grossman endeavors to show, his work, much as Gerleman's, also hinges on the assumption that Esther's own words fall significantly short of conveying that which the text is actually intended to communicate.

While Gerleman reaches this interpretive standpoint by concentrating on Esther's posited interactions with Exodus, Grossman finds a similar position in the universality of shrouded meanings. "We will find it useful," Grossman writes at the very beginning of his book, "to designate the narrative, at the very outset, as one that contains hidden messages; this designation then serves as a point of departure for the process of reading and decoding the narrative" (3). In Esther's case, this hidden meaning carries a particularly striking aspect. Instead of working alongside the plain sense of the text, Esther's concealed sense, Grossman argues, stands in contradistinction to its actual words. "The presence of concealed meanings (which we may assert of every narrative *qua* narrative) does not adequately characterize the book of Esther; rather, its uniqueness lies in the fact that these concealed messages actually assert the opposite of what the revealed plane expresses" (10).

Tellingly, Grossman's interpretation of Esther's text only begins after these fundamental exegetical poles have been established, and, as is so often the case, his specific conclusions come to reflect his starting position. Since, in his view, Esther's hidden plane is destined to overturn its plain sense, he sees the basic level of Esther 2 and the king's indiscriminate collecting of virgins portraying Ahasuerus in a positive light. After suggesting that the king's power is expressed by "provid[ing] the young women of the kingdom with every sort of benefit," Grossman goes on to argue that this episode also highlights Ahasuerus' magnanimousness. "The gathering of the women," Grossman writes, "reflects not only the the king's power but also, as noted, his generosity: the king showers all the young women brought to the palace with perfumes and ointments" (58).

If this surface narrative promotes a magnanimous king, then the hidden level, which is marked by a series of covert but crucial allusions to other biblical texts, undermines the otherwise favorable depiction. "A reader who is open to

---

74 Jonathan Grossman, *Esther: The Outer Narrative and the Hidden Reading* (Winona Lake, IN: Eisenbrauns, 2011).

the hidden reading will sense the biting criticism that pervades the entire chapter [Esther 2]. The author's criticism of the way in which the new queen is chosen hints, as in so many other instances throughout the narrative, by means of an allusion, at a different narrative describing a search for a companion for the king" (58).

For Grossman, the first of these invoked texts comes from 1 Kings 1. Reminiscent of David authorizing a search to find a young woman to keep him warm in his old age, Ahasuerus also has his men seek out a new female companion for the king. As David sends his emissaries throughout his kingdom to look for a pretty young woman, ויבקשו נערה יפה בכל גבול ישראל (1 Kgs 1:3), so does Ahasuerus in Esth 2:2, יבקשו למלך נערות בתולות טובות מראה; in the very next verse, Esth 2:3, "all of the provinces" are invoked, בכל מדינות, much as the passage from 1 Kgs 1:3 speaks of the "entire area of Israel." But it is the differences between these two events, Grossman contends, that holds the key to unearthing the hidden reading and unlocking the true Scroll meaning.

> In contrast [to Ahasuerus' gathering of all the virgins], the proposal of David's servants is that the king's emissaries should go all about the country seeking a fair maiden; the one whom they deem suitable shall be brought to the king's palace. This difference is not trivial – especially from the perspective of the women themselves. The women who spend the night in the palace but ultimately are not chosen as queen may not return to their families or marry another man. After each has had her liaison with the king, she "leaves in the morning for a second harem" (2:14), where she must live as one of the king's concubines. The personal tragedy of each of them is obvious: each woman can only live in hope that one day the king will remember her and call upon her again for another one-time encounter ... The association with the alternative scene, the finding of a companion for David, invites criticism of Ahasuerus and his treatment of women. As the story of David demonstrates, the process could have been undertaken in a different way. (59)

In this line of thinking, the next set of allusions found in Esther 2 references the Joseph story. Both texts record "appointing officers," ויפקד פקידים (Gen 41:34, Esth 2:3), both employ the root for "keeping," ש.מ.ר, and both include a phrase for "pleasing": וייטב הדבר בעיני פרעה (Gen 41:37) and תיטב בעיני המלך (Esth 2:4). While Grossman sees the comparison with David hinging on a divergence, this interaction with Joseph, he argues, revolves around a similarity. "The perspective offered in this comparison gives readers the sense that the king treats the maidens like grain that must be gathered. The 'gathering' of the women from every place to the palace, where they are 'kept' in the hand of Hegai, indeed arouses an image of collecting objects or storing food for times of need" (60).

While appreciating the presence of both this connection to Joseph and the previous link to David, the present critique notes how a more complete read of the Megillah indicates that these allusions are not necessary for sensing Esther's satire of Ahausuerus and his court. As precisely the pericope that Grossman singles out makes so clear, the main thrust of the criticism leveled against the king does not come from an outside text but rather the Esther narrative itself.[75] When a reveling Ahasuerus summons the queen (Esth 1:10–11), his lack of control, and not his wife's intended beauty, comes out for all to see. As his personal insecurity is matched by his utter inability to fashion a response (Esth 1:12–15), Ahasuerus' decision to turn a private slight into unbendable state policy cements the mockery. Since he has no influence over Vashti, then all wives in his empire must always obey their husbands (Esth 1:16–22).

At this point, the underlying similarity between Grossman's and Gerleman's intertextual approaches strikes. Just as Gerleman's predilection for finding internal lacks throughout the Scroll causes him to see unsubstantiated external references carrying Esther's true meaning, so does Grossman's unnecessarily flat read of the Megillah cause him to see the real Shushan action occurring outside the bounds of the specific Scroll text. To appreciate the import of this concern, recall Grossman's point about Gen 41:37 and Esth 2:4. Though the linguistic connections certainly suggest meaningful textual interaction, the differences in narrative environments complicate Grossman's effort to see Esther as a new sort of stored grain. When Joseph recommends that the harvest during the next five years of plenty be gathered and then saved for the coming seven years of famine (Gen 41:33–36), the Pharaoh, all of Egypt, and the whole world are in great and impending danger. The course of action Joseph recommends is thus driven by his desire to encourage the Pharaoh to implement a policy that best addresses the complicated situation and responsibly serves his subjects. By contrast, Ahasuerus has all the virgins in his vast empire gathered to his palace to solve a problem that causes no danger and his own drinking parties generated.

Instead of denying a deliberate allusion between these verses, this critique rather takes issue with Grossman's predetermined view of the connection. Since the Scroll is not here creating a hidden meaning that likens Esther to a piece of food, its plain sense is able to generate the censure of Ahasuerus by repeatedly narrating inversions of the foolish law that his own fabricated crisis brings,[76]

---

75 On precisely this point, see, for example, Loader (*Ester*, 231–32), whose work notes the intertextual connections found in this Esther pericope but still attends to the sharp satire found in the Scroll itself.

76 When Haman returns home after his brief moment of self-control, he takes direction at a most crucial moment from his wife (Esth 5:14; § 2.1). If the prime minister's inability to fight his own battle reminds of the king's complete lack of personal and political control, it also mirrors Ahasuerus' need to take cues from Esther – exactly the opposite of what his supposedly unchangeable law requires (Esth 1:16–22). For after Harbonah has Haman hanged on Mordecai's stake (Esth 7:9–10), the king, still incapable of dealing with the scandalous fallout on his own, must defer to his wife's decisiveness. At her urging, he allows for the Jews to write a law of their own to reverse Haman's still live edict (Esth 8:5–8).

and, as this study returns now to continue demonstrating, this example proves illustrative for Esther's overarching intertextual stance. As opposed to completing narrative aims that the actual Megillah for one reason or another does not itself express, Esther's connections to Joseph rather deepen and expand those sentiments that are already present in the Scroll by providing an instructive backdrop against which the significance of the Shushan events comes into sharpest relief. One last review of previous intertextual scholarship underscores the necessity of this interpretive response.

3.1.3 Berger's Emphasis on Esther and Saul

Though Yitzhak Berger pursues an agenda entirely different from both Gerleman and Grossman, his work is still situated inside a well-known scholarly groove.[77] By highlighting Esther's connections to the Saul and David material, Berger picks up on the prominent connections between Esther and 1 Samuel.[78] His particular conclusion, however, marks a clear break with precedent. Instead of viewing the connections between the Saul narrative and Esther book as indicative of a link between Saul and Mordecai, as most commentators have tended to do,[79] Berger argues that the association is actually between Saul and Esther. In Berger's view, a number of points support such a claim. To begin with, since Mordecai is introduced in language similar to the introduction of Kish (Esth 2:5; 1 Sam 9:1), then the association must be intended for the followers of both characters: as Saul comes after Kish, so does Esther follow Mordecai (628). Moreover, in an interesting refraction of the argumentation developed above, Berger notes how "both Saul and Esther are described as good-looking (1 Sam 9:2; Esth 2:7)" (629).

In addition to these linguistic overlaps, Berger also examines a thematic parallel. "Throughout the two narratives, both Saul and Esther exhibit humility and reserve. Indeed, several specific manifestations of this might be seen to correspond to one another" (629). Much as Saul, Berger notes, complies with his father's wish and searches for the missing asses (1 Sam 9:3–4), so does Esther obey Mordecai's command and refrain from divulging her people's true identity (Esth 2:10–11), and, if Saul stays quiet when meeting young women at a well (1 Sam 9:11–13), then

---

77 Yitzhak Berger, "Esther and Benjaminite Royalty: A Study in Inner-Biblical Allusion," *JBL* 129:4 (2010): 625–644.

78 This interpretive trend was already noted by Berg in 1979. "Most modern commentators follow Josephus, the Talmud and the Targumim which view Haman as descended from Agag, the Amalekite king opposed by Saul (cf. 1 Sam 15). If the latter view is correct, the narrator again cites a genealogy which points to the figure of Saul" (66–67).

79 See, for example, Levenson, *Esther*, 56–57; Moore, *Esther*, 19–20, 35; and Berlin, *Esther*, 24–25.

Esther "takes no initiative even when a fuss is made over her as a potential mate for the king (Esth 2:15)" (629).

Berger sees these lines of continuity extending into Esther 4. As Saul remains silent after being derided (ויהי כמחריש, 1 Sam 10:27), he then brings his people to a victory (1 Sam 11:11) that leads to his Amalekite failure (1 Sam 15:15, 21, 24; Berger, 630). A similar pattern can be found in Esther: if the Jewish queen also initially stays quiet despite Mordecai's pleas (אם החרש תחרישי, Esth 4:14), "a transformation occurs" (630) that engenders a reversal. "Once again," Berger sums up, "all Israel is depending on Benjaminite leadership, and this time a newly energized Esther immediately takes charge (Esth 4:15–16), and will eventually save the Jews from their Agagite adversary" (630).

These links lead to Berger's most significant argument. Since רוח and הצלה (Esth 4:14) are also found in key moments in the Saul story (רוח in 1 Sam 10:10 and 16:1–13, and the root נ.צ.ל in 1 Sam 14:48 and frequently in 1 Samuel 30), their usage in the Megillah, in Berger's view, articulates an unvoiced ultimatum in Mordecai's plea to the Jewish queen. If Esther as a descendant of Benjamin does not agree to deliver her people in Esther 4, then, Berger argues, the Judahites surely will (634–35). As this approach offers a Davidic reading to the "other quarter" from which "relief and deliverance" (Esth 4:14) may come, it places the Shushan heroes in direct conflict with David's famous house. Mordecai, appointed by Saul's descendant Esther, becomes the legitimate successor Saul never had, and, if Solomon's actions toward the beginning of 1 Kings bring death inside the Israelite camp, then Mordecai's victory insures peace for the entire Jewish group (643–44).

Though Berger's work surely deepens the case for Esther's deliberate interaction with the Saul and David material, some important qualifications concerning the interpretive direction he chooses must be raised. In the first instance, while Berger is correct to note the paralleled language in the introductions of both Mordecai and Kish, the case for Saul and Esther's good looks is less convincing. Even though the two verses in question, 1 Sam 9:2 and Esth 2:7, make the same point, they do so with decidedly different language.

Esth 2:7: והנערה יפת תאר וטובת מראה

1 Sam 9:2: בחור וטוב ואין איש מבני ישראל טוב ממנו משכמו ומעלה גבה מכל העם

The next hesitation refers to the association between 1 Samuel 10 and Esther 4. While this connection is anchored with a specific verbal parallel, ח.ר.ש, the contexts of the two chapters admit of a discord deeper than Berger's work suggests. In Saul's case, the newly anointed king's silence reflects the people's opposed reactions to monarchy. While Samuel continues to register his objections to the royal institution (1 Sam 10:19), both he and the people ultimately accept the newly anointed Saul (1 Sam 10:24). However, in an ominous reminder of previous concerns (1 Sam 8:10–18), some scoundrels reject the Benjaminite ruler. "How can this fellow save us!" (1 Sam 10:27), they proclaim, and, when this dissident group then refuses even to bring tribute, Saul refrains from intervening: ויהי כמחריש (1 Sam 10:27).

As the people's disparate perspectives combine with Saul's hesitation to gesture toward the tormenting oppositions that come to mark Saul's kingship, the action in Esther 4 expresses an entirely different sentiment. While Saul's silence reflects a deep-seated ambivalence about the institution of Ancient Israelite kingship, Mordecai uses the same root to swing Esther into decisive action. These contextual divergences play out in the respective syntaxes. If the Samuel passage uses the participle to characterize that which Saul is doing, ויהי כמחריש, Esther employs a conditional clause in the imperfect, אם החרש תחרישי (Esth 4:14), to stress that which Esther must not do. Moreover, as the cross-currents that come with the establishment of monarchy continue to fluctuate all the way through David and his followers' rules, the Scroll narrative drives toward a Jewish victory that leaves no room for a sequel. To put it differently: instead of worrying that the queen's growing earthly influence might be an affront to God, Esther's decision to follow Mordecai's urgings marks a decisive turn in a story sorely in need of one.

In addition to these contextual considerations, the final point of the present critique responds to Berger's argument for links between Esther 4 and 1 Samuel 14–16 and 30. Once again, the issue hangs on the challenge of determining what actually indicates an intentional linguistic parallel. Though the roots Berger notes (ר.ו.ח and נ.צ.ל) are indeed reused, the forms of the specific words are crucially different. While Esther 4 employs the less frequent רֶוַח, or "relief," the Samuel passages refer to the far more common רוּח, or "spirit." To concretize the difference: of the five times that 1 Sam 16:13–16 uses רוּח, four of them are in construct to God, as רוּחַ יהוה and רוּחַ אלהים are both used twice (1 Sam 16:13, 14, and 1 Sam 16:15, 16), and the one time that רוּחַ stands on its own, it too is a spirit that God has given – רוּחַ רעה מאת יהוה (1 Sam 16:14). As this significant divergence combines with the frequency with which this particular nominal form of the root is used, the philological strength of Berger's case struggles to satisfy the idea at the heart of Leonard's criteria.

This very rejoinder extends to Esther and Samuel's usage of נ.צ.ל, as well. While Esth 4:14 is the only time in the entire Hebrew Bible that the noun הצלה is used, all five instances in which the same נ.צ.ל root is found in 1 Samuel 30 (30:8, 18, 22) come in far more frequent verbal forms. As a result of such considerations, the wide-ranging exegetical conclusions Berger reaches are called into some question. If Leonard's philological tightening suggests that Esther's allusions to the Saul-David material may not be as frequent as Berger thinks, then Sommer and Ben-Porat's scaffolded frame gestures yet again to the possibility of interpretive overextension. For once it is realized that Esther's usage of הצלה does not necessarily invoke each verbal usage of the same root in 1 Samuel, then the notion that the Megillah conjures the entirety of the Saul cycle becomes less compelling. As these considerations once again do not deny an intentional connection between the texts but rather indicate that such a relationship does not extend beyond the second or third referential layer Sommer and Ben-Porat articulate (that is, identifying the source text and then bringing that specific passage to mind), the problems with Berger's intertextual scheme – problems that both Gerleman and Grossman's works also encounter – come to the fore. By paying too little attention to the differences between the verbal parallels he identifies and the contexts in which such linguistic overlaps occur, Berger too affords an intertextual relationship an expansive significance that the text itself does not fully support.

In this way, the unusual nature of research into Esther's intertextuality can be seen. If the impulse to view Esther's connections to Joseph through one predetermined lens has caused that relationship to be understood in narrower fashions, then attempts to analyze Esther's other intertextual connections have seen a lack of methodological control result in conclusions ranging beyond the specific textual evidence presented. In light of these interpretive swings, this chapter concludes Part One of the present study by bringing one more example of Esther's specific textual links with Joseph to show how the present methodology inhabits a sort of intermediate position. Instead of reducing Esther's interaction with Genesis to any one key or suggesting that Esther's narrative meaning is actually found in another text, a third instance of specific connection between the Scroll and Genesis demonstrates how key aspects of Esther's story align themselves with crucial moments in Joseph's tale.

3.2 Joseph and Esther's Paralleled Good Looks

Similar to Joseph and Haman's struggles with their own self-control, Joseph and Esther's good looks are also phrased in nearly identical terms and play key roles in many of the ups and downs that mark the major swings of both stories. To begin exploring this next set of textual overlaps, consider the narrative background that leads up to the description of Joseph's good looks. When he is first introduced, his lower status as a young boy tending the flocks with the sons of his father's less favored wives is emphasized (Gen 37:2); when the very next verse pushes in the exact opposite direction by foregrounding his unexpected favor (Gen 37:3), a hint of the coming ups and downs emerges.[80] For just as his own

---

[80] For more on this point, see Jon D. Levenson, *Death and Resurrection of the Beloved Son: The Transformation of Child Sacrifice in Judaism and Christianity* (New Haven: Yale University Press, 1993), 143–46.

entry into the story balances difficulty against good fortune, so does the preferential treatment he receives from his father both separate him from the rest and, by engendering his brothers' jealousy, plunge him to the bottom of a waterless pit (Gen 37:23–24). Extending into Genesis 39, this distinctive alternation between favor and misfortune next manifests itself as a slave enjoying the trust of his earthly and heavenly masters (Gen 39:1–6), and in the middle of this telling repetition comes the notice of his good looks: "Joseph was beautiful of form and beautiful of appearance," ויהי יוסף יפה תאר ויפה מראה (Gen 39:6).

Lest his handsomeness afford him any respite from the dizzying ups and downs that have up to now defined his character, his attractiveness quickly turns into the source of his next and even deeper fall. When Potiphar's wife in the very next verse (Gen 39:7) begins her fateful approach – an approach that surely hinges on Joseph's unusual handsomeness – she twists both his clothes and the plot by slandering him to jail for his honest uprightness (Gen 39:17–20). Once Joseph is incarcerated, such weighty shifts start anew: as his jailing brings him to the royal cupbearer and baker (Gen 40:1–4), their dreams (Gen 40:5) coupled with his unique interpretive abilities (Gen 40:8–19) spin to set up his ascent over all Egypt. Thus, when Joseph takes his opportunity with the Pharaoh to suggest a set of prescient policies (Gen 41:25–44), the authority he comes to attain suggests that his striking appearance, which ignited this foreign portion of his rollercoaster ride, contains a significance beyond that which initially meets the eye.

If the notice of Joseph's good looks comes in the middle of his already sharp twists of fate, then Esther's appearance is foregrounded at the very moment of her introduction. "He [Mordecai] was foster father to Hadassah – that is, Esther – his uncle's daughter, for she had neither father nor mother. The maiden was shapely and beautiful"; in Hebrew, this final phrase is articulated in language nearly verbatim to Gen 39:6 – והנערה יפת תאר וטובת מראה (Esth 2:7). For a third time, this philological similarity also comes to punctuate a series of plot overlaps that extend beyond the specific scenes that contain the linguistic links.

For just as Joseph's handsomeness sends him past Potiphar's wife and to the top of the Egyptian court, so does Esther's attractiveness rouse the king into placing her into the seat of Persian royalty (Esth 2:17). In a fashion that reminds of Genesis, this upward trajectory, however, is quick to invert, as Esther's initial exaltation turns into the reason for her own grave danger. As Haman brings all the Jews to their knees (Esth 3:8–11; 4:1–3), the queen's proximity to the king, which previously symbolized the status her good looks helped her to achieve, becomes her entire people's only hope. Since, however, she has not been bidden in some thirty days (Esth 4:11), that which Mordecai comes to demand of her (Esth 4:8) quickly flips her good fortune into a clear and present threat: she either must break the unbreakable law by approaching the fickle king or risk her entire family's death at the hands of her people's nemesis (Esth 4:14).

When Esther finally assents to Mordecai's request and agrees to risk her own life for her people's sake (4:16), the criss-crosses with the Joseph story compound. Just as Joseph's principled fall at the hands of Potiphar's wife engenders his ascent in jail and subsequent rise over all Egypt, so does Esther's brave selflessness spin the real peril she stares down into her own incomparable influence over the whole Persian Empire. Upon her courageous approach, her mysterious favor exerts its silent force once again, and the king greets her uninvited advance with an unexpected graciousness (Esth 5:3). When Esther responds by requesting a series of banquets, she begins the process of wrestling the king away from the prime minister he selected and toward the queen he picked. By repeatedly positioning herself alongside Haman (Esth 5:5; 6:14–7:1), the queen emphasizes the momentum shift: if Haman enjoyed the king's ear to such an extent that Ahasuerus did not even bother to understand that which the prime minister was asking (Esth 3:11), the monarch is now so indebted to his wife – just as the Pharaoh is to Joseph – that he repeatedly follows her over both Haman and the evil edict the prime minister leaves as legacy (Esth 7:6–10; 8:3–8; 9:12–16).

Thus, in addition to noting the two protagonists' good looks, this analysis combines with the previous two examples (§ 2.1; § 2.3) to demonstrate that both the plot twists these handsome appearances generate and the unexpected influences they ultimately afford their characters add important layers to the philological connections noted. As both Esther and Joseph rise and fall in the confusing world of foreign courts, reversals of expectations set up ultimate deliverances from perils that previously threatened so intensely. While Grossman, Gerleman, and, to some extent, Berger assume that webs of inner-biblical links alter the force of this literary movement by filling in its supposed blanks, the present analysis operates from the opposite interpretive corner. Instead of upending the sense of the Megillah by completing that which Esther leaves out, Esther's sustained interaction with Joseph underscores how unusual roots, unique syntactical structures, and identical phrases position the internal coherence of the Scroll alongside Joseph's previous precedent.

3.3 Present Intertextual Directions

Taken together, the three textual examples and various reviews of scholarship found throughout Part One articulate the two major points that form the foundation of the present study. In the first instance, though this analysis appreciates that Esther knows and alludes to several biblical texts, attention to the linguistic, thematic, and narrative parallels to Genesis indicates the unique importance of Esther's sustained interaction with Joseph. To use Leonard's helpful phrasing: as the same rare words come to shape paralleled contexts, the main characters in both Egypt and Persia struggle with their own self-control (א.פ.ק) in ways that upend the dangerous expectations of foreign courts; moreover, these stories also pivot on the identical syntaxes that accompany decisive speeches (כי אין) and the unusual political influence that the favor of good looks can generate (יפה תאר ויפה מראה). In this way, the most crucial narrative action in Esther is shown to develop out of its philological links to Joseph and thus call all the events of the Joseph story to mind throughout the telling of the larger Megillah.

While this opening point is textual in nature, the second deals with the way these overlaps have usually been understood. If previous scholarship has separated the multi-facets of these connections to find relatively narrow intertextual purposes behind Esther's links to Joseph, while approaches to Esther's other inner-biblical allusions have tended to detect intertextual aims that range beyond the textual evidence presented, this approach prefers a different course. By cautioning against those interpretations that reduce Esther's allusiveness to any one aspect or view them as necessary for filling in internal gaps, overturning the plain sense of the actual text, or making the Scroll all about an inner-Israelite rivalry that is never mentioned, this reading notes how Esther's intertextual purpose is best appreciated when its narrative cohesiveness is read against Joseph's instructive backdrop. While the exegetical implications of reading Esther in this way are explored in detail in Part Three, the next section turns to compositional considerations to illustrate how the present argument for Esther's deliberate intertextual design must be informed by the diachronic development of the Scroll.

Part Two: **Compositional and Structural Considerations**

4 Esther's Compositional History and the Development of its Allusive Purpose

Since the present study is diachronically-oriented, two interrelated threads that have already been under discussion require further clarification. The first centers around Esther's authorship. While the current work is designed to demonstrate that MT Esther deliberately recalls Joseph, Ancient Near Eastern analogues for the Purim celebration and the ancient Greek versions of the Megillah have long suggested that no singular author wrote the whole Scroll.[81] As this initial concern complicates the current effort to prove authorial intent behind the intertextual design drawn out in Part One, the second deals with the correlated issue of Esther's literary unity. For if Chapters Two and Three argue that Esther's relationship with Joseph encourages the whole Megillah to be read against Joseph's instructive backdrop, then some of the same critical probes that have gestured to Esther's complex compositional history have also caused several leading critics to divide up the literary worth of the Scroll, as well.

Given the complicated and crucial nature of these issues, they stand at the center of this Part Two. Addressing them necessitates the following sequence: this fourth chapter examines how intertextual differences among Esther's ancient versions clarify issues of Esther's compositional development, and Chapter Five explores how MT Esther's allusive purpose also sheds light onto the processes by which the different textual layers came together to create a literarily cohesive story. Since the present methodology insists that this intertextual analysis not be used on its own to reach these diachronic conclusions, Chapters Four and Five consistently work alongside previous proposals for MT Esther's compositional history in their effort to adjudicate among and refine them. Before turning to such issues, however, a rehearsal of Esther's ancient Greek witnesses, in addition to the scholarly proposals that have been generated to account for them, is required.

4.1 Esther's Greek Witnesses

Since LXX Esther has long been understood as a translation of MT, albeit one of an occasionally freer nature, its details need not be rehearsed here; a review of its six Additions, however, is in order.[82] Though these Additions, usually lettered

---

81 Though no definitive background for the Purim celebration has been determined, scholarship has long posited Babylonian and/or Persian roots. For a brief overview of this issue, see, for example, Moore, *Esther*, XLVI–XLIX.
82 Since there are no surviving Hebrew witnesses comparable to these passages, which are found in both the LXX and Alpha Text, their canonical status has varied. While Judaism has

https://doi.org/10.1515/9783111216119-004

A–F, were likely not composed as freestanding documents, they do evince some cohesive shape, as the following outline indicates.

A: Designed as a precursor to MT Esther 1, Addition A narrates a premonitory dream Mordecai has that consists of dragon combat ending in ultimate relief. This Addition goes on to explain an episode familiar to MT readers: Mordecai overhears two eunuchs planning to assassinate the Persian king, reports such insubordination, and is accordingly rewarded with a position in the court. Since Addition A suggests that Haman supported the violent coup, this introduction provides deeper reason for Haman's spat with Mordecai.

B: This second Addition, which comes between MT Esth 3:13 and 14, records the actual text of the heinous edict to which MT only refers. After praising both the king and Haman, the Greek account of this decree goes on with a chilling clarity that charges Haman to destroy all the people, wives and children included, whom Haman identified. While Addition B records the destruction day as the 14th of Adar, MT refers to the 13th.

C: Following Esther and Mordecai's decisive exchange in MT Esther 4, Addition C adds what might be expected in other biblical books – the prayers of the now endangered main characters. Mordecai begins and explains that his refusal to bow down to Haman was not reflective of his own vanity but rather his commitment not to place anyone above the God of Israel. Mordecai then invokes previous covenants before Esther takes the pious stage. Seized with a fear to which MT Esther only hints, the queen also engages in direct appeal. She asks God to deliver her and her people by placing eloquent words in her mouth and turning the king against the very prime minister he selected.

D: The fourth Addition follows directly on C. Since it also narrates Esther's approach to the king, this Addition overlaps in content with MT Esth 5:1–3. While MT Esther positions the king's unexpectedly gracious reception as part of Ahasuerus' unpredictable personality, this Greek version tells of the king's initial anger being inverted when God changes his spirit.

E: Similar to Addition B, Addition E, which comes between MT Esth 8:12 and 13, narrates the actual content of the pro-Jewish counter-edict. The links between B and E continue: if B lavishes praise upon Haman, E condemns him as an outside usurper; while B accuses the people Haman identified of following perverse laws, E speaks of their righteousness and devotion to God, who has kept the kingdom in good order. This Addition closes then with an injunction for the Jews to defend themselves and move against any who do not act accordingly.

F: Addition F brings LXX Esther to a close by referring to Mordecai's dream from Addition A. Interpreting his previous night vision in terms of the events of the story, Mordecai attributes the ultimate rescue to God.

---

always left these Greek passages out of its Hebrew Bible, Jerome, unsure of their originality, situated them at the end of the book of Esther in his Latin Vulgate. The Protestant reformers, acting over 1,000 years later, removed the canonicity of the Additions altogether by placing them in the Apocryphal section. The Catholic Church (Council of Trent, 1546), by contrast, responded with an affirmation of their canonical status.

Despite the cross-connections noted, scholars have long detected different authorial hands behind these passages. For example, A, C, D, and, most likely, F seem to be translations of Semitic originals; B and E, on the other hand, appear to reflect originally Greek compositions.[83] Though it remains unknown when such traditions were composed and under what specific circumstances they found their way into the Greek versions, they all are believed to have been written in full awareness of the larger Esther traditions.[84]

Brought into an LXX version of Esther that charts, for the most part, directly alongside MT, these passages are also found in the Alpha Text (AT).[85] Since this Esther witness is also ancient but diverges in significant ways from MT, attention now turns to it. For as scholarship has long appreciated, once these Additions are removed from AT, an internally consistent story, but one markedly shorter than the MT Esther version, is found.[86] While many of the basic plot elements are similar to the canonical edition, the following differences indicate the gap between this Greek version and Hebrew Esther.

As important parts of MT pivot on the inalterability of Persian Law, this notion is entirely absent from AT – a divergence that this work addresses more completely in the next chapter (§ 5.3). Moreover, though Addition A does recount Mordecai's sussing out of Bigthan and Teresh's coup plot, it is not found where both LXX and MT have it – at the end of Esther 2.[87] In this same vein, while MT narrates Haman casting lots before going to Ahasuerus for permission to exterminate all of Mordecai's people (MT Esth 3:7–8), AT reverses the order: first Haman goes to the king and then, after receiving the king's approval, casts his lot (AT 3:6–13).[88] Such divergences continue. As MT leaves the reader to determine

---

83 For more on the compositional background of these Additions and how they fit into the Esther traditions in which they are embedded, see, for example, Levenson, *Esther*, 27–34.

84 See, for example, Moore, *Esther*, LXIII–LXIV.

85 For a discussion of some subtle but important differences between the Additions in the two Greek versions, see Karen H. Jobes, *The Alpha-Text of Esther: Its Character and Relationship to the Masoretic Text* (Atlanta: Scholars Press, 1996), 165–94.

86 For a discussion of the internal consistency of AT, see David J. A. Clines, *The Esther Scroll: The Story of the Story* (Sheffield: JSOT Press, 1984), 71–92; for a specific illustration of the ways in which AT is shorter than MT, consider Fox's helpful calculations. "Overall, in terms of a word-count, the AT is about 29 % shorter than the LXX, but since there is also material in the AT that is absent in the LXX, the portion of the LXX unparalleled in the AT is higher than 29 %" (*The Redaction of the Books of Esther: On Reading Composite Texts* [Atlanta: Scholars Press, 1991], 11). A complete explanation of this point is found in Fox's Table II (*Redaction*, 48–49).

87 Since LXX Esther recounts this small pericope twice, once in Addition A and once in Esther 2, the AT absence is all the more noteworthy.

88 A brief explanation of the confusing AT versification is in order. Though different systems have been employed, this work follows the New English Translation of the Septuagint (NETS); it also, when quoting the AT in English, uses the NETS translation.

what Mordecai is thinking when Haman is ordered to parade him in celebratory fashion through the Shushan streets (MT Esth 6:11–12), AT narrates his thoughts explicitly (AT 6:16–17), and, while MT narrates Ahasuerus' anger being ignited when he sees Haman lying on Esther's couch (MT Esth 7:8), AT includes the king's explicit concern for Mordecai (AT 7:14). In addition to these divergences and a number of other smaller changes in language and phrasing, the following larger MT Esther chunks have no direct AT equivalents: MT Esth 2:10–16, 19–23; 3:12–14; 4:5–8a; and 5:9, 11.[89]

While the most striking variation may be the way that AT occasionally invokes God directly – an issue that receives sustained discussion in the third and final section of this study (§ 6.3) – the most substantive narrative differences come in the final few chapters. Fox helpfully details these points of variance.

> Major differences between the LXX and the AT are most frequent in the last part of the book, viii 15–52 // 8:1–10:3 ... The AT concludes as follows: After Haman is hanged, the king summons Mordecai and gives *him* (not Esther) Haman's property (viii 15). Then Mordecai asks the king to annul Haman's decree, and the king entrusts Mordecai with the affairs of the kingdom (16–17). Esther requests permission to execute her enemies; she is granted that right and consequently many men are slaughtered (18–21). Then comes Add E, the king's public epistle countering Haman's plot. After this, Mordecai writes a public letter telling the Jews to celebrate their deliverance and explaining the background of his order (33–38). He then goes forth dressed in glory, the inhabitants of Susa rejoice, and the Jews celebrate (39–40). Many of the *Jews* circumcise themselves, meeting with no opposition (41); indeed, the authorities aid them out of fear of Mordecai (42). Haman and the opponents are named in Susa (43). The Jews kill 700 men *and* the sons of Haman, and plunder their property (44). The king exclaims on the extent of the slaughter (45), and Esther asks that the Jews be allowed to annihilate and plunder at will (45). The king agrees, and they kill 70,100 men (46). Mordecai records all these matters in a book, instructs the Jews to celebrate the 14th and 15th of Adar, and sends portions to the poor (47–48). For this reason the holiday is called Phouraia (49). The king imposes taxes and writes of his wealth and glory, and Mordecai praises him and inscribes it all in the books of Persia and Media (50–51). Finally, Mordecai *succeeds* Xerxes, leads the Jews, and bestows honor on his people (52). The book concludes with Add F, the interpretation of Mordecai's dream. (13)

The issue of the AT content can thus be summed up in the following way. Despite important differences of detail, the AT plot line tracks alongside the major movements of MT for much of MT Esth 1–8:1 (AT 1–7:16). Throughout MT Esth 8:2–10:3 (AT 7:17–59, which includes both Additions E and F), however, the situation changes significantly. Though points of contact remain, the end of AT reflects an Esther tradition substantively different from that which is recorded in MT.

---

89 For a very similar list, see Macchi, *Esther*, 46 n118.

4.2 Scholarly Debates

To make sense of these textual variations, scholarship has generated a range of explanations. As De Troyer notes, most proposals have tended to hinge on one underlying issue: while a number of scholars see these differences indicating that AT is a translation of a now lost Hebrew *Vorlage* that was distinct from MT, others feel that AT, despite its variances, is still best explained as dependent on LXX.[90] David J. A. Clines' work, which represents one end of this spectrum, endeavors to keep AT entirely separate from the MT tradition as found in LXX.[91] For according to Clines, even though both MT and AT reach back to a now lost Hebrew pre-Masoretic version, the conciseness of AT 1–7:16 and its substantively different ending indicate that it developed from this common textual ancestor independently.[92]

This position, Clines argues, is confirmed by seven specific textual examples that "contra-indicate" (87) any dependence of AT on LXX. Of this group, Clines feels his final example, which is seen in the different versions of Esth 7:9, "particularly impressive since with one minor exception (the omission of טוב after דבר in the LXX's *Vorlage*) it appears that LXX and AT had before them exactly the same Hebrew text but handled it quite differently syntactically, as well as semantically (note the translations of עשה, בית, and תלה) without any evident tendency that could be called typical of either text" (89). The verses in MT, LXX, and AT read as follows, with the key phrases in Hebrew and their different reflections in Greek bolded.

MT 7:9: ויאמר חרבונה אחד מן הסריסים לפני המלך גם הנה העץ אשר **עשה** המן למרדכי אשר דבר טוב על המלך עמד **בבית המן** גבה חמשים אמה ויאמר המלך **תלהו** עליו

LXX 7:9: εἶπεν δὲ Βουγαθαν εἷς τῶν εὐνούχων πρὸς τὸν βασιλέα Ἰδοὺ καὶ ξύλον **ἡτοίμα-σεν** Αμαν Μαρδοχαίῳ τῷ λαλήσαντι περὶ τοῦ βασιλέως καὶ ὤρθωται **ἐν τοῖς Αμαν** ξύλον πηχῶν πεντήκοντα εἶπεν δὲ ὁ βασιλεύς **Σταυρωθήτω** ἐπ' αὐτοῦ

AT 7:12–13: καὶ εἶπεν Αγαθας εἷς τῶν παίδων αὐτοῦ Ιδου ξύλον **ἐν τῇ αὐλῇ αὐτοῦ** πηχῶν πεντήκοντα ὃ **ἔκοψεν** Αμαν ἵνα κρεμάσῃ τὸν Μαρδοχαῖον τὸν λαλήσαντα ἀγαθὰ περὶ τοῦ βασιλέως ... καὶ εἶπεν ὁ βασιλεὺς **κρεμασθήτω** ἐπ' αὐτῷ

---

90 Kristin De Troyer, *The End of the Alpha Text of the Book of Esther: Translation and Narrative Technique in MT 8:1–17, LXX 8:17, and AT 7:14–41* (Atlanta: SBL Press, 2000), 37–38.

91 Clines, *The Esther Scroll*.

92 While Fox suggests that the substantive similarities between MT and AT end at MT Esth 8:1 (§ 4.1), Clines sees them reaching to MT Esth 8:5. Since, however, the differences begin already in MT Esth 8:1, this analysis follows Fox's suggestion.

As the sense and specific purpose of the Greek verses align, their language diverges, and Clines' point, which sees LXX and AT as two independent translations
of Hebrew originals, comes into clearer focus. For both Clines and the present
work, the corollary to this point is equally if not more important: if it can be
established, as Clines feels his work does, that AT and LXX are genetically unrelated, then unless AT is seen as cutting out large sections of MT or the similarities
between the MT and AT versions are chalked up to coincidence, then AT 1–7:16
without the Additions must be seen as a relatively accurate translation of an early
Esther core from which MT also descended.[93]

Though Fox seconds the general notion that MT and AT developed separately
from a shared Hebrew ancestor, he ultimately comes to a slightly different conclusion. While Clines suggests that AT was entirely independent from LXX Esther,
Fox argues that LXX Esther did exert some influence over AT. According to Fox,
after MT was translated into the Greek Septuagint, a later AT redactor added in
the six Additions and also changed parts of AT in a way that brought some of its
aspects more into line with LXX.[94] "Where AT = MT = LXX, the agreement might
have arisen because all three versions ultimately descend from the same Hebrew
story. But in cases where AT = LXX ≠ MT," Fox continues, "the AT is probably directly dependent on the LXX, since it shows a peculiarity of that version" (44).
The LXX and AT versions of Esth 1:1 present such a case. As MT Esther simply
opens with this verse as opposed to Addition A, it reads: ויהי בימי אחשורוש
(MT 1:1). In some distinction to this Hebrew, however, both Greek verses make
the same addition in nearly identical fashion.

LXX 1:1: καὶ ἐγένετο μετὰ τοὺς λόγους τούτους ἐν ταῖς ἡμέραις Ἀρταξέρξου
AT 1:1: καὶ ἐγένετο μετὰ τοὺς λόγους τούτους ἐν ἡμέραις Ἀσσυήρου

Fox's work thus represents a sort of middle ground. Though AT represents a
translation of a Hebrew *Vorlage* distinct from MT Esther but from which MT also
in the main descended, the final form of AT does admit of some contact with LXX
Esther. In similar fashion, Emanuel Tov also strikes an intermediate position, but

---

93 As several scholars of this mindset have noted, AT 1–7:16 is not understood to represent an
exact translation of this posited early Esther core at every moment, as surely those responsible
for the final AT form made some alterations, additions, and subtractions in both the translation
and redaction phases. However, since the story is internally consistent and tracks along with
much of the basic MT frame, these changes are often thought to be of the minor sort. For a
helpful discussion of some of these potential changes, see, for example, Fox, *Redaction* (42–95),
which detects a series of minor alterations made by AT redactors.
94 For a helpful diagram of this proposed progression, see Fox, *Redaction*, 9.

his work has Fox's terms in reverse.[95] If Fox sees AT as a translation of a Hebrew
Vorlage that was later influenced by LXX Esther, Tov perceives AT to be primarily
a reworking of LXX that subsequently underwent minor revisions due to the
presence of a distinct Hebrew *Vorlage*. The three versions of Esth 1:20 begin to
illustrate Tov's major point, as both Greek versions miss the sense of the Hebrew
but do so in the exact same way. While MT Esther uses a well-known expression
for "everyone," LXX and AT both translate "from rich to poor."[96]

MT Esth 1:20:	למגדול ועד קטן
LXX 1:20:	ἀπὸ πτωχοῦ ἕως πλουσίου
AT 1:20:	ἀπὸ πτωχῶν ἕως πλουσίων

With this basic connection between AT and LXX established, Tov goes on to highlight two more aspects that round out his position. Since AT at times translates
what MT records more faithfully than LXX, AT must have had access at some
point in its development to a Hebrew version of Esther;[97] however, given that AT
is substantively different from MT in its parts that also do not agree with LXX,
the Hebrew version which came to exert some influence over AT must have
differed to some extent from MT. Tov thus concludes: "L [AT] had independent
access to a Hebrew (or Aramaic) text which differed from MT and it probably
revised the LXX towards that text" (6).

Notwithstanding the important differences noted, Clines, Fox, and Tov's analyses all posit the existence of a Hebrew Esther tradition that was similar but not
identical to MT that exerted at least some influence over AT. In contradistinction
to such analyses, De Troyer argues that the textual evidence does not require
recourse to a now lost Semitic text.[98] Instead, De Troyer recommends a textual
reconstruction that generally follows Tov but rejects his notion of a Hebrew version different from MT altering AT after its original creation. Thus, in De Troyer's
estimation, LXX marks a translation of MT, and AT a free and creative recension,

---

95 Emanuel Tov, "The 'Lucianic' Text of the Canonical and Apocryphal Sections of Esther,"
Textus 10 (1982): 1–25.
96 For Tov's discussion of these and other examples, see "The 'Lucianic' Text," 2–3; for Clines'
response, which acknowledges some limited LXX influence over AT in certain instances, see
Esther Scroll, 90–91. Clines' larger reply, however, hinges on his division of AT. Since most of Tov's
examples come from MT Esther 9–10, Clines' analysis of AT, which sees the final AT passages as
compositionally distinct from the rest of AT, allows him to sidestep the potential problems this
admission might otherwise raise and still assert that the "core of the book [AT 1–8:1] is quite
unrelated to the LXX" (85).
97 For a list of examples Tov brings to show that AT must have had access to a Hebrew text,
see "The 'Lucianic' Text," 5.
98 De Troyer, *The End of the Alpha Text of Esther*.

or *Neugestaltung*, of LXX. "We conclude," she writes, "that the *Vorlage* of the AT was the LXX as it now stands, including the entire chapter 8 (together, in our opinion, with chapters 9 and 10)" (397).

To prove such a point, she suggests that many of the features unique to AT, which Clines, Fox, and, to some extent, Tov see as evidence for the presence of a distinct Hebrew *Vorlage*, actually represent a reworking of other LXX passages. A particularly striking case is found in De Troyer's analysis of AT 7:14. The AT phrase in question, which identifies Mordecai as the one who saves the king from the eunuchs' plot, reads as follows: Μαρδοχαῖον ἐβουλεύσατο κρεμάσαι τὸν σῶσαντά με ἐκ χειρὸς τῶν εὐνούχων (AT 7:14). Though the LXX does not have an equivalent section,[99] De Troyer notes how this seemingly new AT composition is not so new at all. "It comes as no surprise that the AT presents Mordecai in this fashion. Indeed the AT appears to be making use of an unexploited LXX parallel, namely LXX 2:21–23. The LXX speaks of the attack of the two eunuchs in both Add. A and LXX 2:21–23. The AT, by contrast, only deals with the attack in Add. A:11–16 and is thus free to draw upon LXX 2:21–23" (284).[100] To illustrate this point, the relevant parts of the verses in question are quoted once again.

> AT 7:14: Μαρδοχαῖον ἐβουλεύσατο κρεμάσαι τὸν σῶσαντά με ἐκ χειρὸς τῶν εὐνούχων
> LXX 2:21: οἱ δύο εὐνοῦχοι τοῦ βασιλέως
> LXX 2:23: τοὺς δύο εὐνούχους

While these LXX verses and their absence in AT 2 have often been seen as evidence for the distinctness of the AT tradition and what may have been behind it, De Troyer's work makes the case for the contrary. Precisely because these verses do not come earlier are they here brought into the Greek text by the AT authors. De Troyer thus completes the point.

> In association with the verb "to save," the AT states that the king was saved ἐκ χειρὸς τῶν εὐνούχων (from the hands of the eunuchs). The passage in AT 7:14 clearly refers to the two eunuchs who contrived to attack the king: LXX 2:21 οἱ δύο εὐνοῦχοι τοῦ βασιλέως and

---

99 For the sake of comparison, the full LXX verse is as follows: και not αι αἱ ἐν αὐτῇ τῇ ἡμέρᾳ ὁ βασιλεὺς Ἀρταξέρξης ἐδωρήσατο Εσθηρ ὅσα ὑπῆρχεν Αμαν τῷ διαβόλῳ καὶ Μαρδοχαῖος προσεκλήθη ὑπὸ τοῦ βασιλέως, ὑπέδειξεν γὰρ Εσθηρ ὅτι ἐνοικείωται αὐτῇ (LXX 8:1).

100 Interestingly, a similar phenomenon, one that sees other biblical texts comprising large aspects of Ezekiel 38–39, has been explored at length by William Tooman. "The Gog Oracles are a pastiche," he writes. "It [Ezekiel 38–39] was composed by combining bits and pieces of preexisting texts. The oracles' author mined texts from across the Torah, Prophets, and Psalms for the language, topics, themes and images to be used as the building blocks of the new composition" ("Transformation of Israel's Hope: The Reuse of Scripture in the Gog Oracles," in *Transforming Visions: Transformations of Text, Tradition, and Theology in Ezekiel*, eds. William Tooman and Michael Lyons [Eugene, OR: Pickwick Publications, 2010]: 50–111; here: 92).

LXX 2:23 τοὺς δύο εὐνούχους. We can conclude, therefore, that the AT makes use of the passage from LXX 2:21–23 which it does not exploit in the parallel passage thereto. (285)

Taken together, these four positions articulate the broad range in which the details of Esther's textual development have been explained. If Clines, Fox, and Tov all see the evidence suggesting the presence of an independent Hebrew *Vorlage*, only Clines and Fox feel that this recreated *Vorlage* predates MT, while Tov views this now lost Semitic edition exerting its influence over AT after AT was already composed; if Tov concludes that the similarities between AT and LXX suggest that AT descended from LXX, De Troyer argues that even the unique aspects of AT are still best explained as dependent on LXX – just in more creative fashion.

4.3 Intertextual Commonalities in MT and AT

While these basic impasses have maintained,[101] the present approach returns its focus to Esther's relationship with Joseph to illustrate an intriguing pattern. As Jean-Daniel Macchi points out, more linguistic connections to Joseph are found

---

101 Suggesting that this problematic aspect reflects the insecure nature of using the Greek evidence to determine Esther's compositional history, Ego (*Ester*) proposes a different course altogether for dealing with Esther's diachronic development. "Da die Forschungen zum Alpha-Text letztlich zu wenig konsensfähig sind, als dass man daraus valide literar- oder redaktionskritische Schlüsse ziehen kann, bleiben die hier präsentierten grundsätzlichen Überlegungen im Wesentlichen der Methodik der 'klassischen Literarkritik' verhaftet, die nach stilistischen und inhaltlichen Brüchen sucht und von diesen Beobachtungen aus Schlüsse auf die Diachronizität des Textes zieht. Ergänzt wird dies durch generelle Überlegungen zur Textentstehung und zu Fortschreibungsprozessen sowie zu möglichen inhaltlichen Profilierungen, die sich in diachroner Perspektive ergeben" (40). While the present approach appreciates Ego's honest assessment of the complexities and confusions that the Greek witnesses have generated and respects the tried and true redactional method her work prefers, it ultimately maintains that a lack of consensus does not provide grounds to turn away from this compelling, if not maddeningly complicated, body of comparative textual evidence. Interestingly, however, a number of her conclusions are actually supported by the comparative Greek evidence. As she searches MT Esther for "offensichtliche sprachliche Differenzen und inhaltliche Widersprüche" (47) and accordingly devises a list of passages that are, to her mind, the result of later *Fortschreibungen* processes, several of the verses she identifies come at moments when AT shows a variant version (Esth 2:6, 10, 22; 5:9; 8:2; 9:3b, 4; 10:1–3; Ego, 47–48) and thus could be further supported by some engagement with AT. In similar fashion, Bezold also prefers Hebrew Esther's internal evidence when considering its literary development. His specific conclusion, however, differs slightly from Ego's. Arguing for an early wisdom tale that pitted Mordecai against Haman but knew nothing of a threat against the entire Jewish people, Bezold isolates Esth 2:5–6, 21–23; 5:9–14; 6; 7:7–10; 8:1–2, 15a; 10:1–3 as an early version likely dated to the late Persian or early Greek period that then grew in the Hasmonean era into the current Esther form (*Ester*, 79).

in MT than AT.[102] While the specifics of these differences come to add a clarifying aspect to the debate concerning Esther's compositional history, two examples of intertextual commonality between MT and AT must first be examined in order to situate the import of the divergences. The opening similarity comes in Esth 2:7: if both MT and AT use two phrases to refer to Esther's good looks, then LXX only records one. Consider the language of the different versions, with the phrase found in MT and AT but not LXX bolded.

MT Esth 2:7:   והנערה יפת תאר **וטובת מראה**
AT 2:7:   καὶ ἦν ἡ παῖς καλὴ τῷ εἴδει σφόδρα **καὶ ὡραία τῇ ὄψει**
LXX 2:7:   καὶ ἦν τὸ κοράσιον καλὸν τῷ εἴδει

Since AT is here more expansive than LXX, and its phrasing represents a direct translation of the only extant Hebrew version of Esther, the case for AT working not just with LXX but rather with a Hebrew *Vorlage* takes initial shape.

Moreover, that language nearly identical to AT 2:7 is found in LXX Gen 39:6, καὶ ἦν Ιωσηφ καλὸς τῷ εἴδει καὶ ὡραῖος τῇ ὄψει σφόδρα, raises two key attendant points. In the first instance, these Greek correspondences suggest that those re-

---

102 Macchi, *Esther.* "The Joseph story," he writes, "is clearly part of the intellectual baggage of the authors of Esther. Like references to the Davidic monarchy, allusions to episodes in the life of Joseph were made explicit by proto-Masoretic editors who introduced expressions drawn from the source text" (60). In addition to serving as point of departure for this particular analysis, Macchi's work provides crucial corroboration: not only does he indicate how MT Esther enhances the textual allusions to Joseph, but so also does his study note how the Hebrew Scroll heightens the importance of Esther's other intertextual connections to Saul, David, Moses, and Daniel, as well (58–62). While this analysis is clearly indebted to Macchi's sharp insight, it ultimately offers two subtle but important refinements. In the first and most important case, the present work emphasizes a gradual buildup of the allusive purpose. While Macchi stresses how the MT editors introduced many of the connections, this analysis demonstrates how a number of allusions to Joseph were already explicit in the early core (§ 4.4.1), which allowed the MT redactors to add in key additional connections that made Esther's relationship with Joseph uniquely productive for the Hebrew Scroll. (Macchi does acknowledge this point on occasion [see, for example, *Esther,* 162 n80], but his work is most interested in the intertextual connections the later MT editors developed.) Though the second refinement, which deals with Esther's connections to Daniel, falls outside the most specific aim of this present discussion, it is still worth mentioning here. Since Macchi dates MT Esther into the Maccabean period (§ 1.3, n43), he senses a firm historical basis for seeing the MT Esther redactors also enhancing Hebrew Esther's connections to Daniel's court narratives (*Esther,* 61–62). (Given the potentially late date for Daniel 1, in particular, his work does leave open the possibility that parts of Daniel may be alluding to Esther [*Esther,* 62, n184]). The present study, however, takes a different course. While noting the connections between Esther and Daniel, this analysis suggests that both the historical and linguistic evidence fall short of fully proving an intentional relationship; as a result, the present work refrains from positing any purposeful heightening of Esther's intertextual connection with Daniel (§ 7.1; § 7.2).

sponsible for AT were likely aware of the links to Joseph found in the Hebrew version of Esther with which they were working and sought to preserve at least certain linguistic connections in their Esther translation. Second, since LXX Genesis confirms that AT is here translating a Hebrew phrase very similar to if not identical with that which is found in MT Esth 2:7, this comparison also suggests that the Hebrew *Vorlage* behind AT was, at least in this instance, very similar to if not identical with MT. A second example continues to gesture in this direction.

In Esther 4, after Mordecai convinces Esther to approach the Persian king despite the danger it will likely cause her, the queen concludes the dialogue in dramatic fashion: "If I am to die, then I will die," וכאשר אבדתי אבדתי (Esth 4:16). As other commentators have noted,[103] and this work explores in detail in Part Three (§ 6.2), these words are strikingly reminiscent of Jacob's in Gen 43:14. For in Genesis, after Israel has been convinced to release Benjamin so that he can approach an Egyptian ruler, Jacob's final words are equally stirring and also employ that same unusual syntax: "If I am to be bereaved, I will be bereaved," כאשר שכלתי שכלתי (Gen 43:14).

While this second example admits of more variance between AT and MT, it once again suggests that AT was working off of a Hebrew *Vorlage*, and that this *Vorlage* contained this particular connection to Genesis, as well. To determine a point of reference for translating this unusual Hebrew syntax into Greek, consider the Septuagint version of the Genesis passage in question alongside the two Greek Esther editions.

LXX Gen 43:14: ἐγὼ μὲν γάρ καθὰ ἠτέκνωμαι ἠτέκνωμαι
LXX Esth 4:16: ἐὰν καὶ ἀπολέσθαι με ᾖ
AT 4:11: εἰ δέοι καὶ ἀποθανεῖν με

As these differences highlight the challenges of understanding the precise sense of this unusual Hebrew syntax and then finding its best expression in Greek, they also suggest that AT, much like LXX Esther, was here working with a version of the Esther story that contained language distinctly similar to, if not identical with, the language found in MT Esth 4:16. Both the LXX and AT phrases begin with versions of εἰ and καὶ, and then employ aorist infinitives followed by first person accusative pronouns. Though LXX chooses a middle of ἀπόλλυμι, while AT prefers an active infinitive of ἀποθνῄσκω followed by the same first person accusative pronoun, the broad similarities but specific differences once again suggest that AT was not dependent on LXX but was rather working off of a Hebrew *Vorlage* that contained some philological connections to Joseph, even if the AT Greek does not here sound any immediate echo to LXX Genesis.

---

103 See, for example, Rosenthal, "Die Josephsgeschichte," 280–81.

4.4 Differences in the Intertextuality of AT and MT

While these initial two cases indicate that AT was likely working off of a Hebrew *Vorlage* and not just LXX, and that this *Vorlage* contained at least some of the linguistic connections to Joseph that are found in MT Esther, two further examples bring attention to instances in which MT Esther shows philological links to Genesis not found in AT. In this vein, consider Gen 39:10 and MT Esth 3:4. As Rosenthal notes,[104] and Chapter Two briefly explores (§ 2.1, n2), the Hebrew versions of these two verses are markedly similar.

Gen 39:10:   ויהי כדברה אל יוסף יום יום ולא *שמע אליה*

Esth 3:4:   ויהי באמרם אליו יום ויום ולא *שמע אליהם*

While much of the connection in Hebrew hinges on that distinctive repetition of "day," the LXX translations of these two verses admit of serious overlap but do not contain this particular aspect. Consider the text of LXX Gen 39:10 and Esth 3:4:

LXX Gen 39:10:   ἡνίκα δὲ ἐλάλει τῷ Ιωσηφ **ἡμέραν ἐξ ἡμέρας** καὶ οὐχ ὑπήκουσεν αὐτῇ

LXX Esth 3:4:   καθ' ἑκάστην **ἡμέραν** ἐλάλουν αὐτῷ καὶ οὐχ ὑπήκουεν αὐτῶν

As this difference indicates that LXX Esther was not as concerned with maintaining each intertextual connection found in the Hebrew text it translates, the presence of ἡμέρα in LXX Esth 3:4 provides further evidence for the fact that the Septuagint was here working off of a Hebrew original – either MT or a text virtually identical to it – that contained this specific linguistic connection to Joseph.

The AT, however, presents an entirely different case. Though the larger context is the same – at this point in AT, Haman has just been promoted, and Mordecai is curiously refusing to bow down – the repetition with which the courtiers address Mordecai is absent. Consider the AT verse in whole:

AT 3:3:   καὶ εἶδον οἱ παῖδες τοῦ βασιλέως ὅτι ὁ Μαρδοχαῖος οὐ προσκυνεῖ τὸν Αμαν καὶ εἶπον οἱ παῖδες τοῦ βασιλέως πρὸς τὸν Μαρδοχαῖον

While it is possible that AT was here streamlining or reworking LXX, the differences suggest that AT was at this point working with a *Vorlage* that simply did not contain the linguistic link to Genesis found in MT Esth 3:4. In addition to removing the repetition that marks Mordecai's subversive behavior in MT, the AT verse also includes a clarifying line – "When the servants of the king saw that Mordecai was not doing prostration before Haman" – that is not present in either MT or LXX.

---

104 Rosenthal, "Die Josephsgeschichte," 279.

In contrast to this AT version, the context of the scene in both MT and LXX makes it clear that the king's courtiers have seen Mordecai's refusal to bow down to Haman, and, as a result, both MT and LXX jump straight to the courtiers' questioning. As this subtle but telling difference indicates, it would be difficult to explain this AT variation without positing that the underlying tradition with which AT was working was here different from that which MT and LXX record. This point is emphasized by the full text of the MT and LXX verses.

MT Esth 3:2–3: וכל עבדי המלך אשר בשער המלך כרעים ומשתחוים להמן כי כן צוה לו
המלך ומרדכי לא יכרע ולא ישתחוה ויאמרו עבדי המלך אשר בשער
המלך למרדכי מדוע אתה עובר את מצות המלך

LXX Esth 3:2–3: καὶ πάντες οἱ ἐν τῇ αὐλῇ προσεκύνουν αὐτῷ οὕτως γὰρ προσέταξεν ὁ βασιλεὺς ποιῆσαι ὁ δὲ Μαρδοχαῖος οὐ προσεκύνει αὐτῷ καὶ ἐλάλησαν οἱ ἐν τῇ
αὐλῇ τοῦ βασιλέως τῷ Μαρδοχαίῳ Μαρδοχαῖε τί παρακούεις τὰ ὑπὸ τοῦ
βασιλέως λεγόμενα.

In both MT and LXX, the same group of people (עבדי המלך אשר בשער and οἱ ἐν τῇ αὐλῇ) are doing obeisance and then speaking to Mordecai; in clarifying that which needs no clarification in MT and LXX, the AT version is thus shown redundant to and therefore likely not dependent on LXX.

While the instances previously examined (MT Esth and AT 2:7; MT Esth 4:16 and AT 4:11) identify verses for which the *Vorlage* behind AT was quite close to if not identical with MT, this example shows the *Vorlage* behind AT likely differing from MT. As MT and LXX invoke the language and story of Joseph with Potiphar's wife by narrating Mordecai's repeated refusals, the AT records a broadly similar but subtly different sequence that includes an explanatory gloss but not the specific Genesis link.

One final example once again indicates how attention to MT Esther's unique intertextual character suggests that a Hebrew text with broad similarities but also occasional differences to MT stood behind AT. Since this next case deals with the end of the Megillah – MT Esth 8:6 and AT 7:18 – it is particularly complicated. While a more complete discussion of Esther's different conclusions comes in the next chapter (§ 5.3), for now it is important to recall two points: first, since the most substantive similarities between MT and AT run only through AT 7:16, this AT verse may very well be a secondary addition into AT; moreover, since AT does not know of the irrevocability of Persian law, a theme so important at this point in MT, the AT storyline here diverges from MT in crucial ways.

In AT, after Haman has been hanged, Mordecai requests that the deposed prime minister's evil edict be revoked, and the king, unencumbered by the clunky legal structure of MT, is able to assent immediately (AT 7:15–17). Thus, when Esther returns to Ahasuerus to ask for permission to punish her enemies (AT 7:18), the need is not nearly as acute as it is in MT. In addition to this important difference, the language of this crucial MT action, which strongly echoes the Joseph story, is notably different in AT. Since the connections between Genesis 44 and Esther 8 have already been detailed (§ 2.3), the relevant passages are here simply recalled.

Gen 44:34: כי איך אעלה אל אבי והנער איננו אתי פן אראה ברע אשר ימצא את אבי

Esth 8:6: כי איככה אוכל וראיתי ברעה אשר ימצא את עמי ואיככה אוכל וראיתי באבדן מולדתי

The Septuagint versions translate these verses in broadly similar fashion:

LXX Gen 44:34: πῶς γὰρ ἀναβήσομαι πρὸς τὸν πατέρα τοῦ παιδίου μὴ ὄντος μεθ' ἡμῶν ἵνα μὴ ἴδω τὰ κακά ἃ εὑρήσει τὸν πατέρα μου

LXX Esth 8:6: πῶς γὰρ δυνήσομαι ἰδεῖν τὴν κάκωσιν τοῦ λαοῦ μου καὶ πῶς δυνήσομαι σωθῆναι ἐν τῇ ἀπωλείᾳ τῆς πατρίδος μου[105]

Despite the differences noted in the AT storyline, the AT version still recounts Esther's return to Ahasuerus; the scene, however, is expressed without the distinctive language noted above. Devoid of the rhetorical flourishes that mark the MT and LXX versions of both Genesis and Esther, AT 7:18 sees Esther get right to the point: καὶ εἶπεν Εσθηρ τῷ βασιλεῖ τῇ ἑξῆς Δός μοι κολάσαι τοὺς ἐχθρούς μου φόνῳ. "Then Esther said to the king on the next day, 'Allow me to punish my enemies with bloodshed.'"

Providing further evidence for AT working off of a distinct Hebrew *Vorlage* as opposed to LXX, these divergences between AT and the MT/LXX Esther versions suggest the following basic compositional frame. As the specific verbal parallels between MT Esther and AT at 2:7 and MT Esth 4:16 and AT 4:11 indicate, both MT Esther and AT were working off of Hebrew *Vorlagen* that were very similar, if not identical, and also contained some basic connections to Joseph. Since, however, the relationship with Joseph found in AT is less developed than it is in MT, a point that MT Esth 3:4 and 8:6 illustrate, AT 1–7:16[106] without the Additions thus likely represents a more faithful version of the earlier Esther tradition that the MT authors

---

105 An important point is worth reiterating here: that both LXX Genesis and LXX Esther translate the כי איך phrases and first person imperfects with πῶς γὰρ followed by a first person future middle once again indicates that LXX Esther was working off of MT – or something nearly identical to it. Thus, even if the connection between the Greek witnesses is less compelling and may not cause a reader of LXX Esther to recall LXX Genesis, the broad similarities still indicate the specific parallels found in their respective Semitic *Vorlagen*.

106 For Fox, the original ending of AT is not found at AT 7:16 but rather in AT 7:18–21 and 33–38 (*Redaction*, 38–40); Macchi, in somewhat similar fashion, sees the ending reaching into 21bβ, 33b, 34a (*Esther*, 44, n109). While their arguments are cogent and hinge for the most part on the

independently expanded.[107] This distinctive MT intertextual growth is depicted in the following table.

4.4.1 Table One

	Esth MT	Esth LXX	Esth AT	Gen MT	Gen LXX
Esth 1:3 Gen 40:20	עָשָׂה מִשְׁתֶּה לְכָל־שָׂרָיו וַעֲבָדָיו	δοχὴν ἐποίησεν τοῖς φίλοις καὶ τοῖς λοιποῖς	ἐποίησεν ὁ βασιλεὺς πότον τοῖς ἄρχουσι τῆς αὐλῆς	וַיַּעַשׂ מִשְׁתֶּה לְכָל־עֲבָדָיו	ἐποίει πότον πᾶσι τοῖς παισὶν αὐτοῦ
Esth 1:21 Gen 41:37	וַיִּיטַב הַדָּבָר בְּעֵינֵי הַמֶּלֶךְ וְהַשָּׂרִים	καὶ ἤρεσεν ὁ λόγος τῷ βασιλεῖ καὶ τοῖς ἄρχουσι	καὶ ἀγαθὸς ὁ λόγος ἐν καρδίᾳ τοῦ βασιλέως	וַיִּיטַב הַדָּבָר בְּעֵינֵי פַרְעֹה וּבְעֵינֵי כָּל־עֲבָדָיו	ἤρεσεν δὲ τὰ ῥήματα ἐναντίον Φαραω καὶ ἐναντίον πάντων τῶν παίδων αὐτοῦ
Esth 2:3 Gen 41:34–35	וְיַפְקֵד הַמֶּלֶךְ פְּקִידִים בְּכָל־מְדִינוֹת מַלְכוּתוֹ וְיִקְבְּצוּ	καὶ καταστήσει ὁ βασιλεὺς κωμάρχας ἐν πάσαις ταῖς χώραις τῆς βα-σιλείας αὐτοῦ καὶ ἐπιλεξάτωσαν	–	וְיַפְקֵד פְּקִידִים עַל־הָאָרֶץ ... וְיִקְבְּצוּ	καταστησάτω τοπάρχας ἐπὶ τῆς γῆς ... καὶ συναγαγέτωσαν
Esth 2:7 Gen 39:6	וְהַנַּעֲרָה יְפַת־תֹּאַר וְטוֹבַת מַרְאֶה	καὶ ἦν τὸ κοράσιον καλὸν τῷ εἴδει	καὶ ἦν ἡ παῖς καλὴ τῷ εἴδει σφόδρα καὶ ὡραία τῇ ὄψει	וַיְהִי יוֹסֵף יְפֵה־תֹאַר וִיפֵה מַרְאֶה	καὶ ἦν Ιωσηφ καλὸς τῷ εἴδει καὶ ὡραῖος τῇ ὄψει σφόδρα

---

need for a more decisive AT ending, the present approach exerts somewhat more caution in those AT sections that do not have specific MT parallels.

107 The example of MT Esth 8:6 and AT 7:18 raises another important dimension. While the MT redactors sought to expand the connections to Joseph found in the early Esther core, those responsible for shaping the early core into the final AT form did not share this same allusive purpose, as those passages that are likely secondary additions to AT do not contain any connections to Joseph that are not found in MT. If Fox's recreation is correct (pg. 93, n26), and AT 7:18 is indeed part of the early Esther core, then even though the specifics of this example would be complicated, the basic point, which sees MT enhancing Esther's connections to Joseph while AT showing no interest in doing so, would still hold.

(continued)

	Esth MT	Esth LXX	Esth AT	Gen MT	Gen LXX
Esth 2:12 Gen 50:3	מִקֵּץ הֱיוֹת לָהּ כְּדָת הַנָּשִׁים שְׁנֵים עָשָׂר חֹדֶשׁ כִּי כֵן יִמְלְאוּ יְמֵי מְרוּקֵיהֶן	ὅταν ἀναπληρώσῃ μῆνας δέκα δύο οὕτως γὰρ ἀναπληροῦνται αἱ ἡμέραι τῆς θεραπείας	–	וַיִּמְלְאוּ־לוֹ אַרְבָּעִים יוֹם כִּי כֵן יִמְלְאוּ יְמֵי הַחֲנֻטִים	καὶ ἐπλήρωσαν αὐτοῦ τεσσάρα- κοντα ἡμέρας οὕτως γὰρ καταριθμοῦνται αἱ ἡμέραι τῆς ταφῆς
Esth 3:4 Gen 39:10	וַיְהִי בְּאָמְרָם [כְּ][אָמְרָם] אֵלָיו יוֹם וָיוֹם וְלֹא שָׁמַע אֲלֵיהֶם	καθ᾽ ἑκάστην ἡμέραν ἐλάλουν αὐτῷ καὶ οὐχ ὑπήκουεν αὐτῶν	–	וַיְהִי כְּדַבְּרָהּ אֶל־יוֹסֵף יוֹם יוֹם וְלֹא־שָׁמַע אֵלֶיהָ	ἡνίκα δὲ ἐλάλει τῷ Ιωσηφ ἡμέραν ἐξ ἡμέρας καὶ οὐκ ὑπήκουσεν αὐτῇ
Esth 3:10 Gen 41:42	וַיָּסַר הַמֶּלֶךְ אֶת־טַבַּעְתּוֹ מֵעַל יָדוֹ וַיִּתְּנָהּ לְהָמָן	καὶ περιελόμενος ὁ βασιλεὺς τὸν δακτύλιον ἔδωκεν εἰς χεῖρα τῷ Αμαν	καὶ περιείλετο ὁ βασιλεὺς τὸ δακτύλιον ἀπὸ τῆς χειρὸς αὐτοῦ καὶ ἔδωκε τῷ Αμαν	וַיָּסַר פַּרְעֹה אֶת־טַבַּעְתּוֹ מֵעַל יָדוֹ וַיִּתֵּן אֹתָהּ עַל־יַד יוֹסֵף	καὶ περιελόμενος Φαραω τὸν δακτύλιον ἀπὸ τῆς χειρὸς αὐτοῦ περιέθηκεν αὐτὸν ἐπὶ τὴν χεῖρα Ιωσηφ
Esth 4:16 (AT 4:11) Gen 43:14	וְכַאֲשֶׁר אָבַדְתִּי אָבָדְתִּי	ἐὰν καὶ ἀπολέσθαι με ἢ	εἰ δέοι καὶ ἀποθανεῖν με	כַּאֲשֶׁר שָׁכֹלְתִּי שָׁכָלְתִּי	καθὰ ἠτέκνωμαι ἠτέκνωμαι
Esth 5:10 Gen 43:31 Gen 45:1	וַיִּתְאַפַּק	–	–	וַיִּתְאַפַּק וְלֹא־יָכֹל יוֹסֵף לְהִתְאַפֵּק	ἐνεκρατεύσατο καὶ οὐκ ἠδύνατο Ιωσηφ ἀνέχεσθαι
Esth 6:11 (AT 6:18–19) Gen 41:43	וַיַּרְכִּיבֵהוּ ... וַיִּקְרָא לְפָנָיו	καὶ ἀνεβίβασεν αὐτὸν ... καὶ ἐκήρυσσεν λέγων	καὶ ἔσπευσεν Αμαν ἀναλαβεῖν αὐτὸν ἔφιππον καὶ ἐξήγαγεν Αμαν τὸν ἵππον ἔξω καὶ προσήγαγεν αὐτὸν ἔξω κηρύσσων	וַיַּרְכֵּב אֹתוֹ ... וַיִּקְרְאוּ	καὶ ἀνεβίβασεν αὐτὸν ... καὶ ἐκήρυξεν
Esth 8:2 (AT 7:13) Gen 41:42	וַיָּסַר הַמֶּלֶךְ אֶת־טַבַּעְתּוֹ אֲשֶׁר הֶעֱבִיר מֵהָמָן וַיִּתְּנָהּ לְמָרְדֳּכָי	ἔλαβεν δὲ ὁ βασιλεὺς τὸν δακτύλιον ὃν ἀφείλατο Αμαν καὶ ἔδωκεν αὐτὸν Μαρδοχαίῳ	καὶ ἀφεῖλεν ὁ βασιλεὺς τὸ δακτύλιον ἀπὸ τῆς χειρὸς αὐτοῦ	וַיָּסַר פַּרְעֹה אֶת־טַבַּעְתּוֹ מֵעַל יָדוֹ וַיִּתֵּן אֹתָהּ עַל־יַד יוֹסֵף	καὶ περιελόμενος Φαραω τὸν δακτύλιον ἀπὸ τῆς χειρὸς αὐτοῦ περιέθηκεν αὐτὸν ἐπὶ τὴν χεῖρα Ιωσηφ

(continued)

	Esth MT	Esth LXX	Esth AT	Gen MT	Gen LXX
Esth 8:6 Gen 44:34	כִּי אֵיכָכָה אוּכַל וְרָאִיתִי בְּרָעָה אֲשֶׁר־יִמְצָא אֶת־עַמִּי וְאֵיכָכָה אוּכַל וְרָאִיתִי בְּאָבְדַן מוֹלַדְתִּי	πῶς γὰρ δυνήσομαι ἰδεῖν τὴν κάκωσιν τοῦ λαοῦ μου καὶ πῶς δυνήσομαι σωθῆναι ἐν τῇ ἀπωλείᾳ τῆς πατρίδος μου	–	כִּי־אֵיךְ אֶעֱלֶה אֶל־אָבִי וְהַנַּעַר אֵינֶנּוּ אִתִּי פֶּן אֶרְאֶה בָרָע אֲשֶׁר יִמְצָא אֶת־אָבִי	πῶς γὰρ ἀναβήσομαι πρὸς τὸν πατέρα τοῦ παιδίου μὴ ὄντος μεθ' ἡμῶν ἵνα μὴ ἴδω τὰ κακά ἃ εὑρήσει τὸν πατέρα μου

As this chart shows, five of the thirteen most substantive linguistic connections between MT Esther and Joseph are not found in AT;[108] of the five AT minuses, only one is accompanied by a corresponding absence in LXX Esther (MT Esth 5:10), and two of the AT minuses come when the corresponding LXX Esther verse retains at least some connection to LXX Genesis (MT Esth 2:12, 3:4). Moreover, no apparent pattern emerges among the contextual placements of the five AT minuses: while two occur in LXX and MT contexts that deviate broadly from the AT storyline (MT 2:12 and 8:6) and could thus be explained by these larger plot variations, three instances come amidst general plot agreement between MT/LXX and AT (MT 2:3, 3:4, and 5:10). Since these considerations make it difficult to explain the intertextual gap between MT and AT as the result of either direct LXX influence or purposeful AT subtraction, this intertextual attention suggests the basic independence of the AT and LXX translations and thus reinforces those compositional models that see the final MT form as an independent expansion of an early Esther tradition generally reflected in AT 1–7:16 without the Additions.

4.5 Pluses and Minuses in MT and AT

Before turning to explore the processes by which these secondary MT intertextual additions were combined with the early Esther core and the literary integrity of the resulting narrative whole that was created, one crucial complexity must be

---

108 While some commentators, Rosenthal, in particular, posit other linguistic connections between Esther and Joseph – for example, Esth 1:5//Gen 50:3, Esth 2:18//Gen 43:34, and Esth 10:3//Gen 41:43; 43:12 – the present analysis views the thirteen listed here as the strongest and most important cases of philological borrowing.

considered. While the present work has up to now been focusing on MT pluses – that is, those Hebrew passages that have no equivalent in AT – and explaining them as redactional additions to MT, Karen Jobes' detailed study emphasizes a counter-balancing point: the AT also contains passages that are not found in MT and can at times be explained as deliberate alterations made by those responsible for AT.[109] Her analysis of Esth 1:21 provides a compelling example. While all three Esther versions clearly reflect the same basic sense, they do so in somewhat different terms. If MT expresses the king's opinion through the well-known Hebrew idiom "in the eyes of," then LXX removes the eye idiom entirely, while AT refers to the king's heart. The specific language of the verses is as follows:

MT 1:21: וייטב הדבר בעיני המלך
LXX 1:21: καὶ ἤρεσεν ὁ λόγος τῷ βασιλεῖ
AT 1:21: καὶ ἀγαθὸς ὁ λόγος ἐν καρδίᾳ τοῦ Βασιλέως

On first glance, this variation seems to be best explained by positing a minor difference in the MT and AT *Vorlagen*. Since LXX eliminates the synecdoche altogether, the AT plus, ἐν καρδίᾳ, could be seen as a translation of a related but different Hebrew phrase found in a hypothetical Hebrew version from which AT was working: וייטב הדבר בלב המלך.[110] That the actual Hebrew phrase, וייטב הדבר בעיני המלך, or some very similar version of it, is found twelve other times in the Hebrew Bible but never once translated with ἐν καρδίᾳ only appears to provide further support for the notion that AT was here working off of a *Vorlage* slightly different from MT.

However, as Jobes points out, two considerations militate against such a conclusion. First of all, the hypothetical Hebrew phrase, וייטב הדבר בלב המלך, never once occurs in the biblical text, and, since the entire AT exhibits a clear *Tendenz* that steers away from maintaining Hebrew synecdoche and metonymy in its Greek version,[111] a different explanation for this textual variation surfaces. Thus, even though AT here has a phrase that is not found in LXX and rendered differently from the language of MT, it seems possible if not likely that this variation reflects not a divergent *Vorlage* but rather the translation style and literary preferences of the AT authors.

---

109 Jobes, *Alpha-Text*.
110 As Jobes notes, this position has been forwarded by Carey A. Moore, "A Greek Witness to a Different Hebrew Text of Esther," *ZAW* 79:3 (1967): 351–58. For Jobes' critique, which is here spelled out, see *Alpha-Text*, 123–24.
111 As Jobes details, the AT preference for avoiding Hebrew synecdoche is found in the following six passages: MT Esth 1:10d; 2:9a; 3:11f; 5:8b; 6:9c; and, possibly, 7:9d. For Jobes' fuller discussion, see *Alpha-Text*, 122.

Jobes extends this analytic line to Esther 2, as well. After noting a series of pluses found in this MT chapter,[112] she suggests that much as the difference between MT and AT at 1:21 gestures to the specific translational technique of AT, then so may the discrepancies between MT and AT throughout Esther 2 reflect a set of purposeful AT minuses that those responsible for AT removed from the *Vorlage* they shared with MT. For Jobes, this possibility seems all the likelier given that most of this chapter, and especially the omitted parts in AT,[113] are dedicated to aspects of the Hebrew Megillah that receive less attention in AT – the opulence of the Persian court, and the importance of queen Esther, for example.

Since such a recreation would push against the general argument forwarded here, which is inclined to view these differences as purposeful MT pluses as opposed to deliberate AT minuses, it must be examined more closely. At the center of Jobes' point is the presence of clear AT *Tendenzen* that, in her view, ought to be seen as considered literary choices and not just rote reflections of the earlier textual tradition those responsible for AT supposedly inherited. While appreciating the spirit of Jobes' position, the present analysis suggests that the same basic literary consideration Jobes extends to AT must also be applied to MT; for in the case of the differences found between AT and MT in Esther 2, that which is found only in MT also plays a pivotal role in the internal literary purposes of the Hebrew text.

In this vein, consider MT Esth 2:10 and 2:20 – two verses that have no parallel in AT. In the first case, Esth 2:10, Esther is said not to have revealed her people in the harem, just as Mordecai told her; in the second, Esth 2:20, Esther once again conceals her true identity, but this time after she has reached the queenship. Though it is true that such redundancies could have been deleted by the AT authors, the opposite possibility also presents itself. Since the hidden nature of Esther's identity plays a key role in setting up her later ability to defeat Haman and deliver her people,[114] these unique MT passages can just as easily be seen as reflecting an important MT *Tendenz* and thus used as evidence to support not their excision from AT but rather their secondary insertion into MT.

When this consideration is then coupled with the additional connection to Joseph found in this unique MT section (Esth 2:12), the argument for seeing MT Esther 2:10–16 and 19–23 as deliberate MT growth – and not purposeful AT sub-

---

112 According to Jobes' calculations, some 50 % of the crucial MT Esther 2 scenes are not expressed in AT 2, as MT Esth 2:10–16 and 19–23 do not find direct expression in AT (*Alpha-Text*, 131).

113 For the specific phrases from MT Esther 2 that are not found in AT, see Jobes, *Alpha-Text*, 130.

114 As the Introduction makes clear (§ 1.2), Beal, in *The Book of Hiding*, sees the notion of hidden identity as so central to MT Esther that he devotes his entire interpretive program to it.

traction – is compounded. As a result, while the present approach appreciates Jobes' argumentation and certainly recognizes that some of the differences between MT and AT in language and phrasing may very well reflect the AT authors' translation and literary choices, it continues to suggest, along with Fox and Clines, that most of the substantive MT pluses are best seen as secondary Hebrew additions as opposed to purposeful AT deletions. Since the following chapter notes how an investigation of further and more sizable differences between MT and AT also points in this direction, this suggestion continues to find corroboration.

5 The Redactional Stages and Narrative Cohesiveness of MT Esther's Final Literary Form

With MT Esther's basic authorial lines sketched, the literary cohesiveness of the Hebrew Scroll and the processes by which the different MT textual layers came together must now be examined. While the compositional seams gestured to above have been used as evidence for a set of corresponding literary disjunctions, this intertextual analysis once again engages with previous proposals to demonstrate that the narrative unity reaching across the distinct authorial sections of MT Esther's final form was provided by one major Hebrew redaction. As these considerations continue to underscore the importance of dealing with diachronically defensible textual layers when pursuing author-oriented intertextual analyses, so do they also indicate how MT Esther's secondary additions increased not just its linguistic connections to Joseph but its structural links, as well. Since these specific issues have not yet been appreciated in scholarship, this chapter brings Part Two of the present study to a close by noting how previous efforts to read the Scroll allusively have tended to overlook these crucial historical and compositional components.

5.1 Attempts to Divide the Literary Integrity of the Hebrew Scroll

A review of key scholarly attempts to carve up the narrative cohesiveness of the Hebrew Scroll commences this effort. On the one hand, W. Lee Humphreys' influential take on Esther dovetails with important aspects of the conclusions reached in Chapter Three.[115] Much as the above analysis argues for a compositional seam at the beginning of MT Esther 8, so does Humphreys posit a break between Esther and Mordecai's tale and the institution of the Purim festival.[116] On the other hand, however, a critical difference also emerges. While Humphreys sees this authorial division resulting in a sharp ideological clash between Esther's distinct compositional sections, attention to the comparison with Joseph demonstrates how the disparate parts of the Hebrew Scroll are in fact literarily connected.

---

115 W. Lee Humphreys, "Life-style for Diaspora: A Study of the Tales of Esther and Daniel," *JBL* 92:2 (1973): 211–223.
116 "There was once an independent Jewish tale," Humphreys writes, "of the adventures of Esther and Mordecai, which was not yet linked to Purim, and which had the form of a court tale" (214).

https://doi.org/10.1515/9783111216119-005

According to Humphreys, if Esther and Mordecai's tale paints with an early universalistic brush designed to highlight how Jews can navigate skillfully through foreign courts, then the later Purim tradition depicts a violent Jewish particularism that upends the cosmopolitan nature of the story leading up to it.[117] By drawing a comparison here to the book of Daniel – which is also, according to Humphreys, comprised of early universalist tales (Daniel 2–6) that were then later combined with nationalistic notes (Daniel 7–12)[118] – Humphreys claims to find support for his bifurcated read of Esther.

> In this instance [the Book of Daniel], as in the case of the tales of Esther and Mordecai, tales that had their origin in the post-exilic diaspora and that present a style of life for the diaspora Jew which affirms most strongly that at one and the same time the Jew can remain loyal to his heritage and God and yet can live a creative, rewarding, and fulfilled life precisely within a foreign setting, and in interaction with it, have been taken over into a new framework that stresses an exclusiveness and even a nationalistic stance over against and in conflict with the foreign context of the Persian and hellenistic diaspora.[119] (223)

---

117 While "the tale [of Esther and Mordecai] does not permit any tension to develop between their double loyalty to king and co-religionists" ("Life-style," 215), the Purim tradition later affixed to it certainly does. "The utilization," Humphreys writes, "of the tale of Esther as a festal legend for Purim gave added emphasis to the conflict between Jew and pagan and to the joy at the defeat of the latter" (222).

118 Despite this basic similarity, Humphreys notes some differences between Esther and Daniel, as well. The court tales in Daniel 2–6, for example, contain a distinctive devotional component that is not present in the Esther and Mordecai story. "Here," Humphreys writes, referring to the Daniel 2–6 collection, "there are marked developments beyond the tale of Esther and Mordecai. Daniel and his companions do not have expressed links with their fellow Jews, and they are not the source of deliverance for their co-religionists (cf. also the Joseph narrative). Furthermore, the Jewishness of the hero is stressed and even provides a hinge for the plot. The courtier is quite passive, he is delivered not only through his own skills in the ways of court intrigue, but primarily through the miraculous intervention of his deity, to whom the courtier is completely loyal, and who thus appears as sovereign deity of all men and nations. Aspects characteristic of the piety of the Jew are stressed in this connection (Dan 1:8–20; 2:19–23; 3:13–18; 6:10). In this stress on the devotion of the hero characteristic elements in the tale of the courtier are submerged. The God of Daniel is the central figure and not the courtier" (220–21).

119 For an entirely different take, see Anderson's controversial essay, "The Place of the Book of Esther." After pointing out how Esther and Mordecai rise in Persia through potential violations of Jewish Law – intermarriage and dietary laws, for example – Anderson suggests that the point of such narrative twists is quite different from Humphreys' universalism. "These things, however," he writes, referencing the aforementioned illegalities, "are dictated by the necessity of the plot. Far from advocating a policy of compromise and intermarriage, the book intends to show that the action of both Esther and Mordecai, though governed by calculating expediency, had as its object the preservation of the cultural and racial integrity of the widely dispersed Jewish people (cf. 10:3)" (35). Despite this disagreement, Humphreys' work has still had a sustained impact on scholarship. Consider, for example, the following comments in Day's commentary. Though she refrains from

Picking up on and updating this analytic line, Clines returns to the Greek evidence surveyed above to refine Humphreys' suggestion even further.[120] While Humphreys assumes that two textual blocks were rather artlessly joined without examining the historical processes through which the different textual strands might have been combined, Clines argues for a series of Hebrew redactions that both account for the comparative evidence presented by AT and maintain the narrative divide Humphreys identifies. For Clines, the issue is accordingly twofold: since AT has neither the irrevocability of Persian law nor the distinct ending found in MT, these two features must have come into MT separately, given that, at least to his eye, the legal theme is woven nicely into the earlier tale, while the violence and style of the Purim tradition stand in direct tension to Esther and Mordecai's story.

Splitting up these unique MT Esther features causes Clines to recreate Esther's textual development in the following way. An initial Hebrew redaction of the early Esther core added in the irrevocability of Persian law and many of the smaller MT Esther 1–8 passages that are not present in AT 1–7:16. According to Clines, these initial MT redactors understood the base Esther narrative well and, by preserving the debonair atmosphere of the earlier tale, brought the original story to an appropriate conclusion in MT Esth 8:15–17. "The gladness and joy," Clines writes of these verses, "the feast and holiday, signify that the matter is settled, not that their [the Jews'] fate still hangs in the balance. So clear is it that the Jews are destined for life that pagans spontaneously attach themselves to the Jewish community" (*Esther Scroll*, 65).

While Clines' hypothetical intermediate version of a Hebrew Esther enjoyed this fitting conclusion, a second Hebrew redaction spoiled this cohesive story by affixing to it the uncouth Purim tradition found in MT Esther 9–10. "Far from presenting a vivid, subtle and dramatic story such as chs. 1–8 contained," Clines claims, "9.1–19 is striking for its poor construction, its inferior narrative development, and its logical weaknesses ... From 9.20 onwards," he continues, "it is downhill all the way, from a dramatic, narrative, or even logical, point of view" (39, 50).[121]

Humphreys' literary-critical conclusions, she seconds the emphasis Humphreys places on assimilation. "Unlike the roughly contemporaneous works of Ezra and Nehemiah, the book of Esther does not suggest that the goal of proper Jewish living is to return to Judah; instead, it promotes the idea that Jews can live personally fulfilling, and even socially successful, lives in exile from Palestine" (*Esther*, 13). After briefly noting how this echoes Joseph, Daniel, Tobit, and Jonah, Day continues along a line similar to Humphreys: "The message is that when living in a foreign environment, one need not totally separate from the dominant culture but become involved in it. With such involvement," she concludes, "it is possible even to become politically well placed and economically prosperous in foreign society" (13).

120 Clines, *Esther Scroll*.

121 According to Clines, MT Esther's final chapters are also comprised of originally different compositions. While MT Esth 9:1–19 represents one block, then 9:20–10:3 represents a second. For the details of Clines' position, see *Esther Scroll*, 50–63.

For Clines, the "maladroitness" (40) of this second MT redaction is seen in six narrative discontinuities that arise between MT Esther's last two chapters and the rest of the story. While the end of Esther 8 leaves both Haman's and Mordecai's decrees valid, Clines sees Esther 9 proceeding as if Haman's decree had been abolished. The second discrepancy is also related to the decrees: while the Jewish edict of Esther 8 calls for the Jews to assault any armed force that might attack them, the events of Esther 9 show the Jews striking pro-actively before any hostile force materializes. Clines' third, fourth, and fifth points deal with the usage of particular words and phrases,[122] and the sixth difference relates to the motif of Ahasuerus' generosity. If the king's magnanimity in Esther 1–8 is always the result of a "previously narrated request made by the queen," then his benevolent action in Esther 9 is "unmotivated by any request on Esther's part" (47).[123] Clines thus concludes:

> The narrator of ch. 9 has presented a Jewish massacre of anti-Semites rather than Jewish self-defense against an imperially sponsored pogrom. It cannot have served his purpose either as storyteller or as propagandist to have made this massacre the sequel of the conflicting decrees, and we can only conclude that the author of ch. 9 imperfectly understood the thrust of the plot of chs. 1–8. He knew chs. 1–8 only superficially as a story of Jewish triumph over a heathen plot – which indeed it is – and lacked the subtlety to imagine a victory that could not be quantified by a body-count. (40)[124]

While the present analysis agrees that MT Esther 9–10 are secondary and likely the result of a complicated compositional process in their own right, it once again turns to the comparison with Joseph to caution against Humphreys' and Clines' efforts to separate these chapters on literary grounds from the plot developments leading up to them.

5.2 Interlocking Inversions in MT Esther and Joseph

As Humphreys and Clines divide the literary connectivity of the Megillah, Meinhold's work identifies twelve narrative components found in both Joseph and

---

122 For the details of the linguistic discrepancies Clines detects and the other disjunctions noted above, see *Esther Scroll*, 39–47.
123 While the present approach responds to Clines' work by demonstrating an opposed perspective in the next two subsections, Fox, who reaches a similar conclusion to the one that is ultimately forwarded here, takes on a number of Clines' points directly. For these more specific rebuttals, see Fox, *Redaction*, 110–15.
124 For an opposing perspective on these final chapters, see Jobes, *Alpha-Text*, 132. According to her, despite the obvious disjunctions between the endings of MT Esther and AT, both versions contain a sequence of twelve events that occur in the same order, which suggests that the original Esther core must have, at least in some way, extended into these final events.

Esther that gesture to their internal cohesiveness.[125] Since Meinhold sees these overlaps reflecting the parameters of the *Diasporanovelle* genre, he begins by noting how both Joseph and Esther commence with scenes that prepare their entire stories for what is to come.

> Die Vorgeschichte (Gen 37:1–35) ist eine Art Einleitung. Sie erfüllt die Funktion, für die gesamte Geschichte das Terrain zu bereiten. Familiäre Beziehungen und Verwicklungen bestimmen diesen Abschnitt. Joseph – noch der jüngste Sohn Jakobs – wird von seinem Vater mehr geliebt als seine Brüder. Daß Joseph zudem die Reden seiner Brüder dem Vater hinterträgt und durch Träume und deren Erzählen den Anschein von Hochmut erweckt (Gen 37:5–8, 9 f.), macht die Gründe aus, weshalb er von seinen Brüdern gehaßt wird. Es entwickeln sich Konflikte, im Verlauf derer Joseph aus dem näheren Familienzusammenhang und dessen sozialer Verwurzelung (als Ackerbau treibende Kleinviehnomaden) ausscheidet (Gen 37:28, 36), um nach Ägypten, also ins Fremdland, in eine (welt-)politische Situation gebracht zu werden. (I, 311)

By introducing the interlocking nature of Joseph's plot, Joseph's *Vorgeschichte* both foretells how his brothers will ultimately bow down to him (Gen 37:7–9) and launches a series of events that will paradoxically spin to bring him low. For when Joseph's brothers, already jealous of the favor he enjoys from their father (Gen 37:4), hear the contents of his suggestive dreams, their antipathy deepens (Gen 37:5–11). After his father then sends him on that ill-fated mission to check up on his brothers (Gen 37:12–14), the fratricidal strife boils over to toss the very brother who seemed destined for great things to the bottom of a dry well (Gen 37:24).

As Joseph is then rescued by outsiders and taken down to Egypt (Gen 37:28, 36), his enslavement in a foreign land engenders the next reversal. As the master notices his slave's unusual favor and places Joseph over his whole household (Gen 39:3–5), Joseph's proximity to Potiphar attracts his master's wife whose wrongful accusation lands him in jail (Gen 39:8–20). While Meinhold views this integrated sequence as being comprised of three formal components, "der kleine Aufstiegsbericht" (Gen 39:1–6), "die Standhaftigkeitsprobe (Gen 39:7–12)," and "die Standhaftigkeit trägt der Hauptperson Schwierigkeiten und Gefahren ein (Gen 39:13–20a)" (I, 313–15), his larger point also comes into focus. By introducing the difficulties that Joseph's own favor paradoxically brings, the *Vorgeschichte* in Genesis 37 prepares the terrain for both the subsequent challenges Joseph faces and successes he enjoys.

In Esther, a similarly interlocked dynamic is initiated in its opening scene. There, when Vashti rebuffs her drunken husband, the king is left in angered disbelief (Esth 1:12). Since, however, Ahasuerus proves unable to fashion a response himself (Esth 1:13), his councilors are forced to step in with a crude twist: if the queen

---

125 Meinhold, "Die Gattung," Parts I and II.

disobeyed the king, then every woman in the empire must always obey their husband; if Ahasuerus' wife refused to come before him, then every virgin must come at his beck and call (Esth 1:16–22). Thus, when Esther is ordered to do exactly that which Vashti refused (Esth 2:8), her agreeable approach to Ahasuerus upends Vashti's displeasing refusal to land the young Jewish woman in the very seat Vashti once inhabited.

In addition to stressing how this rising action, or *Aufstiegsbericht*, parallels Joseph's first ascent in Egypt (II, 78–79), Meinhold's analysis goes on to note how this initial Esther movement also spurs further similar events. After Esther attains the queenship by inverting that which Vashti did (Esth 2:17), her elevated position flips again; though it surely connotes her great fortune, her proximity to the king soon becomes her own immediate danger. As Haman's evil edict is sealed (Esth 3:8–13), and Esther's perch now represents her entire people's only hope, she is called upon to approach the king yet again – but this time she is the one breaking the fearful Persian law by coming despite not being invited (Esth 4:11–16), exactly the inverse of what Vashti was punished for (Esth 1:12). When the king receives Esther with an unexpected graciousness (Esth 5:2–3), and her moment of danger paradoxically comes to propel her rise even further, the opening Shushan event, as Meinhold suggests, is shown to set up later Scroll twists that influence key movements in Esther's plot.

Once again, Meinhold's genre emphasis has him break this sequence up. While Esth 3:1–4a,c serves as "die Standhaftigkeitsprobe" and thus represents a formal parallel to Joseph's trial with Potiphar's wife in Gen 39:7–12, then Esth 3:4b, 5–15, which emphasizes the difficulties that Mordecai's steadfastness brings, finds reflection in Joseph's tumble into incarceration at the dishonest hands of Potiphar's wife (Gen 39:13–20a).[126] By continuing to prefer how these events consistently intertwine with all that is around them, the present approach shifts the emphasis of Mein-

---

126 Or, as Meinhold calls it, "die Standhaftigkeit trägt der Hauptperson Schwierigkeiten und Gefahren ein" (II, 81). At this point, a key critique of Meinhold's work presents itself. For as others have pointed out, by breaking up the plot elements of both stories, his comparison is occasionally forced to rearrange the order of the very elements he identifies. (On this point, see, for example, Berg, *Book of Esther*, 133–36.) Consider the very component under present discussion – that is, the difficulties that the main characters experience as a result of the steadfastness they show. While this narrative stage fits on this occasion nicely into Meinhold's pre-arranged scheme, as it is preceded by the "Standhaftigkeitsprobe" and followed by the main characters' efforts to ward off the very difficulties that have just been introduced (II, 82), the return of this same stage later in Esth 5:9–14 throws the flow of the genre argument Meinhold's work pursues off balance. Given that this problem repeats throughout Meinhold's analysis, as, for example, the next stage in Esther's plot development jumps significantly ahead of the development in Joseph (II, 83), the rigidity of Meinhold's genre approach is once again shown to get in the way of the textual insights his work points out.

hold's insights. Instead of picking the stories apart to isolate and then compare individual components, this analysis appreciates how both Joseph and Esther's larger plots develop around a series of key inversions that spiral out of previous reversals and then move to set up the next set.[127]

5.3 The Narrative Connectivity of Multiple Conflicts in Esther 8–10

While these narrative connections are all found in MT Esther 1–8, and thus could be construed as support for the redactional conclusions and literary divisions Clines proposes, an analysis of the final Scroll chapters demonstrates how MT Esther 9–10 also tie themselves into this inverted action.[128] Consider, in this vein, the irrevocability of Persian law. Though this peculiar feature, which is entirely absent from AT,[129] plays an important role throughout MT, it exerts particular influence over the final few Hebrew chapters. After Mordecai has been honored and Haman impaled (Esth 7:10), a palpable highpoint in the Scroll drama is attained. Since Esther 3, precisely this conflict between the Jewish courtier and Amalekite prime minister has animated so much of the story: it imbues Mordecai's second refusal in Esther 5 with significance and makes the humorous action in Esther 6 more than just funny. However, even as this direct confrontation is resolved in Mordecai's favor, the peculiar MT legal feature presents the Hebrew Scroll with a second tension that keeps the rest of Mordecai's people very much in harm's way.[130] Thus,

---

127 Ego, in her commentary, is perhaps the latest to stress the significance of inversions in Esther. Though she does so without extended reference to Joseph, her work is still particularly instructive; for a helpful overview of her take on this crucial point, see her exposition on the topic (*Ester*, 16–24).

128 Though coming at this issue from a different angle, White Crawford has also forwarded a very similar position. By attending to the structure of the banquets which run from MT Esther 1 all the way to Esther 9 – and, thus, crucially across Clines' authorial divisions – she concludes in helpful fashion. "Although the author may have used sources in composing his work, the book is now a unified literary piece with a distinct and meaningful structure." (*Esther*, 856). Much of this chapter and the next are devoted to demonstrating how Esther's relationship with Joseph articulates and sharpens this very point.

129 Interestingly, though the irrevocability of Persian law found in MT Esther 8 is directly expressed in LXX Esth 8:8, it is not found in the opening LXX chapter despite being initially introduced in MT Esth 1:19. Consider the relevant verses: while MT 1:19 makes the point clear, ויכתב בדתי פרס ומדי ולא יעבור, LXX curiously translates ולא יעבור with καὶ μὴ ἄλλως χρησάσθω, "and let it not be applied differently." The whole LXX phrase is as follows: καὶ γραφήτω κατὰ τοὺς νόμους Μήδων καὶ Περσῶν καὶ μὴ ἄλλως χρησάσθω (LXX 1:19).

130 The analysis pursued here follows key aspects of Macchi's work. While the immediate intertextual point of this chapter – which comes to note how the MT inclusion of the irrevocability

after Haman is hanged, Esther, realizing her work is not yet done, returns yet again to her husband and, falling at his feet on her people's behalf, hopes that Jacob's syntax (§ 2.3) will beat back the danger of Haman's lingering edict (Esth 8:5–6).

When Ahasuerus assents, the unusual Persian legislative structure prevents the king from simply canceling that which Haman decreed (Esth 8:7–8), and the scribes must be summoned so that Mordecai can dictate a counter-decree (Esth 8:9–13). While Clines sees the tale reaching its correct conclusion in the verses that directly follow (Esth 8:15–17), the textual evidence suggests an alternate take. As the MT narrative twists its way through unchangeable decrees and their counters, the AT account reads quite differently. In this Greek witness, once the evil prime minister is hanged, the king expresses his rage at Haman before promoting Mordecai. Since this version of the story does not know of the legal restraints found in MT, Mordecai simply asks Ahasuerus to remove the evil edict, and the king agrees without complication.

> And the king said to Esther, "He even planned to hang Mardochaios, who saved me from the hand of the eunuchs? Did he not know that Esther is of his race?" So the king called Mardochaios and granted him all that belonged to Haman. And he said to him, "What do you want? I will do it for you." And Mardochaios said, "That you revoke Haman's letter." So the king entrusted to him the affairs of the kingdom. (AT 7:14–17)

Thus, by the time Esther joins this AT scene, the majority of the tension has been diffused. Though she requests to "punish her enemies with bloodshed" (AT 7:18) and then accordingly strikes them "in great numbers" (AT 7:20), such action is not necessary for the resolution of any major narrative problem: Haman has already lost, and, since his heinous decree is not compounded by the inalterability of Persian law, the Jews are no longer endangered by the now defunct edict. As a result, when the king's unprompted concern for the Jewish cause repeats alongside the outsized Jewish aggression,[131] the jagged literary edges Clines so harps on

---

theme provides yet another structural parallel to Joseph (§ 5.3) – is not taken up by Macchi, the general scheme he proposes for understanding the literary worth of MT Esther is here seconded. Consider his insightful summary remarks, which also note how MT Esther pivots around two related but ultimately independent tensions. "From [MT] Chapter 3, two plots intermingle. The first is a conflict to the death between two courtiers, Mordecai and Haman" (*Esther*, 53). After singling out some of the scenes pointed to here, Esth 7:10, for example, that are particularly important for the working out of this conflict, Macchi then identifies a second tension running throughout MT Esther. "A second plot concerns all the Jews. The complication is linked to the proclamation of a decree of annihilation (3:7–12)" (53).

131 "And the king said to Esther, 'How have your people here and in the surrounding countryside fared?' And Esther said, 'Let it be granted to the Judeans to destroy and plunder whomever they want.' And he agreed. And they killed seventy thousand one hundred men" (AT 7:45–46).

come to the fore. "The narrative [in AT]," Clines correctly observes, "has given no reason for the king to suspect that the Jews were in any danger" (*Esther Scroll*, 82).

While Clines is right to note the clumsiness of this doubled AT sequence, the paralleled action in MT is far from gratuitous.[132] For in the Hebrew version, even though at this point the prime minister is no longer, the Jews are still faced with a pressing dilemma: they must either strike out or be struck themselves by Haman's still valid decree. After the Jews of Shushan kill 500 men on the thirteenth of Adar (Esth 9:5–6), those outside the city continue in more brutal fashion. "The rest of the Jews, those in the king's provinces, likewise mustered and fought for their lives. They disposed of their enemies, killing seventy-five thousand of their foes; but they did not lay hands on the spoil" (Esth 9:16). While Clines' literary divisions insist that these scenes are narratively detached from MT Esther's earlier events, the phrasing of this disquieting verse points to its connection. The Jews' effort to fight for "their lives," עַל נַפְשָׁם, articulates the point: while Haman's stunning end brings the court drama with Mordecai to conclusion, the unchangeable edict keeps the second major conflict of the story – the legal one – very much alive by holding the Jews firmly in the firing line.[133] That the Jews' unusually violent assault rebounds Haman's initial aggression back against his supporters reflects the internal inversions previously discussed (§ 5.2);[134] that this must play out to ensure the Jews' actual safety shows the events of this penultimate Hebrew chapter important for resolving a tension that aspects of the entire MT story develop.[135]

---

132 For more on the way in which Clines problematically allows his take on AT to influence his reading of MT, see Loader's critique, which points out how once Clines' opinion concerning the weaker character of the later MT chapters is questioned, then his claim that the later AT chapters are also secondary loses much of its force (*Das Buch Ester*, 211–13). While the present approach appreciates the spirit of Loader's work, it does ultimately suggest that the final AT events are likely secondary – a point that comes out not through their stylistic deficiencies but rather through the unusually substantive disjunctions between it and MT.

133 Since Macchi also appreciates how these two tensions running throughout MT Esther are ultimately independent (see pg. 109, n15), he also sees the story requiring the same two moments of resolution identified here. "A first denouement takes place with Haman's execution (7:5–10). The plot takes another twist when the king declares that the decree cannot be revoked (8:3–8). The final denouement only takes place with the writing of the counter-decree (8:9–14) and the massacre of the Jews' enemies (9:1–19)" (*Esther*, 53).

134 Interestingly, this action presents another subtle but crucial difference to the action in AT. While MT keeps the Jews' aggression reserved for their enemies (Esth 9:1–2, 5, 16), the Greek witness has the Jews striking more indiscriminately (AT 7:46) – an account that does not present the same sort of specific inversion that is such a hallmark of the larger MT Esther narrative.

135 On this general point, see Berlin, who writes the following about Esther 9: "To put the world right, as the Book of Esther does, requires the removal of evil, of the enemy" (*Esther*, 82). Fox, in his critique of Clines' work, articulates a similar perspective. "The Aftermath's [MT Esther 9–10] report of Jewish victory is necessary in the MT, for it could by no means be taken for granted

5.4 Complex Conflicts and Multiple Resolutions in Joseph

Much as the defeat of Haman in Esther 7 and Jewish victory in Esther 9 combine to bring the two major conflicts of the Hebrew Scroll to their ultimate resting points, so can a similar sort of layered conclusion be found in the Joseph story. While MT Esther revolves around personal spats and legal tensions, Joseph balances familial strife with a food shortage, and, if Haman's defeat marks a turning point even though the legal conflict is still lingering, then so does Joseph's self-identification (Gen 45:1 f.) represent an obvious climactic moment despite key aspects of the two most salient tensions persisting.[136]

To appreciate this point, consider the concern Joseph shows for his father directly after he reunites himself with his brothers. "I am Joseph," the vizier finally explains. "Is my father well?" (Gen 45:3). Then, after reiterating his identity and accounting for God's role in this spiraling drama (Gen 45:4–8), the vizier speaks of Jacob yet again. "And you must tell my father everything about my high station in Egypt and all that you have seen; and bring my father here with all speed" (Gen 45:13). When word reaches Jacob, this unsettled thread continues to throb. As the brothers recount to their father that Joseph is still alive, Israel can barely stand the surprise and realizes he must act with all alacrity. "His heart went numb, for he did not believe them. But when they recounted all that Joseph had said to them, and when he saw the wagons that Joseph had sent to transport him, the spirit of their father Jacob revived. 'Enough!' said Israel. 'My son Joseph is still alive! I must go and see him before I die'" (Gen 45:26–28).

When the meeting between father and son finally occurs, a telling textual echo reinforces how this subsequent development helps to complete the multi-stage resolution that begins in Gen 45:1. Much as Joseph, in the direct aftermath

---

that no one would dare assail the Jews now that they were allowed to defend themselves. They were still a scattered minority and vulnerable to massed assault, and their enemies still had the right to attack them" (*Redaction*, 111). In fact, Fox pushes the issue even farther: since he contends that the inclusion of this motif in MT requires the ending found in the Hebrew version of the Scroll, he argues that the redactor (R-MT) who introduced the legal unalterability must be the same person responsible for the creation of MT Esther's final chapters (*Redaction*, 115). As a later section of this chapter demonstrates (§ 5.5), the comparison with Joseph offers further support for Fox's notion of a single redaction making the most sense of MT Esther's final form.

136 Though any number of debates continue to animate Joseph scholarship, it is rather settled that Gen 45:1 represents a turning point. Consider, for example, Claus Westermann's comment: "The Joseph narrative reached its climax in ch. 45" (*Genesis 37–50: A Commentary*, trans. John J. Scullion [Minneapolis: Fortress, 1986], 153), or Levenson's remarks, "Judah's repetition of the same offer (44:32–34) brings the entire tale to its climax: it prevents the enslavement of Benjamin, and, by destroying Joseph's carefully constructed persona, forces him to reveal himself to his brothers, for he 'could no longer control himself' (45:1)" (*Death and Resurrection*, 162–63).

of his own decisive self-identification, embraced Benjamin who then wept on his neck (Gen 45:14), then so does Joseph here embrace his father's neck and begin to cry. In both cases, the language is markedly similar:

Gen 45:14:	ויפל על צוארי בנימן אחיו ויבך ובנימן בכה על צואריו
Gen 46:29:	ויפל על צואריו ויבך על צואריו עוד

As the verbal parallels cause the previous brotherly scene to be recalled in this father and son moment, the connection between the initial breakthrough and this later working out of the remaining tension clarifies.

If the doubled problems in the Megillah are resolved in sequential fashion – first comes Esther and Mordecai's defeat of Haman (Esth 7:10), and then the rescue of the entire Jewish nation (Esther 9) – the Joseph story here admits of an interesting variation. As key components of the familial conflict do not meet final resolution at the initial breakthrough in Gen 45:1, so do some of the serious problems that the famine has created also require further attention after Joseph and his brothers reunite.

Though this question of food security appears settled shortly after Joseph identifies himself, as the Pharaoh promises to provide Joseph's family with the best of the land (Gen 45:17–20), the following chapter describes a different scene, which causes some of this tension to be stoked yet again. For after Joseph and his father come together in a fashion that recalls Joseph's encounter with Benjamin (Gen 46:29–30), the vizier then curiously prepares his family for a meeting with the Pharaoh that will ostensibly cover what was already determined.

> I will go up and tell the news to Pharaoh, and say to him, "My brothers and my father's household, who were in the land of Canaan, have come to me. The men are shepherds; they have always been breeders of livestock, and they have brought with them their flocks and herds and all that is theirs." So when Pharaoh summons you and asks, "What is your occupation?" you shall answer, "Your servants have been breeders of livestock from the start until now, both we and our fathers" – so that you may stay in the region of Goshen. (Gen 46:31–34)[137]

When Joseph then presents his family to Pharaoh (Gen 47:2), a hint of drama still remains. Will the Pharaoh, despite his previous reassurances, now reject his vizier's family? Will the brothers once again play spoiler to their father's reunified family? When all goes to plan, and the brothers say their lines correctly so that the Pharaoh can reauthorize his Goshen allowance (Gen 47:3–6), the full reach of

---

137 Those open to different source-critical models have long detected a compositional seam here. For a fuller discussion of this point, see, for example, E. A. Speiser, *Genesis* AB I (Garden City: Doubleday, 1964), 346–47, or Westermann, *Genesis 37–50*, 150–63.

the threat that the famine has generated finally comes to relax.[138] Though the world continues to suffer (Gen 47:13), "Joseph sustained his father, and his brothers, and all his father's household with bread, down to the little ones" (Gen 47:12).[139]

As both MT Esther and Joseph are shown to narrate complex resolutions to doubled problems, the multifaceted structural links between the Hebrew Scroll and Joseph come to the fore. Much as the plots of the two stories consistently build through sequences of interlocking inversions, so do the reversals in both Joseph and MT Esther revolve around two related but ultimately distinct tensions. Since key components of these structural overlaps in MT Esther hinge on the irreversibility of Persian law, a theme entirely absent in AT, the thrust of the present chapter is highlighted. In addition to increasing the linguistic links to Joseph, as the previous chapter demonstrates, Esther's MT redactors reworked the early textual core they received by heightening the structural parallels to Joseph, as well.[140]

One final example of a difference between MT Esther and AT underscores the import of MT Esther's additional organizational links to Joseph. As others have occasionally noted, the dramatic reversal in MT Esther 6 can function as a sort of narrative midpoint: in Hebrew Esther's macro structure, a series of seven events lead up to this crucial scene, and a sequence of seven opposed actions

---

138 A last refraction of these tensions is found in Gen 50:15–21. While often seen as a central theological message (see, for example, von Rad, "Joseph Narrative," 297), these verses also reflect the lingering problem of the familial conflict. Now that Jacob has died, the brothers are concerned that Joseph may finally unleash any anger that he may have been hiding for the sake of his father. "When Joseph's brothers saw that their father was dead, they said, 'What if Joseph still bears a grudge against us and pays us back for all the wrong that we did him!'" (Gen 50:15). When Joseph tells them to "have no fear" (Gen 50:19), yet another resting point is felt.

139 General support for seeing these verses in Genesis 47 tying up important threads of the earlier conflicts can be found in works as divergent as Westermann, *Genesis 37–50*, and Römer, "The Joseph Story," as both consider Gen 47:1–12 to be part of a fuller version of the tale (Westermann, 164–72; Römer, 189).

140 An important caveat is here worth underscoring. Since the theme of an unalterable law is also attested in Daniel 6 and thus likely reflects aspects of or ideas about the Persian legal system that were generally known in the Persian and Hellenistic periods (for a review of this point, see, for example, Ego, *Ester*, 346–47), the present analysis in no way means to suggest that developing this structural parallel to Joseph ought to be seen as the only consideration for its inclusion in MT. Rather, this line of argument appreciates that this tradition likely predates MT and was then brought into the canonical version for reasons that reflect any number of concerns in addition to the intertextual purpose stressed here – the sardonic illustration of the Persian bureaucracy, as well as an effort to portray certain aspects of governmental life in detail. By attending, however, to the ways in which the different ancient versions of Esther create more connections to Joseph as they mature, this work still maintains that this MT feature helps to sustain and heighten the structural relationship to Joseph, even if its inclusion reflects multiple immediate purposes.

follow.[141] This analytic line is bolstered by the way in which the action of Esther 6 is framed. On the one side comes Mordecai's second refusal to bow down, a disrespect that sends the prime minister into a rage that only his wife's plan can calm, and, on the other, Haman's parading of Mordecai is followed by the queen's second banquet, the very scene in which Esther identifies Haman as the guilty party.

Though AT also narrates both Haman's repeated attendance at Esther's two banquets and the intervening discussion he has with his wife and friends (AT 5:15–24; 6:23), this Greek witness does not recount the prime minister's second encounter with Mordecai. In AT, after Esther responds to the king's query by requesting a second banquet (AT 5:17–19), Haman simply returns home.

> So Haman went into his home and gathered together his friends, his sons and Zosara his wife. And he boasted saying how the queen had invited no one on her special day "except the king and me only. Tomorrow also I have been invited. Yet this alone distresses me: whenever I see Mardochaios the Judean in the court of the king, and he does not bow down to me." (AT 5:20–22)

While this narrative setup depends on a number of previous instances and also looks forward to important events still to come, the absence of the repeated encounter with Mordecai indicates how this Greek structure is not as tightly interlocked as the Hebrew. For in MT, when Haman leaves the first banquet only to see Mordecai for a second time, a host of echoes ring. While the language references Joseph (וַיִּתְאַפַּק, Esth 5:10; § 2.1), the Hebrew Scroll action also recalls Mordecai's initial insolence and Haman's overblown edict (Esth 3:2, 5–6). The internal Megillah connections that Haman and Mordecai's second encounter spurs continue: when a furious Haman returns home, his wife, in an inversion of the opening decree of the book, instructs him (Esth 5:9–14; 1:16–22), and, in similar fashion, the solution Zeresh proposes and Haman giddily accepts (Esth 5:14) is itself an inversion of that which the prime minister previously determined – that Mordecai cannot pay for his disrespect alone (Esth 3:6).

Though the constituent parts of these flips are still present in AT, they are not as immediately recalled in this Greek version without the coordinating scene of Haman and Mordecai's second meeting in MT Esther 5. While Haman's complaint (AT 5:22) reminds of Mordecai's disobedience, his agitation seems disconnected from the particular events around it; for if the chance run-in with Mordecai in MT Esth 5:9 provides the perfect trigger for Haman's subsequent anger, his repeated attendance at Esther's banquets in AT, which left the insatiable prime minister marveling at his own status (AT 5:13–20), does not directly lead to the

---

141 See, for example, Levenson, *Esther*, 5–8, which itself picks up on Fox, *Character*, 157.

frustration he returns home to express. As a result, by the time AT 6 rolls around, and Mordecai is promoted with all of Haman's awards, the reversal in AT is shown to reach back to Esther 3 but not directly through the preceding events as it does in MT.

As Meinhold's work points out, Mordecai and Haman's second encounter in Esther 5 heightens the difficulties that come from Mordecai's sustained steadfastness and corresponds in a number of ways to Joseph's plot development. While Mordecai's continued dissent, which seems to endanger the Jews further, actually spins into Haman's fall, so does Joseph's repeated refusal to sleep with Potiphar's wife throw him into a jail that ultimately catapults him over all of Egypt.[142] In this way, the aim of the present chapter once again sharpens into focus – and this time from a new angle. Much as the irrevocability of Persian law adds a second conflict to provide MT Esther with a narrative cohesiveness that mirrors aspects of Joseph's complex literary structure, so does this smaller MT addition in Esther 5 also enhance the structural connections between the Hebrew Megillah and Genesis story. Thus, even if some of Clines' rougher edges can be found in the compositionally distinct sections of MT Esther, the final canonical form coheres literarily in a way that resembles Joseph's interlocking structure and sequence of multiple resolutions.

5.5 Compositional Histories and Author-oriented Intertextuality

Though previous attempts to read Esther intertextually have tended to sidestep the thorny compositional issues Part Two has addressed, this analysis suggests that author-oriented approaches to Esther's intertextuality must consider these decisive historical factors. For when they are taken into account, a compelling pattern emerges. While an early Esther tradition – that is, the basic AT 1–7:16 frame without the Additions – referenced Joseph in a noticeable but less concerted way, those who had a hand in shaping MT into its final form consistently reworked the tradition they inherited to deepen the linguistic and structural ties between the Esther story they created and the Joseph story they knew.

The present work thus refines its own diachronic argument. Both MT and AT were working with very similar if not identical early Hebrew traditions concerning Mordecai and Esther's exploits; these early traditions, which are reflected in

---

142 In Meinhold's scheme, these actions in MT Esth 5:9–14 and Gen 39:13–20a are both placed in a similar narrative role: "Die Standhaftigkeit trägt der Hauptperson Schwierigkeiten und Gefahren ein" (I, 315; II, 83).

AT 1–7:16 without the Additions, likely date to the middle part of the Persian period shortly after Xerxes' reign ended. As these tales circulated in the latter part of the Persian period or beginning of the Hellenistic era, they were combined with differing final traditions, as the divergent endings of MT and AT show. In this same period, those responsible for MT also expanded and altered the *Vorlage* from which they were working by, among other things, highlighting Esther's significance and introducing the irrevocability of Persian law in ways that increased the philological and structural connections to Joseph.

If Clines argues that the MT pluses found throughout MT Esther 1–8 represent an initial redaction while the addition of Esther 9–10 a second and, according to him, literarily inferior one (§ 5.1), then attention to Hebrew Esther's relationship with Joseph has once again proven instructive. Since the secondary additions found in both MT Esther 1–8 and 9–10 develop new linguistic and structural connections to Joseph, this shared intertextual purpose found across MT Esther's different secondary insertions suggests that one major redaction best explains the textual growth of the Hebrew Megillah. As Fox reaches a very similar conclusion without even considering intertextual issues, the present analysis is further supported.

> A single redactor shaped the entire MT by adapting and supplementing the Hebrew proto-AT, or – to be cautious – proto-Esther, their common forerunner. In chs. 1–7 this author-redactor is closely reworking an older story, most of it ready to hand. In ch. 8 he continues the narrative, but now treats his source much more expansively. In ch. 9 he is composing a new ending with a liturgical purpose, building upon a few hints supplied by his source. The MT is a unity insofar as a single redactor has imposed his will and his intentions on an earlier text. (115)[143]

In addition to shedding important light on key aspects of Esther's compositional development, this attention to Esther's diachronic development also presents another challenge to the previously surveyed attempts to read the Scroll allusively. Though Gerleman and Grossman claim to read Esther's referential quality in

---

[143] While Fox speaks of one redactor, the present approach suggests it likely that this work was completed by a group of redactors and scribes working in cohesive fashion at the same time and place, and, if Fox sees this singular MT redactor composing much of Esther 9–10, this work tends to see the Hebrew redactors reworking pre-existent Purim traditions into their present canonical position. For a similar perspective, consider Berlin's remarks about the literary cohesiveness and compositional development of Esther's concluding chapters. "The etiology of Purim in chapter 9, at least until verse 29, was probably written at the same time as the rest of the book. I am not saying that the story did not exist independently, in one form or another, prior to its appearance in the Masoretic Text. My point here is that I see the present form of the story along with the etiology of Purim as the work of the Masoretic author. This author reshaped the earlier story for use as an explanation of and as encouragement for the perpetual celebration of Purim" (*Esther*, 83).

diachronic fashion, their lack of direct engagement with questions of Esther's authorship causes them to reach historically unreliable conclusions. This problem begins to play itself out in the links Gerleman draws between Purim and Passover, which Gerleman sees as a key component of the connections between Esther and Exodus. "Die Estererzählung," Gerleman writes, "mündet in die Feier und Einsetzung eines Festes aus. Sie ist von vornherein als die Festlegende von Purim angelegt worden. Daß wir in dieser Architektonik der Erzählung eine Angleichung an die Struktur der Exodusgeschichte und der dazugehörenden Passahfestschilderung sehen sollen, ist schon gesagt" (*Esther*, 22).

While Gerleman correctly notes how the current form of MT Esther flows into its final celebrations, his analysis does not address the historical reality that AT presents – an oversight that is all the more surprising given that his work openly recognizes the import of Moore's pivotal analysis (39–40).[144] Since the different end to AT indicates that the MT Purim tradition was originally distinct from the rest of the Esther story, Gerleman's argument is confronted with a problematic historical reality: either MT Esther's narrative sections and concluding Purim passage independently developed as desacralizing accounts of the exodus story, or the desacralizing aim that he claims is so central to the story only came in after the Esther and Mordecai stories were fused with the concluding Purim section.

This sort of critique also extends to highlight complications in Grossman's work. While the differences between his hidden reading and the present intertextual approach have already been discussed (§ 3.1.2; § 3.3), the point at issue here is Grossman's assumption of unified composition – an assumption that influences his strategy for dealing with the complexities of Esther 9. Suggesting, for example, that the second fast the queen calls in Esth 9:31 does not refer to the previous events in the Scroll narrative, Grossman argues that the actual connection is to the "fasts that the Jews had taken upon themselves in commemoration of the destruction of the Temple" (*Esther*, 205).

However, since the linguistic link to the outside verse – Zech 8:9, in this case – consists only of אמת and שלום and is thus not strong enough to support a claim for deliberateness on its own, Grossman has to fall back on the larger frame he has created. Given that the whole Megillah is by nature concealed literature, this verse must also be referring to something beyond itself.[145] At this juncture, how-

144 Carey A. Moore, "A Greek Witness to a Different Hebrew Text of Esther," *ZAW* 79 (1967): 351–58, was the first to refute the previously held belief that AT was a Lucianic recension by demonstrating the ancient quality of this Greek witness.
145 When discussing Esther 9:15–32, Grossman writes, "Some perceive this unit as a technical, historical note meant to connect the plot of the story with the festival of Purim; as a result, the unit's literary shape often remains neglected. However, like every other chapter of the book of Esther, this chapter integrates concealed messages; beyond the technicalities of the acceptance

ever, Grossman's lack of historical specificity calls his conclusion into question. For even if the earlier parts of Esther are shown to be interested in delivering hidden messages – a point that this study doubts on the detailed grounds laid out above (§ 3.1.2) – such evidence would not suggest that this later and compositionally distinct passage is necessarily doing so, as well. Though Grossman circumvents such a critique by sidestepping the debates concerning Hebrew Esther's authorship, the evidence presented by the Greek witnesses raises a firm objection to the one-dimensional diachronic assumption his work follows. In this way, the corollary to the critique of Humphreys' and Clines' works finds expression: much as authorial seams do not automatically create literary disjunctions, so must literary cohesiveness not be used to block clear evidence for compositional complexity.

In contradistinction to these approaches, the present focus on Esther's diachronic development has suggested a gradual buildup of the allusive purpose. While the original Esther core contained some connections to Joseph, the MT redactors increased and enhanced both the linguistic and structural links to the Genesis tale. By recalling, for example, Joseph's repeated refusals in Genesis 39 in Mordecai's initial dissent in Esther 3, connecting Haman's one-time show of self-discipline in Esther 5 to Joseph's fights with his own self-control in Genesis 43 and 45, and including a second legal conflict that requires its own distinct resolution, the MT redactors turned an inchoate allusive relationship into an unusually productive intertextual association that brings the entire Joseph story to bear on the telling of the whole Megillah. With the deliberateness of these textual features established in historically-sensitive fashion, the next and final section turns to explore the interpretive implications that this sustained and purposeful interaction has for the meaning of Hebrew Esther.

---

of the Festival lies a fierce debate about the status of Jews in exile in general and their position vis-à-vis their brothers and sisters in Yehud in particular" (*Esther*, 195).

Part Three: **The Theology of Esther and Contrast of Daniel**

6 The Theological Implications of Esther's Relationship with Joseph

At this juncture, a brief rehearsal of the findings helps situate the import of the analyses that come in this final section. In Part One, three specific textual examples were examined to demonstrate Esther's uniquely close linguistic, thematic, and narrative relationship to Joseph; by surveying the scholarly literature on the topic, the opening section also noted how past criticism has fallen short of appreciating the full depth and breadth of these connections, which consistently position Esther's happenings against Joseph's instructive backdrop. Part Two then turned to specify the deliberateness of these links by attending to the multi-layered compositional history of the Scroll. As the comparative evidence provided by Esther's ancient Greek witnesses shows, the MT Esther redactors, though not the first to associate Esther with Joseph, repeatedly sought to enhance the structural and philological contacts with Joseph that were already present but not as developed in the early Hebrew version of Esther from which they worked.

With such key points established, these final two chapters deal with two last and particularly crucial issues. In the first instance, this present chapter details one more example of specific linguistic borrowing to explore the fuller interpretive implications of reading MT Esther alongside Joseph's instructive precedent. While this effort sheds fresh light onto Esther's much-debated theological stance, the next and final chapter of this study turns to the book of Daniel for a point of comparison. Given that scholarship since Rosenthal has tended to see the connections between Esther and Joseph spanning to Daniel, as well, Chapter Seven accordingly reviews the evidence presented by the court narratives to determine whether some of the intertextual designs detected in the Scroll can be found in Daniel 1–6, too.

6.1 Koller's Politics of Exile

An analysis of Aaron Koller's take on the Megillah kicks off this final effort.[146] His book, which sees the Scroll through a thoroughly political lens, ties two distinct scholarly threads together. In the first instance, his interpretive slant extends out of Humphreys' influential essay.[147] Suggesting that the Scroll was written in the diaspora and for a diasporic audience, Koller extends Humphreys' basic environ-

---

146 Aaron Koller, *Esther in Ancient Jewish Thought* (Cambridge: Cambridge University Press, 2014).
147 Humphreys, "Life-style."

https://doi.org/10.1515/9783111216119-006

mental emphasis to contend that Esther's disinterest in land and law is an argument for a particular way of life. When living outside of Israel, Koller suggests, Jews must make the compromises necessary to stay close to power so that they are positioned to intervene when the tide inevitably turns against them.

To some extent, the second scholarly discussion that Koller's work picks up on also has roots in Humphreys' seminal article. While Humphreys sees a parallel between Esther and Daniel – in both cases, tales of universal appeal were brought into more nationalistic frames – Koller follows Matthew Rindge's more recent effort to foreground a contrast between the two books.[148] If Daniel 2, in Rindge's estimation, references Joseph in a way that criticizes the Genesis character, then an assimilated Esther alludes to Joseph, who, for Rindge, represents the ideal of acclimation, to bolster the stance of compromise the Scroll takes.

Given the crucial role Rindge's work plays in Koller's argument, a brief rehearsal of Rindge's essay is in order. After noting 18 specific literary similarities between Genesis 41 and Daniel 2, as well as a number of larger-scale thematic points of contact ("Jewish Identity," 88–90), Rindge suggests that the differences between the chapters coalesce into three distinct patterns that consistently portray Daniel as superior to Joseph. According to Rindge, the first pattern centers around dream interpretation. Since Daniel must not only interpret the king's dream but also discover the contents of the dream, Rindge perceives Daniel's interpretive abilities outstripping Joseph's (90–92). While the second divergence reflects the characters' piety, the same basic outcome, which sees Daniel best the Egyptian vizier, is reached: "Whereas Joseph claims that God is the source of his interpretation (Gen 41:16), Daniel's prayer demonstrates such a belief" (93).

The third and final set of differences reflects the two characters' attitudes toward their respective foreign surroundings, and, once again, Rindge sees Daniel coming out on top. While Joseph's interpretation of the Pharaoh's dreams allows for the Egyptians to survive, "Daniel's interpretation declares the future collapse of Nebuchadnezzar's kingdom" (95). Moreover, though Joseph ascends higher than Daniel, "the author of Daniel 2," who was invested in forwarding a model that championed maintaining a distinct Jewish identity in foreign lands, "would most likely understand Joseph's promotion as a decline" (96). Rindge thus concludes: "In his ability to interpret dreams, his piety, and his resistance to foreign imperial rule, Daniel is consistently presented as a 'new and improved' version of Joseph" (98).[149]

---

148 Matthew S. Rindge, "Jewish Identity under Foreign Rule: Daniel 2 as a Reconfiguration of Genesis 41," *JBL* 129:1 (2010): 85–104.

149 Rindge's larger aim is to place this comparison in context with other texts of the Second Temple period. "On one end of the spectrum is 1 Maccabees, which enjoins rejection of foreign culture and empire ... If 1 Maccabees occupies one end of the spectrum, the depiction of Joseph in Genesis 37–50 lies at the opposite extreme. As was noted above, Joseph is presented as an

Accepting Rindge's basic premise, Koller incorporates the book of Esther into this comparative spectrum. If the author of Daniel 2 intended to present an alternative to Joseph's assimilationist stance, Koller feels that the authors of Esther endeavored to counter Daniel's position by supporting the exilic model Joseph supposedly embodies. While Rindge focuses on Daniel's altering of Joseph, Koller attends to Joseph's character and all the ways in which he consistently sacrifices his Jewish identity in order to gain power in a foreign land. For Koller, two points articulate this movement most directly, and the first revolves around Joseph's active forgetting of his past.

> Once in Egypt, he turns his back on his family with a shocking finality. Apparently convinced that all members of his household were at least complicit in the vicious treachery committed against him – including his father, who had, after all, *sent* him to check on his brothers – he lives a life in Egypt of remarkable solitude. As a slave, then as a prisoner, then as an interpreter of dreams, and finally as a prince, he cuts a figure of austere aloneness. He is accompanied by no one, has no friends, cultivates no relationships. Alone he fails, alone he rises; failure and success are his alone. Not only does he not develop new relationships within Egyptian society, but he actively dissolves his old ties to his family and his ancestry. Or, perhaps, he perceives that these ties have already been dissolved, and he sets about eradicating them from his identity altogether. He names his first son "Manasseh," from a Semitic root meaning "to forget," and he explains: "for the Lord has made me forget all my toils *and my whole family*" (Genesis 41:51). The second son, on the other hand, is named "Ephraim," "for the Lord has made me prosper in the land of my affliction" (41:52). (*Esther*, 83)

This process of removing himself from his own family of origin has an added layer of significance, as, according to Koller, it affords Joseph the necessary space to rise in the foreign land he comes to call home. Koller sees this dynamic playing out in both the Pharaoh and Joseph's worldly powers: since Joseph swears by the Egyptian ruler (Gen 42:16), Joseph must have placed the Pharaoh in God's position,[150] and, in this same vein of placing humans into the divine's place, Koller suggests that Joseph himself also occasionally operates in God's sphere (84–85). Thus, with his Israelite past forgotten and his Egyptian authority cemented, Joseph, Koller argues, is presented as the symbol of ideal acculturation. "Joseph is an extreme example of a Jew who, while remaining a Jew, has given up much of his overtly Jewish identity in order to take part in the political life of his new land" (85), and, in this regard, "Esther adopts Joseph as a role model whole-heartedly" (85).

---

archetypal assimilationist" (99–100). In this environment, Daniel 2 thus represents a mediate position, a "'moderate' resistance to this religio-cultural assimilation" (103).

150 "Biblical characters," Koller asserts, "typically swear by God, or by the life of God, but Pharaoh here has replaced God. In Joseph's mind, Pharaoh plays that role: he is the all-powerful sustainer of life" (84).

With both Joseph and Esther stationed on the assimilationist side, the contrast between Joseph and Esther, on the one hand, and Daniel, on the other, is established. In both religious and political terms, "Daniel represents the other pole: a Jew who never sacrificed anything" for his foreign environment (85). From his food preferences to the interpretive help he receives from God, from discussing religion with the king to persuading Nebuchadnezzar to admit the God of Israel, Daniel insists on his own heritage regardless of the cost. "The author of Esther," Koller concludes, "vehemently disagrees with this approach. His characters, as has been seen above, sacrifice nearly everything, from their names to their choices of food and spouse ... the book of Daniel takes exile to be a thoroughly lamentable and hopefully brief episode in the history of the Jews. In Esther, on the other hand, diaspora life is simply a reality to be navigated" (85).[151]

In many ways, Koller's work, which sees Esther's interaction with Joseph as central to the purpose of the Scroll, represents yet another important development in the scholarly understanding of the relationship; in other ways, however, it too falls short of appreciating the fuller significance of the intertextual interaction. By lining up the biblical characters for direct comparison and then viewing their similarities and differences through only this political lens, Koller's approach misses a number of narrative connections that engage aspects found across Joseph and Esther that extend beyond this one predetermined area. As one final instance of literary borrowing shows, Esther's connections to Joseph do not reduce to social examples for others to follow but rather position the Egyptian events as an instructive backdrop that expresses continuity between that which already occurred in Genesis and that which is presently happening in the Megillah.

6.2 Joseph's Divinely Initiated Patterns Reflected in Esther's Paralleled Movements

To explore such a point, recall Genesis 43, on the one hand, and Esther 4, on the other. In Canaan, Jacob is facing a terrible dilemma: he must either risk Benjamin, whom he believes to be the only remaining son to his beloved wife, by sending

---

151 At this point, a serious historical problem develops in Koller's work. Since Koller sees Daniel 2 as a key component of Daniel's rejection of Joseph, his intertextual argument hinges on Esther's authors being aware of not just some of Daniel's court narratives but this particular tale, as well. However, given that the present literary form of Daniel 2 requires a Hellenistic date, Koller's intertextual position is compromised by his own interest in dating Esther to the Persian period (37). While the following chapter notes how large sections of Daniel 2 may very well have been composed in the Persian era and thus could have conceivably been known by Esther's Persian authors, the key historical implications of Koller's claim, which would require

him down in his other sons' increasingly questionable care to the dangers of Egypt or deal with the painful consequences of a worsening food shortage. While the immediate cause for Jacob's impossible choice is the famine, Levenson has shown how this larger sequence stems at a deeper level from the difficulties that God's unusual preference for Jacob's second-youngest son has brought.[152] For back in Genesis 37, when Joseph first realizes his unusual status, the initial result of his favor is far from the greatness of which he dreamt. Though his brothers' jealousy is the most obvious reason for his unexpected misfortune in a pit, Joseph must at this early juncture share a portion of the blame. By repeatedly reporting his self-aggrandizing dreams to those who ought to be above him (Gen 37:5–11) without any concern for how his surprising status might come across, Joseph shows himself to be as ill-prepared for his leading role as his brothers are unable to accept their supporting one.

Upon Joseph's arrival in Egypt, such unexpected twists of fortune continue. If his favor with God initially causes him to rise in Potiphar's house (Gen 39:2–6), then so does it once again forcefully turn back against him. His proximity to Potiphar's wife – itself a result of the esteem he has mysteriously just found – presents him with the opportunity that so enticed him two chapters earlier: take the master's wife, she offers, and surely the master will be soon to follow (Gen 39:7–12).[153] This time, however, Joseph's reaction is quite different. Instead of jumping at the opportunity to place himself above the rest, he remains steadfastly loyal to the one above him (Gen 39:8–10), even at great personal cost to himself (Gen 39:20). At this point, the direction of Joseph's up and down trajectory – a trajectory that will ultimately force his father to send Benjamin away so that lasting familial reunification can be attained – starts to take shape. If Joseph as a seventeen-year-old excitedly placed his own good fortune over his older brothers' fates, he now sees his unusual favor requiring an uprightness to his superior regardless of the consequence.[154]

---

careful redactional approaches that identify certain verses of Daniel 2 as later insertions, must at the very least be engaged – something Koller's work never actually does. For a basic discussion of these issues and a brief review of their scholarly history, see the analysis below (§ 7.1).

152 Levenson, *Death and Resurrection*, 143–69.

153 On this point, see Levenson, *Death and Resurrection*, 156, which points to the well-known parallel in 1 Kgs 2:13–25. In this context, the present analysis would also call attention to Esther 7, where Ahasuerus ultimately decides to rid himself and his empire of the evil prime minister only when the king misunderstands Haman's pathetic fall to Esther's couch as an attempt to usurp his throne by taking a pass at the queen.

154 Suggesting a parallel to the Egyptian "Tale of Two Brothers," Westermann interprets in similar fashion. "The reason for Joseph's refusal is clear: he may not, he will not commit a breach of trust (also H. Gunkel), not only because he knows very well that he would put his own position in jeopardy, but also because he cannot do this to his master who has promoted

As this action shows Joseph's character movement in full swing, the final phase in this arc completes the personal transformation that God's election has brought about. After Joseph's refusal of Potiphar's wife has him tossed into jail for righteousness (Gen 39:20), his divine favor kickstarts yet another improbable rise (Gen 39:20–23). Using his next ascent to interpret the cupbearer and baker's dreams correctly (Gen 40:7–22), he waits to be called before the Pharaoh where he is once again confronted with a set of two dreams – the very same design that started this entire sequence in the first place. This internal echo causes a natural comparison between the scenes in a way that highlights Joseph's maturation: if Joseph in Genesis 37 was only able to see what his own dreams meant for him, he now interprets the Pharaoh's in a way that addresses the danger facing the entire world; if the teenage Joseph foregrounded the exultation that the chosen would receive, despite his dreams depicting a host of other supporting characters, he now places both his own abilities and the plenty of the present in the service of all for the challenging times to come (Gen 41:25–36).

That this action helps to make sense of and validate God's election of Joseph, which at the outset seemed to cause more chaos than good,[155] completes the link for the present analysis. For when the brothers are then forced to descend to Egypt to collect the grain that Joseph's unusual gifts have allowed him to store, the vizier uses the elevated position into which his favor propelled him to deter-

---

him and shown such confidence in him. It is the same reason in the Egyptian parallel. He respects the limit because he sees behind it the benevolence he has found in his master's eyes (v. 4). Joseph therefore emphasizes his responsibility: '... He has withheld nothing from me ...' The narrator is deliberately setting side by side the responsibility of the eldest brother in ch. 37 and the responsibility of one in administrative office" (*Genesis 37–50*, 66).

155 Since this analytic line continues to follow Levenson, consider his insightful remarks. "The choice of Joseph is the engine both of the decline in the family's fortunes and of its ascent from the pit of jealousy, conspiracy, deception, despondency, and, ultimately, destitution into which it had fallen. But the family ascends farther than it had declined. The chosenness of Joseph proves more an asset than a liability, and the wisdom and justice of the God who chose him, so easily doubted at the beginning of the tale, are richly vindicated at its end" (*Death and Resurrection*, 168). For a somewhat different take, see von Rad's work, which turns to Gen 50:20 to suggest not a validation of divine election but rather an irreconcilable mystery between God's purpose and human action. After quoting the famous verse, "You meant evil against me, but God meant it for good," von Rad develops his argument. "Here the problem of the relationship between human intentions and the divine control of events is still more keenly felt: God has all the threads firmly in his hands even when men are least aware of it. But this is a bare statement of fact, and the way in which God's will is related to human purposes remains a mystery. Thus the statements of what 'you meant' and what 'God meant' are in the last analysis irreconcilable ... The purposes of God and man are set over against each other, and the purposes of God prevail" ("The Joseph Narrative and Ancient Wisdom," in *The Problem of the Hexateuch and Other Essays*, trans. Trueman Dicken [New York: McGraw Hill, 1966]: 292–300; here: 297).

mine whether his brothers are equipped to reunite themselves with the one they so wronged (§ 2.1). Since this testing requires that the brothers show their new-found commitment to protecting Benjamin – that is, the very opposite of what they did to Joseph – the agonizing decision Jacob faces in Genesis 43 is shown to reflect not just the food shortage directly in front of him but also the long and aching tendrils that Joseph's favor paradoxically created.

Though the drama of the story depends on Jacob at this point not seeing all these interconnections, his response to the first of Judah's two powerful speeches (Gen 43:3–10; § 2.3) reveals how the results of the earlier fratricidal tension still ring loudly in Jacob's head. Instead of worrying about the imminent threat of starvation, Jacob relents to the obvious reality Judah demonstrates – the brothers can either return to Egypt with Benjamin, or they all must stay in Canaan and risk starvation (Gen 43:3–10) – without concern for food but rather fear of losing yet another son. "If it must be so," Jacob concedes resignedly,

> do this: take some of the choice products of the land in your baggage, and carry them down as a gift for the man – some balm and some honey, gum, ladanum, pistachio nuts, and almonds. And take with you double the money, carrying back with you the money that was replaced in the mouths of your bags; perhaps it was a mistake. Take your brother too; and go back at once to the man. And may El Shaddai dispose the man to mercy toward you, that he may release to you your other brother, as well as Benjamin. As for me, if I am to be bereaved, I shall be bereaved. (Gen 43:11–14)

While the Hebrew syntax of Jacob's final phrase, "If I am to be bereaved, I shall be bereaved," is highly unusual, כאשר שכלתי שכלתי (Gen 43:14), it is repeated exactly at a moment of equal importance in the Megillah. In a fashion similar to the other examples of specific literary borrowing discussed throughout this study, this philological link is also accompanied by a number of telling narrative parallels. Much as Joseph's unusual distinction repeatedly turns to trouble him – first with his own family and then on Potiphar's estate – so does the unexpected favor of an orphaned Jewish girl in Persia initially elevate but then flip against her. After Esther's familiarly phrased beauty (Esth 2:7//Gen 39:6; § 3.2) raises her into Ahasuerus' court (Esth 2:17), her proximity to the king, which up to this point has expressed the mysterious good favor she received from both Hegai and then Ahasuerus (Esth 2:9, 15, 17), quickly becomes the source of her acute danger. Since her connection to Ahasuerus is the Jews' only hope, she, Mordecai contends, must jeopardize her own life on behalf of her now threatened people (Esth 4:8).

Keeping the Genesis story in mind continues to present the Megillah action with instructive parallels. Much as Joseph in Genesis 37 is only able to see his dreams evincing his own greatness, so can Esther at this moment only hear Mordecai's words for what they might mean for her. Though Mordecai stresses the communal nature of the danger by asking Esther "to plead with [the king] for her people" (Esth 4:8), Esther responds in a single and selfish dimension. "All the king's courtiers," she returns through the intermediary Hathach, "and the people of the king's provinces know that if any person, man or woman, enters the king's presence in the inner court without having been summoned, there is but one law for him – that he be put to death. Only if the king extends the golden scepter to him may he live. Now I have not been summoned to visit the king for the last thirty days" (Esth 4:11).

However, in much the same way that a dry pit and wrongful bondage begins the process of turning Joseph's youthful selfishness into a more mature wisdom, so does the threat of immediate destruction bring about the sea change in the queen. For when Mordecai reminds Esther of the hazard her own distinction can bring, his warning triggers an unexpected character transformation. "Do not imagine," Mordecai rejoins, after initially failing to spur Esther into action, "that you, of all the Jews, will escape with your life by being in the king's palace. On the contrary, if you keep silent in this crisis, relief and deliverance will come to the Jews from another quarter, while you and your father's house will perish" (Esth 4:13–14).

If Joseph's refusal to put himself over Potiphar's house paradoxically punishes him for demonstrating an unexpected commitment to the one who elevated him, then Esther suddenly upends the selfishness of her previous obstinacy only to imperil herself. "Go," she now commands Mordecai, "assemble all the Jews who live in Shushan, and fast in my behalf; do not eat or drink for three days, night or day. I and my maidens will observe the same fast. Then I shall go to the king, though it is contrary to the law; and if I am to perish, I shall perish!" (Esth 4:16). That her final phrase, "If I am to perish, I shall perish," reuses Jacob's exact syntax punctuates the larger narrative resonances traced above: וכאשר אבדתי אבדתי (Esth 4:16).[156]

If the buildups to these phrases overlap, then so do their aftermaths also correspond, and, if the particular linguistic connection under present discussion – Esth 4:16 and Gen 43:14 – is reflected in AT and thus likely part of the early Esther core that the MT redactors maintained, then the present analysis turns now to show that this example is embedded inside a series of other philological links that the MT redactors likely added in their effort to position this specific parallel inside an increasingly meaningful intertextual frame. After Jacob nervously re-leases Benjamin and the brothers make their way south, the vizier sees his only

---

156 Though the expressions, "If I am to be bereaved, I shall be bereaved" (Gen 43:14) and "If I am to perish, I shall perish" (Esth 4:16), sound relatively normal and grammatical in English, the syntax employed in both cases is highly unusual in Biblical Hebrew. After כאשר, usually a temporal conjunction, is employed to introduce a conditional clause, two suffix conjugation verbs express subjunctives that both turn out to be counterfactual.

full brother and struggles to maintain his own self-control (וַיִּתְאַפַּק, Gen 43:29–31); in similar fashion, after Esther agrees to approach the king despite the obvious danger it places her in, she calls for a series of banquets that causes Haman's swings of emotion to fall in and out of check (וַיִּתְאַפַּק, Esth 5:9–14; § 2.1). Such parallels continue: after Joseph uses Benjamin's presence in Egypt to make him appear the guiltiest party, Judah must return to the vizier and somehow try to convince him not to detain the one Jacob had been so desperate to protect (כִּי אֵיךְ, Gen 44:34); in the Megillah, after Esther's banquets present her with the opportunity to dethrone the prime minister (Esth 7:3–10), she must also return to the king to find a way past an edict that cannot legally be changed (כִּי אֵיכָכָה, Esth 8:6; § 2.3).

Since these last two instances of linguistic borrowing, א.פ.ק and כִּי אֵיךְ, are not found in AT 1:7–16 and therefore likely secondary MT additions, the multiple layers of the relationship and the consistency with which Joseph is referenced in the Hebrew Megillah suggest a significance that extends beyond genre similarities, interpretive mindsets, or social goals. As Esther's key movements repeatedly conjure equally important moments in Joseph, the events of the Megillah are shown to extend out of the narrative arc that Genesis initiated. Since God's powerful preferences and occasional activities play key roles in bringing about these twists in Joseph (Gen 39:2–5, in particular), the parallels found in Esther articulate the contours of a distinct theological position. In the Scroll, even when the heavenly presence remains out of reach, the earthly patterns God enacted in the Egyptian past continue into the confusing silence of the Persian present.[157]

---

157 In somewhat similar fashion, Macchi also finds theological meaning in Esther's interaction with Joseph. To his eye, however, the religious worth of the relationship is found not in the continuation of previous and divinely initiated patterns but rather in the way that both stories supposedly force their readers to look for God's trace silently encoded in the narratives. "By not making explicit mention of divine action," Macchi writes, "the MT uses a literary technique that aims to direct the reader to discern divine will and action behind events and human actions. An analogous process is found in the Joseph story (Gen 37–45). Practically no action of God is mentioned explicitly. Yet, the fortuitous things that happen to Joseph are reported, and his dreams can be understood as the expression of an act of God. It is only at the end of the narrative that Joseph addresses his brothers, and explicitly interprets what has happened as a result of divine will 'Do not be tormented over having sold me here, for it is God who sent me ...' (Gen 45:5). Hinting at, rather than overtly mentioning divine action is astute, for this forces the reader to interpret the significance of the narrative and its theological meaning" (*Esther*, 72). In addition to noting how this admittedly creative take still falls into the hewn interpretive grooves of Scroll scholarship that have tended to mix finding God where the divine is not with the faithful readings of later generations (§ 1.1), the present work also seconds the spirit of Wetzel's response. For as Wetzel notes, even though Joseph "shares with MT Esther a lack of overt divine appearances or communication between God and the characters in the story, MT Esther goes much further by eliminating references to God from the narrator's comments as well" (*Violence*

For if Joseph's favor paradoxically separates him from his father and then forces Jacob to risk Benjamin, then so does Esther's status in Persia keep her away from Mordecai and cause her to endanger her own life. Moreover, if the threat against Benjamin unexpectedly spins into lasting familial reunification and relief from the deadly famine, then so does the peril Esther faces ultimately set up her ability to dethrone the prime minister and deliver the Jews from a threat that should have been unavoidable. In this way, the exact opposites of the fears both Jacob and Esther so earnestly express come to pass: Jacob is not further bereaved but rather reunited with both Simeon and Joseph in a land that will support them, and Esther does not lose her life but rather elevates Mordecai along the way to rescuing her entire nation from a murderous cliff. Thus, as opposed to reading God's presence into a purposefully silent Hebrew Scroll or relying on the unarticulated faiths of Esther's characters or later readers, the parallels traced here indicate how the Megillah invokes Joseph to develop a specific theology of divine absence. Since both God's presence and choices remain beyond immediate detection in Shushan, the earthly designs Joseph's previous divine election engendered are shown to extend into yet another story of foreign chaos turning into unexpected deliverance.

6.3 The Significance of Divine Absence in MT Esther's Theology

Since this interpretive line sees Esther purposefully exploring moments of prolonged divine absence, a final review of the Greek witnesses confirms the importance of God's silence in the Hebrew Scroll by showing it to be the result of a considered authorial choice. As this last examination of key AT and LXX verses demonstrates, the early Esther core from which the MT redactors worked likely contained at least some of the direct references to God found in AT 1–7:16, thus suggesting that those responsible for MT knew of and purposefully removed this overt religious language in their reworking of the earlier Megillah tradition.[158]

---

and Divine Victory, 166, n31). By also emphasizing this crucial distinction, this analysis thus seeks to show how Esther's relationship with Joseph does not import Joseph's theological posture into the Megillah. Instead, Esther explores how the providential line God creates with Joseph can extend even when God's immediate presence remains out of sight.

158 For an opposed perspective, see, for example, Jobes' work, which suggests it "more natural that religious language was added in the Greek versions to clarify, expand and specify points in the biblical Hebrew text that cry out for theological exposition" (*Alpha-Text*, 212). For an even more developed position, consider Melton's work, *Where is God*, which follows De Troyer's previously discussed historical recreation (§ 5.2). Since Melton sees AT, which has the most directly

To approach such a point, note how three distinct categories of direct divine references are found in Esther's Greek witnesses: instances that are only found in AT (AT 4:9, 11; 6:17; 7:2), instances that are found in both AT and LXX (AT 4:5// LXX 4:8; AT 6:1//LXX 6:1; and AT 6:22//LXX 6:13), and one passage that is only found in LXX (LXX 2:19–20). Since those examples that are only found in AT are particularly illuminating for the present purposes, this analysis now turns to a comparison of the AT, MT, and LXX versions of Esther 4.

In AT, after Esther sends word to Mordecai, asking him to remove his sackcloth and come to see her (AT 4:4), Mordecai sends an impassioned message back. "Do not turn away from going to the king," he begins, "and flattering his person for the sake of me and my people, remembering your humble days when you were being brought up by my hand, because Haman, who is the second in command, has spoken to the king against us to put us to death. Therefore call upon God, and speak about us to the king, and deliver us from death!" (AT 4:4–5).

Despite the obvious divine difference, this AT section reflects a close connection with the MT version. In both cases, Mordecai discovers Haman's terrible edict and then proceeds to convince the initially recalcitrant queen that she must act on her people's behalf. While the corresponding LXX chapter shows an even closer connection to MT, two of the features found in AT but not MT are present in LXX. Much as AT recounts Mordecai, in his first exchange with Esther, reminding the queen of her earlier days (AT 4:4), so does LXX record that distinctive opening back and forth in similar fashion. "Remember your humbled days," Mordecai addresses Esther through the messenger, "when you were brought up by my hand, for Haman, the second to the king, has spoken against us to put us to death" (LXX 4:8). Moreover, if Mordecai in AT concludes his initial plea by invoking God (AT 4:5), so does Mordecai in LXX also at this point reference the divine. "Call upon the Lord," the Jewish courtier says, "and speak to the king about us, and deliver us from death" (LXX 4:8).

In both of these LXX phrases, the language is very similar to, and at times even identical with, the corresponding AT passages. Consider the verses in full:

AT 4:4: μνησθεῖσα ἡμερῶν ταπεινώσεώς σου ὧν ἐτράφης ἐν τῇ χειρί μου
LXX 4:8: μνησθεῖσα ἡμερῶν ταπεινώσεώς σου ὡς ἐτράφης ἐν χειρί μου

Such notable similarities are also found in the different Greek versions of Mordecai's invocation of the Lord.

---

religious language of all three ancient versions, as a recension of LXX, she thus concludes that over time the three versions of Esther became increasingly more religious in nature (70).

AT 4:5:   ἐπικαλεσαμένη οὖν τὸν θεὸν λάλησον περὶ ἡμῶν τῷ βασιλεῖ καὶ ῥῦσαι ἡμᾶς ἐκ θανάτου

LXX 4:8: ἐπικάλεσαι τὸν κύριον καὶ λάλησον τῷ βασιλεῖ περὶ ἡμῶν καὶ ῥῦσαι ἡμᾶς ἐκ θανάτου

Since both the specific language and general sense of these AT and LXX verses demonstrate a clear connection, it is possible to explain these specific instances not as original AT passages but rather the result of later LXX influence.[159]

While such an interpretation would exclude these verses from the early Esther core and suggest that the MT redactors were not aware of them, this analytic line cannot be extended to the divine references found at the end of this AT chapter. Consider the pertinent AT verses, which pick up at Mordecai's second attempt to move the queen into action. "So Mardochaios sent to her [Esther] and said to her, 'If you ignore your nation and do not help them, then surely God will be to them a helper and deliverance, but you and your father's household will perish'" (AT 4:9), and "Then the queen sent saying, 'Proclaim a religious service, and petition God earnestly, and I and my girls will do likewise'" (AT 4:11). For both of these verses, the LXX, by contrast, follows right along with MT. "Mardochaios said to Hachrathaios, 'Go, and say to her, 'Esther, do not say to yourself that you alone of all the Judeans in the empire will be safe. Because even if you keep silent at this time, from elsewhere help and protection will come to the Judeans, but you and your father's household will perish'" (LXX 4:13), and: "Then Esther sent the messenger who had come to her back to Mardochaios, saying, 'Go, gather the Judeans that are in Susa, and fast on my behalf, and neither eat nor drink for three days, night and day. I and my attendants will also abstain from food. And then I will go to the king, though it is against the law, even if it be that I perish'" (LXX 4:15–16).

If AT 4:9 and 4:11 indicate AT reflecting a tradition that speaks openly of God in a way that is distinct from LXX, then so do AT 6:17 and 7:2 confirm the independence of this textual strand and demonstrate such language to be firmly embedded within the AT storyline. In AT 6, though the same basic reversal found in MT is narrated, a set of subtle but internally consistent differences to MT is found. While MT and LXX never express the characters' mindsets amidst the stunning twist of fate, AT repeatedly does. First comes Haman's sharp disappointment:

---

159 Even Clines accepts this basic interpretive line (*Esther Scroll*, 107–112). Since the idea of LXX exerting some influence over AT is counter to his most fundamental aim, Clines argues that these few instances of possible LXX contamination "is quite untypical of the book [AT] as a whole" (111) and thus does not disrupt his general position of an entirely independent AT. Fox's work, which is open to some limited contact between AT and LXX, also views these examples as reflective of LXX influence in a way that fits more comfortably within his overarching program (*Redaction*, 120–21).

"Now when Haman realized that it was not he himself who would be extolled, but that it was Mardochaios, his heart was utterly broken, and his spirit became feeble" (AT 6:13). When this Greek narration then turns to Mordecai, it picks up right where the Jewish protagonist left off in AT 4 – afraid for his life as a result of Haman's murderous edict. Thus, since Mordecai does not yet understand why Haman is commanding him to remove his sackcloth (AT 6:15), Mordecai's fear maintains until the shock of the king's garments is coupled with an explanation from above.

> And Haman took the robe and the horse, showing reverence to Mardochaios even on the very same day on which he intended to impale him. And he said to Mardochaios, "Tear off the sackcloth." And Mardochaios was distressed as one dying, and with anguish he took off the sackcloth and put on the garments of glory. And Mardochaios thought he saw a sign, and his heart was toward the Lord, and he was mystified in silent fear. (AT 6:14–17)

Though this AT appeal has no parallel in LXX, the explicit mention of Mordecai's internal reaction continues into the following AT chapter. At the beginning of AT 7, after Esther has called her second banquet since she hesitated at the first, she now realizes that she must finally speak up against the king's hand-picked prime minister. While this action also occurs in MT and LXX, AT narrates a crucial difference, as the queen's fear, which is only hinted at by the course of actions in MT and LXX, is here directly revealed. "As the drinking advanced [at Esther's second banquet], the king said to Esther, 'What is the danger, and what is your petition? Up to the half of my kingdom!' Esther struggled with her reply, because the adversary was before her eyes, and God gave her courage as she called upon him" (AT 7:1–2). As this divine reference once again has no LXX equivalent, the entire AT passage is shown to fit nicely in its present literary context by linking to the previous glimpses into the other characters' mindsets – something MT and LXX consistently refrain from doing.

Though these divergences could be interpreted as AT pluses, the present approach sees no reason to exclude them from the early Esther core from which both AT and MT worked. Not only do they fall inside the general parameters of the posited early textual tradition, but so also does their excision from MT make clear sense given the designs of Esther's Hebrew redactors. By removing all direct divine language while increasing the intertextual links to Joseph, the MT redactors sought to invoke God's action in the past in order to explore the theological possibilities of divine absence in the present. In this particular way, then, this analysis once again aligns itself with Clines.[160]

---

[160] While this line of argument, which sees those responsible for MT removing the religious language of the early Esther core, has also been forwarded by Macchi, its implications have not yet been fully appreciated, as even this deliberate effort to remove God's direct presence has

The pluses of the AT can more readily be explained by supposing that MT represents a systematic attempt to remove religious language than by supposing AT to represent a systematic attempt to introduce religious language. For at no point is the religious language of the AT at all unnatural or forced, whereas the absence of such language from the MT has very frequently seemed to commentators unnatural or at least due to a deliberate avoidance of usual Hebrew manners of speech. (112)[161]

While previous attempts to read the Megillah have tended either to read God's activity onto Esther's page or find the characters' and readers' elusive beliefs, this comparison with AT suggests a different interpretive result. As the enhancement of Esther's connections to Joseph and the decision to keep from language about God and faith are shown deliberate and unique to the Hebrew Scroll, they accordingly combine to play a crucial role in MT Esther's overarching purpose. While Joseph is able to navigate the Egyptian court with heavenly favor, Esther and Mordecai must work their way through a Persian maze devoid of all divine involvement. Despite the challenges that this confusion creates, however, the parallels reaching across the two stories emphasize that even when God's presence

---

been viewed in terms of God's activity and later readers' faithful responses. "These modifications," Macchi writes of the MT redactors' likely removal of the references to God found in AT, "are part of a global editorial strategy aimed at not making explicit reference to divine action. The editors do not deny the possibility of divine intervention; the narrative even suggests it. Yet, they want to make readers think about the forms of divine action and the theological issues that are hidden behind the narrated events" (*Esther*, 181). While the present analysis underscores both Macchi's historical point, which sees the MT redactors removing Esther's earlier references to God, and his effort to find, counterintuitively, theological meaning in this concerted editorial decision, it suggests a more specific purpose. By eliminating all direct references to God and increasing the intertextual links to Joseph – a point Macchi also expertly notes (§ 4.4) – those responsible for the final shape of the Hebrew Scroll sought to explore a theology of divine absence that illustrates how the patterns God initiated in the past continue into the present even when God's presence remains obscured.

161 Though Clines does not consider MT Esther's intertextual character, he develops yet another reason to see these differences between AT and MT as purposeful MT minuses as opposed to AT pluses. While the present study has focused on those instances of religious language that invoke the God of Israel, Clines notes how AT also occasionally invokes non-Jewish divinities (AT 4:7; 6:23; 7:22). Since these references are also not present in MT, Clines thus concludes: "It would indeed be simpler to suppose that the MT represents a deliberate excision of *all* religious language, from whatever perspective, than to suppose a supplementer who added not only the references to God's activity from a Jewish perspective but also such passages as 4.7 and 6.23 from a pagan perspective" (*Esther Scroll*, 109).

remains obscured, the providential patterns that led to deliverance in a previous foreign land still maintain in the present.[162]

---

162 This explanation answers a key question raised by Fox. While Fox considers it possible that the MT redactors excised all religious language from the *Vorlage* off of which they were working, he feels that such an interpretive line requires a reason that has not yet been demonstrated. "The excision of religious statements [in MT] would be a far more radical act than simply not writing them into a story to start with. It would be a bold *theological* statement, but one that would require some guidance or clarification beyond what is offered by MT-Esther" (*Redaction*, 120–21). As this analysis shows, however, there is indeed a reason for this excision. By increasing the links to Joseph and removing the direct references to God, MT Esther intentionally expresses how that which God previously enacted continues into the present even when God remains out of sight.

7 Daniel's Position in Joseph and Esther's Intertextual Chain

Since the majority of this study has been dedicated to exploring the unusually important relationship Esther develops with Joseph, one final matter must be addressed. As scholarship since Rosenthal has appreciated, aspects of the connection between Esther and Joseph extend to the court narratives of Daniel 1–6, as well. Similar to both Joseph and Esther, these tales also tell of Jews rising in foreign courts to deliver themselves and their people from imminent dangers. Much as Esther solidifies its interaction with Joseph through specific linguistic connections, so are some philological similarities to both Esther and Joseph found in this Daniel collection. Thus, this last chapter explores the form and function of these connections to determine whether certain aspects of Esther's relationship to Joseph – which, up to this point, has been understood as a uniquely productive association – can also be found in Daniel.

To begin this final investigation, issues of dating for Daniel 1–6 are addressed so that questions of relative chronology between the court narratives and the two texts at the center of this study can be explored. Once this historical background is set, attention then turns to the textual evidence that links Daniel 1–6 with both Esther and Joseph, and the cases are examined, once again according mainly to Leonard's criteria, for evidence of authorial intent. At that point, the major analysis of the chapter can be pursued, as Daniel's relationship with Joseph is compared to Esther's in order to determine how they both engage with the same Genesis text.

7.1 The Dating of Daniel's Court Narratives

While the compositional history of the entire Daniel book presents any number of difficulties, scholarship has reached some generally accepted parameters for Daniel 1–6. As an introduction to the major characters and themes of the narratives that immediately follow, Daniel 1 is usually thought to have been written in full knowledge of the larger Daniel 2–6 collection;[163] the individual tales that comprise Daniel 2–6, however, seem to have developed independently over a longer period

---

[163] That Daniel 1 serves as an introduction to this Aramaic collection is of course complicated by the Hebrew of this opening chapter. While scholarship has generated a host of possibilities to explain this peculiarity, several recent commentators have proposed a relatively straightforward explanation. This introductory chapter was originally written in Aramaic but then translated into Hebrew once the final five Hebrew chapters of the Daniel book were added to the opening court narratives. On this particular point, see, for example, Carol Newsom, *Daniel* (Louisville: West-

https://doi.org/10.1515/9783111216119-007

of time. Some tales, with their clear dependence on Nabonidus (556–539 BCE), admit of Neo-Babylonian roots; others, Daniel 2, for example, hinge on a Hellenistic context – at least in their present canonical form.

Given the integral role Daniel 2 plays in this narrative section, John J. Collins has argued that the later provenance of this chapter requires dating the whole Daniel 1–6 collection to the Hellenistic period.[164] While Collins' approach preserves the textual integrity of Daniel 1 and 2, Reinhard Kratz has forwarded a different model that separates out certain verses from these opening chapters.[165] Noting how very little in Daniel 2–6 actually requires the late date Collins has advocated, and that those verses that do may even stand in some tension to their immediate literary environments, Kratz proposes that the fourth kingdom in Dan 2:40–44, which clearly refers to the Greek era, is a secondary addition into an earlier Persian period collection of court stories that was neither eschatological in nature nor knew of Greek rule.[166]

Since the present approach appreciates the force of Kratz's argument and recognizes that the frame of Daniel's court stories without the introductory Daniel 1 may very well have been composed and circulated in the Persian period, which is precisely when this study sees the early Esther tradition first being developed and written down (§ 1.3; § 5.5), it proceeds along two distinct tracks. While a *terminus post quem* in the Persian period for much of Daniel 2–6 still allows for the original authors of this textual unit to have known and intentionally invoked Joseph, it does not present a firm basis for a relative chronology with Esther. As a result, more caution in terms of historical directionality is exerted when Esther and Daniel's textual links are examined.

7.2 Daniel and Esther

With these basic historical matters sketched, attention can now turn to the specifics of Daniel's textual contact with Esther. To foreground the conclusion: while Koller simply assumes that Esther was aware of and purposefully referring to

---

minster John Knox, 2014), 8, or John J. Collins, *Daniel: A Commentary on the Book of Daniel* (Minneapolis: Fortress Press, 1993), 24–39. For a survey of previous explanations, see Collins, 12–13.

164 Collins, *Daniel*, 35–37.

165 Reinhard G. Kratz, *Translatio Imperii: Untersuchungen zu den aramäischen Danielerzählungen und ihrem theologiegeschichtlichen Umfeld* (Neukirchen-Vluyn: Neukirchener Verlag, 1991).

166 On this particular point, see Kratz, *Translatio*, 55–70, in particular; for Collins' response, which explores some challenges in Kratz's reconstruction and thus prefers maintaining the integrity of the present Daniel 2 form, see *Daniel*, 36–37.

Daniel,[167] the details provide a different picture. Much as the historical evidence is unable to determine any clear relative chronology, so does the textual evidence fall just short of clearing the high authorial intent bar.

To begin this examination, consider how Daniel 5 opens with a motif that is productive in the Megillah – banquets thrown by a fictitious foreign king. "King Belshazzar gave a great banquet for his thousand nobles, and in the presence of the thousand he drank wine" (Dan 5:1). In similar fashion, Esth 1:3 speaks of Ahasuerus: "In the third year of his reign, he gave a banquet for all the officials and courtiers – the administration of Persia and Media, the nobles and the governors of the provinces in his service." Despite Daniel's change to Aramaic, some basic philological connections are still discernible. Both kings give banquets, בלשאצר מלכא עבד לחם (Dan 5:1), and עשה משתה (Esth 1:3), and, in both cases, the feasts are for the nobles of the kingdom, לרברבנוהי אלף (Dan 5:1), and לכל שריו ועבדיו (Esth 1:3).[168]

At the Persian banquet, Ahasuerus waits until he has had something to drink before sending his order for the queen to be brought before him. "On the seventh day, when the king was merry with wine, he ordered Mehuman, Bizzetha, Harbona, Bigtha, Abagtha, Zethar, and Carcas, the seven eunuchs in attendance on King Ahasuerus, to bring Queen Vashti before the king wearing a royal diadem, to display her beauty to the peoples and the officials; for she was a beautiful woman" (Esth 1:10–11). In similar fashion, Belshazzar at the Babylonian party also waits for his wine to kick in before he orders for the vessels from Jerusalem to be brought to him. "Under the influence of the wine, Belshazzar ordered the gold and silver vessels (למאני דהבא וכספא) that his father Nebuchadnezzar had taken out of the temple at Jerusalem to be brought so that the king and his nobles, his consorts, and his concubines could drink from them" (Dan 5:2).[169]

These broader linguistic and thematic similarities continue. Belshazzar's party, which begins so merry, deteriorates with the same speed and intensity as Ahasuerus' does. In Esther 1, when Vashti refuses her happily intoxicated husband's summons, the king suddenly becomes enraged. "The king was greatly incensed, and his fury burned within him" (Esth 1:12). In Daniel 5, as the guests of the Babylonian court are enjoying their drinks and praising their gods, a mysteri-

---

167 On the historical problems that this uncritical claim generates, see pg. 100–01, n151, above.

168 Rosenthal, who sees Daniel "als drittes Glied in der Kette des Vergleichs" ("Die Josephsgeschichte," 281), also notes this connection.

169 The emphasis on the vessels in this verse also finds an echo in the opening banquet in Esther, where Ahasuerus' golden vessels receive special attention with similar language. "Royal wine was served in abundance, as befits a king, in golden beakers (בכלי זהב), beakers of varied design" (Esth 1:7). On this point, see Rosenthal, 281.

ous hand appears (Dan 5:4–5), and the mood of the once merry king changes just as rapidly. "The king's face darkened, and his thoughts alarmed him; the joints of his loins were loosened and his knees knocked together" (Dan 5:6). Moreover, just as Ahasuerus turns to his counselors for guidance in his moment of rage, "Then the king consulted the sages learned in procedure" (Esth 1:13), so too does Belshazzar look to his advisors for help in deciphering the bizarre writing in his moment of alarm: "The king called loudly for the exorcists, Chaldeans, and diviners to be brought" (Dan 5:7).

When Belshazzar's advisors are unable to help (Dan 5:8), the queen's intercessions bring Daniel to interpret the cryptic markings (Dan 5:10–13). Such action engenders Daniel's rise in the Babylonian court all over again: as Daniel arrives before the troubled Babylonian king, the foreign ruler explains his problem and offers a handsome reward. "Now if you can read the writing and make known its meaning to me, you shall be clothed in purple and wear a golden chain on your neck and rule as one of three in the kingdom" (Dan 5:16). When Daniel correctly deciphers the damning message (Dan 5:26–28), the fictitious Babylonian monarch keeps his word despite the indictment Daniel has interpreted, and the handsome Israelite is honored just as the king had promised. "Then, at Belshazzar's command, they clothed Daniel in purple, placed a golden chain on his neck, and proclaimed that he should rule as one of three in the kingdom" (Dan 5:29).

This verse and the movement surrounding it find reflection in two different occasions in the Megillah: Esther 8, and the narration of Mordecai being honored in Persia, and Haman's ironic misunderstanding of the king's intent in Esther 6. After Esther has outsmarted Haman and revealed him to be the author of the murderous decree leveled against the Jews (Esth 7:6), Ahasuerus orders him to be hanged (Esth 7:9). Though the evil Persian prime minister has been deposed, his edict still remains valid, and Esther must approach her husband with one last request (Esth 8:5–6). When the king once again agrees to Esther's demand, a Jewish counter-decree is dictated (Esth 8:7–14), and Mordecai then emerges as honored as Daniel. "Mordecai left the king's presence in royal robes of blue and white, with a magnificent crown of gold and a mantle of fine linen and purple wool" (Esth 8:15). To highlight the philological resonances, Esther's Hebrew is worth comparing with Daniel's Aramaic; once again, the specific similarities are in bold.

Esth 8:15: ומרדכי יצא מלפני המלך בלבוש מלכות תכלת וחור **ועטרת זהב** גדולה ותכריך בוץ **וארגמן**

Dan 5:29: באדין אמר בלשאצר והלבישו לדניאל **ארגונא והמונכא די דהבא על צוארה**

The sort of clothing Daniel receives in 5:29, purple to represent the royal, ארגונא in Aramaic, is reminiscent of the purple mantle of fine wool that Mordecai is wearing, ותכריך בוץ וארגמן, and the golden chain around Daniel's neck, והמונכא

די דהבא על צוארה, finds echo in the golden crown Mordecai has on his head, ועטרת זהב.

These types of connections are also found in Esther 6. There, as Haman comes to the king's chambers for permission to execute Mordecai (Esth 6:4), Ahasuerus, having just learnt that Mordecai saved his life from Bigthan and Teresh's planned insurrection (Esth 6:2), is seeking to reward the very man his prime minister is conspiring to kill (Esth 6:3, 10). Convinced, however, that the king must be referring to him, Haman begins rattling off all of the many honors he fully expects to receive. In addition to receiving a royal horse and a royal diadem upon his head (Esth 6:8), the insatiable prime minister also needs public adoration and suggests that this man be taken through the city in royal garb to cries of his royal favor (Esth 6:9).

A set of linguistic similarities once again accompanies these larger narrative overlaps. Haman's suggestion to the king, that the man whom he wishes to honor be clothed in royal garb, והלבישו את האיש (Esth 6:9), is phrased in similar fashion in Dan 5:29, והלבישו לדניאל, and the public affirmation Mordecai ultimately receives, "And they shall proclaim before him: This is what is done for the man whom the king desires to honor!" (Esth 6:9), connects to the public declaration of Daniel's rule in 5:29. "They proclaimed that he should rule as one of three in the kingdom." Consider these phrases in both Hebrew and Aramaic:

| Esth 6:9: | וקראו לפניו ככה יעשה לאיש אשר המלך חפץ ביקרו |
| Dan 5:29: | והכרזו עלוהי די להוא שליט תלתא במלכותא |

Given these philological and contextual connections, a case for a set of intentional allusions, regardless of the direction of influence, seems to grow. At this point, however, a key consideration gives reason for pause. In all three examples of the linguistic contact here surveyed – Esth 1:3//Dan 5:1, Esth 8:15//Dan 5:29, and Esth 6:9//Dan 5:29 – which likely represent the instances that contain the strongest philological links between Daniel and Esther,[170] paralleled connections are also found in Joseph.[171] Consider the following verses:

---

170 For a fuller list of the connections between Esther and Daniel, see Macchi, *Esther*, 61–62. As his list indicates, a number of broader thematic associates are present, but most links to Esther are found in Daniel 1, 2, and 5.

171 This is also the case in Esth 1:5, 2:12//Dan 1:15, 18//Gen 50:3, though the merits of this linguistic connection in terms of Esther and Daniel remain less than fully convincing. One other instance of a potential three-way connection, Esth 2:7//Dan 1:4//Gen 39:6, is discussed in more detail below (§ 7.3).

Esth 1:3:	בשנת שלוש למלכו **עשה משתה לכל שריו ועבדיו** חיל פרס ומדי הפרתמים ושרי המדינות לפניו
Dan 5:1:	**בלשאצר מלכא עבד לחם רב לרברבנוהי אלף** ולקבל אלפא חמרא שתה
Gen 40:20:	ויהי ביום השלישי יום הלדת את פרעה **ויעש משתה לכל עבדיו**
Esth 8:15:	ומרדכי יצא מלפני המלך בלבוש מלכות תכלת וחור **ועטרת זהב** גדולה ותכריך בוץ **וארגמן** והעיר שושן צהלה ושמחה
Esth 6:9:	ונתון הלבוש והסוס על יד איש משרי המלך הפרתמים **והלבישו את האיש** אשר המלך חפץ ביקרו **והרכיבהו על הסוס** ברחוב העיר וקראו לפניו ככה יעשה לאיש אשר המלך חפץ ביקרו
Dan 5:29:	באדין אמר בלשאצר **והלבישו לדניאל ארגונא והמונכא די דהבא על צוארה והכרזו עלוהי** די להוא שליט תלתא במלכותא
Gen 41:42–43:	ויסר פרעה את טבעתו מעל ידו ויתן אתה על יד יוסף **וילבש אתו בגדי** שש וישם רבד הזהב על צוארו וירכב אתו

Since most all of the specific linguistic links between Daniel and Esther in these verses are also found in the Genesis passages listed, another possible explanation arises. Given that the case for Daniel knowing and purposefully invoking Joseph is quite strong, a point the next subsection demonstrates (§ 7.3), the connections between Daniel and Esther could very well be incidental to both of their respective interests in referencing Joseph. In an effort to clarify this issue, three instances of linguistic overlap between Esther and Daniel that do not have any counterpart in Joseph are now examined. These examples are as follows:

Esth 1:10:	ביום השביעי **כטוב לב המלך ביין אמר** למהומן
Dan 5:2:	**בלשאצר אמר בטעם חמרא** להיתיה
Esth 2:6:	אשר **הגלה** מירושלים עם **הגלה אשר הגלתה עם** יכניה **מלך יהודה**
Dan 5:13:	הוא **דניאל די מן בני גלותא די יהוד די היתי מלכא אבי מן יהוד**
Esth 6:1:	בלילה ההוא **נדדה שנת המלך**
Dan 2:1:	**ושנתו נהיתה עליו**

Though these examples are likely the clearest points of linguistic contact between Esther and Daniel that do not share connections with Joseph,[172] the textual evidence in all three cases seems to fall just short of proving authorial intent. While Esth 2:6 and Dan 5:13 represent the strongest case, the formulaic nature of the phrase, which reads as though it may contain aspects of frozen forms, gives rea-

---

172 Consider, for example, two other cases Macchi notes. Much as the word for eunuch, סריס, is found throughout Esther, so is it also present throughout Daniel 1, and, if Mordecai is said to have "sat at the palace gate," ישב בשער המלך, in Esth 2:19 and 21, then so is Daniel found in a similar spot: ודניאל בתרע מלכא (Dan 2:49). While סריס is not entirely convincing on its own and is also repeatedly found in Joseph, "sitting at the gate" is also not necessarily indicative of an intentional connection, as there is nothing terribly unusual or distinctive about the phrase.

son for hesitation.[173] In the case of Esth 6:1 and Dan 2:1, the differences between Hebrew and Aramaic complicate any claim for specific borrowing, and the expression itself seems simply to be the way of articulating sleeplessness. Finally, though the wine link between Esth 1:10 and Dan 5:2 is, as the above analysis highlights, surrounded by a number of contextual links, the philological connection – בְּיָין הַמֶּלֶךְ לֵב כְּטוֹב and חַמְרָא בִּטְעֵם – is too distant to support a claim for deliberateness. As a result of these considerations, the general position forwarded by Berg and Collins, which suggests that these admitted points of overlap are best explained as shared motifs reflecting similar cultural situations and literary tropes, is here seconded.[174]

7.3 Daniel and Joseph

If diachronic and textual uncertainties prevail when Daniel and Esther's connections are assessed, then Daniel's relationship with Joseph takes on a different complexion. To anticipate the conclusions once again: much as the relative chronology between these two texts can be clearly established (§ 7.1), so also is the textual evidence far more indicative of a deliberate set of allusions. This examination begins with Daniel 1 and 2, where a number of the specific linguistic connections to the Joseph story are found.[175] After removing the Israelites from their homeland, Nebuchadnezzar starts a search for the wisest and most handsome men among the displaced Judeans (Dan 1:1–4). When Daniel is then situated in Nebuchadnezzar's court with the other good-looking and wise Jews of the Babylonian exile (Dan 1:6–7), he takes his opportunity with the handsomeness and favor given to him by God. Adhering to a strictly vegetarian diet, he makes himself even better looking than before and attracts the attention of the foreign king (Dan 1:12–15). Not to disappoint, Daniel's exceeding wisdom, which seems to be exactly that which his good looks are expressing, cements his status as the best of the lot and

---

173 In the main, this hesitation reflects Sommer's "central methodological principle" (*Prophet Reads Scripture*, 32) that cautions against using "stock vocabulary" for proving authorial intent.
174 "The Joseph story," Berg writes, "and the book of Esther share general features of setting and events which also are found in the tales of Daniel 2–6. These general correspondences probably result from the use of stock settings and type-scenes to portray the problems of diaspora life and the possibilities for a successful life under foreign rule" (*Book of Esther*, 145). Since this analysis comes to offer a slightly different take on Daniel's relationship with Joseph, it aligns itself more closely with Collins' suggestion. "The similarities," Collins writes, "between Daniel and Esther can be attributed to their common setting to a greater degree than is the case with the Joseph story" (*Daniel*, 40).
175 Rosenthal, "Die Josephsgeschichte," 278: Gen 40:22//Dan 5:1; Gen 41:2//Dan 1:15; Rosenthal, 282: Gen 41:15//Dan 5:15; Gen 41:38//Dan 5:11; Gen 41:42//Dan 5:29.

confirms his rise in the Babylonian palace (Dan 1:17). As Daniel's foreign ascent reminds of the two stories under discussion here, a linguistic connection concretizes this broader link: Daniel's good looks, which, like Joseph and Esther's, also play such a pivotal role in his selection, are phrased in nearly identical terms, טובי מראה (Dan 1:4).[176] If Joseph separates himself from the Egyptian wise men with his exceeding wisdom, then Daniel is not only better looking but also wiser, and even Nebuchadnezzar, the eternal enemy of the Jews, must choose him (Dan 1:19).

Though Daniel 2 was surely composed by a different author,[177] the textual links with Joseph continue into this chapter. When Joseph is first presented to the Pharaoh, the Egyptian ruler addresses the handsome Israelite standing before him with a turn of phrase productive throughout the whole story: "I have dreamt a dream," חלום חלמתי (Gen 41:15). Such words recall Joseph's: after his father gives him that multi-colored coat, and his brothers hate him for the special familial status he enjoys (Gen 37:3–4), his dream sequence commences with a nearly identical linguistic construction. "Joseph dreamt a dream" (Gen 37:5), ויחלם יוסף חלום, as once again a verbal form of the root ח.ל.מ is paired with its cognate accusative. When Joseph then narrates this to his brothers, such language is found yet again. "Listen to this dream that I have dreamt!" שמעו נא החלום הזה אשר חלמתי (Gen 37:6). Even though "this dream" is no longer the formal object of "I have dreamt," the echo of this verse and the one directly preceding it rings strongly in the Pharaoh's narration in Genesis 41.

As is so frequently the case in this story, Joseph's dream sequence is doubled, and his second dream is introduced and then narrated with nearly identical language. After being sarcastically rebuked by his spiteful brothers for the contents of his seemingly self-serving first dream (Gen 37:8), Joseph compounds the problem by explaining his second to them, as well (Gen 37:9). This passage also contains that distinctive cognate accusative phrase: "Again he dreamt a dream," ויחלם עוד חלום (Gen 37:9). Once again, Joseph then echoes this narration of events in his own reporting to his brothers, "I have dreamt a dream again!" חלמתי חלום עוד, which employs exactly the same language that Pharaoh will use to address Joseph just a few chapters later. To continue this initial round of internal ricochets, this phrase is also picked up by Jacob, who, like his older sons, chastises Joseph for the sugges-

---

176 This could, of course, be seen as a potential point of contact between Esther and Daniel: והנערה יפת תאר וטובת מראה (Esth 2:7) and וטובי מראה (Dan 1:4). However, the present analysis would once again suggest that this case is not definitive, as Esther and Daniel's shared language could be explained as two independently developed allusions to Joseph – an explanation that follows a much more historically defensible line.

177 The implications of this crucial point for the present analysis are explored in full in the following section (§ 7.4).

tive content of his night visions. "What is this dream that you have dreamt?!" מָה הַחֲלוֹם הַזֶּה אֲשֶׁר חָלָמְתָּ (Gen 37:10).

What's more, in a third scene, precisely this expression is used by both the cupbearer and baker. This time, Joseph, now the newly-appointed chief guard of the Egyptian prison, notices that his two new prisoners seem out of sorts (Gen 40:6). When he then approaches them to find out what is wrong, they respond in familiar fashion. "We dreamt dreams," they begin, "and there is no one to interpret them" (Gen 40:8). In Hebrew, the same cognate accusative phrase once again marks the opening clause, חֲלוֹם חָלָמְנוּ. Invoking this threefold repetition – first Joseph and his family, then the cupbearer and baker, and finally the Pharaoh himself – Daniel 2 also begins with a verbal form ח.ל.מ. and its cognate accusative, "Nebuchadnezzar dreamt dreams," חָלַם נְבוּכַדְנֶצַּר חֲלֹמוֹת (Dan 2:1). Such similarities to Genesis continue. In the same way that the Pharaoh's dreams "agitated his spirit," וַתִּפָּעֶם רוּחוֹ (Gen 41:8), so too do Nebuchadnezzar's agitate his, וַתִּתְפָּעֶם רוּחוֹ (Dan 2:1). Moreover, much as the Pharaoh's agitation pushes him to call on his wise men and sorcerers to interpret his confusing dream (Gen 41:8), so does Nebuchadnezzar pair a verbal form of ק.ר.א with חַרְטֻמִּים to call on his wise men and sorcerers for help interpreting his troubling dream (Dan 2:2).

Gen 41:8:	וַיִּשְׁלַח **וַיִּקְרָא** אֶת כָּל **חַרְטֻמֵּי** מִצְרַיִם וְאֶת כָּל חֲכָמֶיהָ
Dan 2:2:	וַיֹּאמֶר הַמֶּלֶךְ **לִקְרֹא לַחַרְטֻמִּים** וְלָאַשָּׁפִים וְלַמְכַשְּׁפִים וְלַכַּשְׂדִים לְהַגִּיד לַמֶּלֶךְ חֲלֹמֹתָיו

In both cases, the native wise men's inability to interpret their ruler's dreams creates the opening for Israelites to rise.[178] When the Egyptian sorcerers fail the Pharaoh, the restored cupbearer intercedes to bring Joseph to the royal court (Gen 41:9–14); in similar fashion, when the Babylonian sorcerers fail their king, Arioch intervenes so that Daniel can be brought before Nebuchadnezzar (Dan 2:13–25). Much as these lead-ups exhibit linguistic and narrative similarities, so too do the exchanges Joseph and Daniel have with their respective foreign rulers admit of overlap. When the Pharaoh addresses Joseph with that distinctive phrase, "I have dreamt a dream," חֲלוֹם חָלַמְתִּי, he then goes on to explain why he has had Joseph rushed out of jail and brought to the seat of power. "I have heard that you listen to dreams to interpret them" (Gen 41:15). While the Pharaoh offers Joseph this initial praise, the Israelite protagonist is just as quick to move the credit back

---

178 According to Humphreys, the connections between Daniel 2 and Joseph's rise in Egypt are reflective of both narratives belonging to the court contest genre. Distinct from court conflicts, which tend rather to see one courtier in direct dispute with another, these contests show one courtier's ability to do that which others cannot. "Like Joseph in the court of Pharaoh, Daniel beats the native courtiers at their own game" ("Life-style," 219).

to God. "It is not I!" Joseph exclaims in response, "But rather God who will look after the Pharaoh's well-being" (Gen 41:16).

In Daniel 2, when Daniel is presented to the Babylonian king after the wise men cannot make sense of the monarch's dream, Nebuchadnezzar addresses a handsome Israelite much as the Pharaoh did. "Can you really make known to me the dream that I saw and its meaning?" (Dan 2:26). If Joseph responds with humble piety, then so too does Daniel explain to Nebuchadnezzar that only God can complete the impossible task the Babylonian ruler is demanding. "The mystery about which the king has inquired – wise men, exorcists, magicians, and diviners cannot tell to the king. But there is a God in heaven who reveals mysteries, and He has made known to King Nebuchadnezzar what is to be at the end of days" (Dan 2:27–28).

Moreover, the interpretations given by these two handsome Israelite men also show broad similarities. Just as Joseph turns the Pharaoh's seven cows and seven ears into state policy (Gen 41:25–36), so does Daniel turn the four materials of Nebuchadnezzar's dreamed statue into world politics (Dan 2:31–45). This link is completed when both foreign rulers accept the interpretations provided by their Jewish wise men and then honor them in their respective foreign courts (Gen 41:37–45; Dan 2:46–49). Joseph becomes second-in-command over all of Egypt for his interpretative abilities, and Daniel becomes governor over the whole province of Babylon for his.[179] As these linguistic links and contextual overlaps between Daniel 1 and 2 and Joseph fulfill the spirit of Leonard's philological and contextual criteria, both chapters are shown to interact purposefully with the Genesis story.[180]

---

[179] For more on the relationship between Daniel 2 and Genesis 41, see Michael Segal, "From Joseph to Daniel: The Literary Development of the Narrative in Daniel 2," *VT* 59 (2009): 123–49. While Segal's major aim is to demonstrate the secondary nature of Dan 2:15–24a, he also claims that the earlier version of Daniel 2 used Joseph as a sort of model. "In light of all these parallels," Segal concludes, referencing many of the similarities noted above, "it has been correctly suggested that the Joseph story serves as a literary model for the Daniel tale, and was probably chosen since the former describes an Israelite or Jew in the Diaspora, who was able to succeed in the court of the foreign king" (142).

[180] In addition to the works by Collins, Koller, Rindge, and Segal noted above, a number of other scholars have also reached this conclusion. Given that similar philological and contextual connections to Joseph are also found in Daniel 5 (see pg. 154, n13), this conclusion has also frequently been extended to Daniel 5, as well. For a recent and brief overview of the approaches scholarship has developed to make sense of these connections, see, for example, Newsom, *Daniel*, 12–15.

7.4 Daniel's Place in Joseph and Esther's Distinctive Relationship

With these textual analyses complete, Daniel's place in Esther and Joseph's intertextual association can now be explored. To begin, however, another historical notice must be addressed. Since Daniel 1 and 2 both contain references to Joseph, the canonical ordering of the book gives the impression of a sustained and sequential set of allusions. The compositional history of the book, however, suggests the opposite sequence. Since Daniel 2 – or at least the vast majority of it – was written before most if not all of Daniel 1, the authors of Daniel 1 likely created their intertextual links to Joseph after those in Daniel 2 had already been developed. The result, which connects this opening chapter to the larger collection by picking up on and enhancing the intertextual character of the collection the Daniel 1 authors both introduced and compiled,[181] resembles the allusive growth seen across Esther's versions.

At the same time, however, a key difference is detected. As the early Esther core already contained structural links to Joseph in the form of interlocking narrative reversals, the MT redactors were able to increase such structural connections by adding in a second major plot tension, the irrevocability of Persian law, which, at least in part, mirrors the doubled food and familial conflicts in Joseph (§ 5.2; § 5.3). In Daniel's case, however, those responsible for the compilation of Daniel 1–6, who were likely also involved in the composition of Daniel 1, did not alter the unusual structural foundation of the textual units they received and, as a result, maintained a collection of individual tales that is organized in a fashion entirely different from the more cohesive Joseph story.

While realizing that this difference is likely far more reflective of the limits of redactional intervention than the intertextual considerations under present discussion, this analysis still notes that the structural differences between Daniel and Esther – whatever their most immediate causes might be – substantively affect the allusive natures of the two books. Due to Esther's organizational similarities with Joseph, for example, the up and down sequence of events that follows Esther's good looks is able to ricochet continuously against the topsy-turvy movement in Joseph that begins with his identically phrased handsomeness (§ 3.2); in similar fashion, the structural overlaps between Esther and Joseph's plots also let

---

181 This position concerning the authorship of Daniel 1 and the important role the authors of Daniel 1 played in compiling the court narratives has been accepted across scholarship. Consider, for example, how even though Kratz and Collins diverge on the general compositional development of Daniel 1–6, they both in the main agree on this point (Collins, *Daniel*, 35; Kratz, *Translatio*, 36–38).

the ramifications of Haman's moment of self-discipline and the seldom-used root
(א.פ.ק) to express it interact with the elongated test Joseph devises that hangs on
the vizier's ability to maintain control over his emotions (§ 2.1).

In Daniel, however, such extended points of narrative contact that surround
the specific linguistic connections noted are not able to develop as directly. While
the dream narratives in Daniel do work together in their present form, the plot
movements surrounding them do not intertwine as closely as the action does in
Joseph. In Joseph, this dream motif runs throughout the whole story. Creating the
threefold self-referential quality noted above (§ 7.3), which links Joseph's opening
dreams to the cupbearer's, baker's and Pharaoh's, the recurrences also help to
maintain connections across the distinct elements of the plot: as Joseph is thrown
into a pit because of his dreams, so do the dreams of others unexpectedly spin
to elevate him over all Egypt. In Daniel, however, while this motif punctuates
different moments throughout the court narratives, the events that express it
do not require each other as immediately as they do in Joseph. For even when
Daniel and the dream motif return in Daniel 4, the action picks up in an entirely
new context, as the sudden change to first person narration suggests.

> I, Nebuchadnezzar, was living serenely in my house, flourishing in my palace. I had a dream
> that frightened me, and my thoughts in bed and the vision of my mind alarmed me. I gave
> an order to bring all the wise men of Babylon before me to let me know the meaning of
> the dream. The magicians, exorcists, Chaldeans, and diviners came, and I related the dream
> to them, but they could not make its meaning known to me. Finally, Daniel, called Belteshaz-
> zar after the name of my god, in whom the spirit of the holy gods was, came to me, and I
> related the dream to him, [saying], "Belteshazzar, chief magician, in whom I know the spirit
> of the holy gods to be, and whom no mystery baffles, tell me the meaning of my dream
> vision that I have seen." (Dan 4:1–6)[182]

On the one hand, echoes to Daniel 2, and even back to the Joseph story, surface.
Once again, a foreign ruler dreams, and his wise men cannot make sense of it,
and, once again, the ruler must call in a good-looking Israelite to interpret the
troubling visions.[183] While Joseph finds an interpretation helpful to both him and

---

182 *The Prayer of Nabonidus* has long convinced scholars that the events of Daniel 4 were originally related to Nabonidus, the Babylonian king who ruled from 556–539 BCE, and only ascribed
to Nebuchadnezzar at a later date. "Since Nabonidus was not a king whose memory had much
cultural resonance for Jews except during the time of his actual reign, it is not surprising that
many of the stories originally told about him were transferred to the more historically significant
Nebuchadnezzar" (Newsom, *Daniel*, 9). Such obvious historical confusion suggests that even
though this chapter contains traditions that date back to the Babylonian period, the form recorded in Daniel 4 is far removed from the original events of the 6th century BCE. As this once again
points to a date in the Persian period, the relative chronology with Joseph is preserved.
183 For the ways in which Daniel's rise in Daniel 4 also represents a narrative of court contest,
and how this helps to make sense of some of its connections to Joseph, see pg. 120, n178.

the Pharaoh, Daniel finds revenge against the Babylonian king. After Nebuchadnezzar recounts the contents of his dream, something he strangely refused to do in Daniel 2, Daniel must make its challenging interpretation known.

> You will be driven away from men and have your habitation with the beasts of the field. You will be fed grass like cattle, and be drenched with the dew of heaven; seven seasons will pass over you until you come to know that the Most High is sovereign over the realm of man, and He gives it to whom He wishes. And the meaning of the command to leave the stump of the tree with its roots is that the kingdom will remain yours from the time you come to know that Heaven is sovereign. Therefore, O king, may my advice be acceptable to you: Redeem your sins by beneficence and your iniquities by generosity to the poor; then your serenity may be extended. (Dan 4:16–24)

On the other hand, however, even though this sequence reminds of Daniel 2, the development in Daniel 4 is not linked as tightly to that which came before it as the thoroughly intertwined action of Joseph's dream sequences (§ 7.3; § 5.2). To illustrate this point, consider Genesis once more. When the Pharaoh dreams, Joseph's opportunity to interpret them depends entirely upon the cupbearer and baker's previous night visions, and, in similar fashion, Joseph is only in a position to interpret the cupbearer and baker's dreams because of his foolish recounting to his brothers of his own suggestive dreams. In some contrast, even if Daniel is called to Nebuchadnezzar in Daniel 4 because of his rise in Daniel 1, a detail the text never explicitly clarifies, such an interconnection would not demand the strange contents of the foreign ruler's dream – and certainly not their bizarre reflection in reality. Moreover, even if the contents of Nebuchadnezzar's dream in Daniel 2 evinces the arrogance for which he is being humbled in Daniel 4, the Babylonian king would not need to be driven from men and growing eagle hair (Dan 4:30) for this process to play itself out.

Thus, though the dream stories that wind through Daniel's court narratives contain moments of resonance among them, their details and larger plot sequences do not directly interlock with and depend on each other. That this stands in contradistinction to the way that different scenes in both Joseph and Esther are internally interwoven indicates how the textual connections to Joseph found in Daniel are not able to sustain the kind of elongated parallels Esther's structural similarities to Joseph allow. As a result, even though key parts of Daniel 1–6 and Esther invoke the Joseph story while narrating stories of Jewish rises and deliverances in foreign courts, their respective relationships to Genesis are best seen as operating at different levels of significance.

7.5 Daniel and Isaiah, Esther and Joseph

In a fashion particularly illustrative for the present study, Jennie Grillo has recently argued that the allusive purpose in Daniel 1–6 indeed does grow alongside its compositional history.[184] While the present work has focused on Joseph as intertext, Grillo takes Isaiah to reach a conclusion strikingly similar to the position this work has sought to forward with respect to MT Esther. If Daniel's early court narratives occasionally create some resonances with Isaiah, particularly in Daniel 2, 3, and 6,[185] then the redactional layer found in these narratives, which, for Grillo, is found in Daniel 1 and the "date notices" and "hymnic snatches interposed throughout the tales" (365),[186] increases the frequency and force of the intertextual relationship with Isaiah that the earlier individual stories initiated.

For Grillo, this concerted interaction with Isaiah that the Daniel 1–6 redactors developed is found in three main areas. First, the very opening of Daniel 1 is intended to invoke Isaiah 39:6–7. Commenting on this connection, Grillo writes,

> Isaiah's warning has two elements: all the precious things of Hezekiah's ancestral treasuries will be carried away to Babylon (Isa 39:6/2 Kgs 20:17), and the sons of the royal house will be taken away to be servants in the palace of the king of Babylon (Isa 39:7/2 Kgs 20:18). The book of Daniel, correspondingly, begins with the news that Nebuchadnezzar has now carried away the vessels of the Jerusalem temple to the treasury of Babylon (1:1–2), along with sons of the royal household taken to serve in the palace of the king (1:3–4). (367)

Next, Grillo sees the imagined exilic forecast in Isaiah 39 as the perfect sort of model for the exilic setting that the beginning of Daniel is seeking to depict. While other biblical texts – Esther and Joseph among them – would have surely provided a firmer guide to actual exilic realities, Daniel's "mental journey all the way back to a claimed historical setting in Babylon" (372), Grillo suggests, can only really be guided by the figure of Isaiah.

The final way in which this later redaction of Daniel 1–6 shows its indebtedness to Isaiah is through the "chronological scaffolding in the redactional notices that follow on from 1:1 in 1:21, 6:1 and 6:29" (375). In Grillo's view, this macrolevel paralleling with Isaiah is found in two components. First, as Dan 1:21 makes clear, the Nebuchadnezzar to Cyrus scheme follows Deutero-Isaiah's structure,

---

184 Jennie Grillo, "'From a Far Country': Daniel in Isaiah's Babylon," *JBL* 136:2 (2017): 363–80.

185 Grillo's work here relies heavily on past scholarship – Seow, Fröhlich, and Bentzen's studies, in particular. For a fuller discussion of these points and the complete bibliographical references, see Grillo, 366.

186 Following Kratz, *Traslatio*, Grillo identifies Daniel 1 in addition to a smattering of verses throughout the 2–6 collection as the products of the same redactional activity that brought the court collection together. For the details of her position, see "From a Far Country," 365.

and, in the posited threefold empire arrangement that this Daniel 1–6 redaction developed,[187] an Isaianic influence can be found. While the traditional sequence is likely to have gone from Assyria to Media to Persia, Daniel substitutes Babylon for Assyria. Though others have suggested Chronicles and Jeremiah as potential reasons for this shift, Grillo once again turns to Isaiah, this time to 13:1–14:23. "The most explicit and purposefully exegetical substitution of Babylon for Assyria in fact lay nearer to hand for the collector, in the book of Isaiah" (376).

As Grillo's compelling analysis goes on to note, three major implications develop out of the intertextual connections that the redactors of Daniel 1–6 created with Isaiah. In the first place, such connections help to situate all of the many links between Daniel 8–12 and Isaiah. For much as the redactors of Daniel 1–6 were, at least in part, initially spurred to pursue these textual links to Isaiah by the present but still somewhat less developed associations found in the earlier Persian period court narrative collection, then so were the authors of Daniel 8–12 pulled all the more to Isaiah as intertext by the full-fledged allusive quality of the later redacted Daniel 1–6 textual unit.[188]

If this gradual intensification of the allusive purpose in the book of Daniel is precisely the sort of intertextual character that the present work has found in MT Esther, then so do the next two conclusions Grillo reaches also resonate with this study. In Grillo's estimation, the interaction with Isaiah that the redactors of Daniel 1–6 worked out hinges on a crucial aspect – all of Isaiah, as opposed to just the specifically invoked verses, must be conjured when reading Daniel's court narratives.[189] Finally, Grillo's third and last implication is, perhaps, the most instructive for the present study. Once the totality of the relationship between Daniel 1–6 and Isaiah is appreciated, a deeper intertextual purpose, one that touches on the Daniel 1–6 redactors' fundamental intent, surfaces. By providing a "canvas"[190] on which Daniel's Aramaic tales are best seen, the references to Isaiah demonstrate how the Daniel redactors sought to present their new literary work

---

187 Once again, Grillo's analysis is here building off of Kratz's work in *Translatio*; for the specific references, see Grillo, 375, n40 in particular.

188 For a more complete bibliography of the connections that the later apocalyptic stories develop with Isaiah, see Grillo, 365–66, n6 specifically.

189 This is seen most clearly in Grillo's emphasis on Daniel's interaction with Isaiah 39, which, according to Grillo, encourages the reader to focus not just on this Isaiah chapter but also the sustained exilic focus that directly follows it.

190 Grillo employs this term (380) following Mark S. Smith's essay, "What is a Scriptural Text in the Second Temple Period? Texts between Their Biblical Past, Their Inner-Biblical Interpretation, Their reception in Second Temple Literature, and Their Textual Witnesses," in *The Dead Sea Scrolls at 60: Scholarly Contributions of New York University Faculty and Alumni*, eds. Lawrence Schiffman and Shani Tzoref (Leiden: Brill, 2010): 271–98.

in terms of a previous design. While Grillo concludes her essay by suggesting that Mark Smith's analysis of Second Temple literature, which sees the authors of this period consistently painting amidst the landscape of their literary predecessors, aptly applies to Daniel 1–6, then the present work notes how Grillo's conclusions concerning Daniel's usage of Isaiah can be extended to Esther's relationship with Joseph, as well. "Isaiah's word to Hezekiah," she writes, "establishes at the start of the book of Daniel an open door into the larger narrative world of Deutero-Isaiah, where Israel's exilic experiences can be told anew on an ancient pattern" (380).

Since the MT Esther redactors also set out to tell their exilic experiences anew against the backdrop of an ancient pattern, one last point is worth underscoring. If Daniel's connections to Joseph have been shown to grow as the court collection matured, though not in a way that exerts a sustained influence over all of Daniel 1–6, then Grillo's essay provides what might be an explanation as to why. While maintaining and developing the relationship with Joseph was likely important to the Daniel 1–6 redactors, enhancing and increasing the intertextual interaction with Isaiah seems to have been of even greater significance. Therefore, much as those responsible for MT Esther surely interacted with other biblical texts but developed links to Joseph in a particularly instructive way, then so did the Daniel 1–6 redactors invoke several biblical texts while still foregrounding the unique importance of Isaiah for their court narrative collection.

This final chapter thus comes to a close with a summary observation. While Esther scholarship has long been preoccupied with the ways in which God's peculiar absence in the Scroll sets the book apart from its biblical environment, this analysis gestures to the ways in which the Megillah fits nicely within its Second Temple context. Just as other texts of this period do, so does Esther reference other biblical texts, encourage the larger contexts of those intertexts to be recalled throughout its entire telling, and, in so doing, position its own story, albeit replete with fresh and distinct details, as a continuation of previously enacted patterns. In this way, the theological stance that this study has sought to show Esther articulating is supported. Though the specifics of Esther's religious posture are surely unique to the Scroll, the processes by which Esther explores its fascination with divine absence are firmly embedded within the literary and religious culture that produced it.

8 Conclusion: Esther's Intertextual Reflections and Theological Additions

Since the present study has sought to demonstrate that Esther's theological purpose comes out most poignantly when the Megillah is viewed alongside the intentional relationship it develops with Joseph, some final remarks concerning author-oriented intertextuality and theologies of divine absence bring this work to a close. In the first half of this Conclusion, the methodological implications that Esther's relationship with Joseph has for the historical study of inner-biblical allusions are probed and three refinements to established principles are suggested. In the second half, scholarship on divine absence is explored; for even as this fascinating area has drawn increased attention from both theologians and historically-minded biblical critics alike, the perspective offered by the Scroll has tended to be overlooked. Tracing some of the reasons for this unusual oversight, the final section of this Conclusion thus gestures to areas for further study by insisting that Esther, the only biblical book never to mention God, must be considered in this scholarly discussion.

8.1 Three Refinements to Author-oriented Biblical Intertextuality

In his article on which the present work has extensively relied, Leonard includes a criterion for determining intentional references that has become commonplace – the abundance of deliberate allusions in a particular passage can help to tip the scale in otherwise "borderline" cases.[191] "An implication flowing from the [cumulative] principle outlined here," Leonard reasons, "is the notion that strong evidence for allusions in some cases can lend support to less certain allusions elsewhere. Each additional connection found in a text provides supporting evidence for affirming less obvious allusions" (253). While appreciating the clear and compelling spirit of this point, the following intertextual reflections commence by noting how the implementation of this theoretical principle – the actual effort to prove the authorial intent of less certain cases by appealing to stronger ones – has occasionally brought about uncertain results.

---

191 Leonard, "Identifying Inner-Biblical Allusions," 253. This "borderline" term was first coined in this context by James L. Kugel, "The Bible's Earliest Interpreters," *Prooftexts* 7:3 (1987): 269–83, in his review of Michael Fishbane's *Biblical Interpretation in Ancient Israel* (New York: Oxford University Press, 1985).

https://doi.org/10.1515/9783111216119-008

In this context, Grossman's analysis is worth recalling. Consider, for example, his claim that the Esther book repeatedly invokes the Jerusalem Temple. The philological evidence he presents, however, is less than fully compelling: of the 49 times תכלת is used, 42 instances come in a Temple context; as for בוץ, four of its seven usages are in relation to the Temple, and 28 of 39 for ארגמן. Since such correspondences are not definitive in their own right, Grossman stakes the majority of his claim on the word בירה.

> It is probably not coincidental that the only other place in the Bible that is referred to as בירה is Jerusalem (and the Temple within it), as, for example, in David's prayer (1 Chr 29:19) … It is not clear when this title began to be used for Jerusalem and for the Temple (it is definitely a later word). However, if the author of Esther was familiar with it as a name for Jerusalem, it is possible that he sought thereby to hint at the tension discussed above: which is the בירה? Which is the royal city – the capital of Ahasuerus's kingdom or the city in which the Temple is located? (*Esther*, 23)

Though the combined philological evidence Grossman compiles could certainly gesture to a set of textual correspondences that may very well have been deliberately placed by any number of authors, uncertainties regarding individual examples and the directions of influence remain. To return to Leonard's helpful categories: the language Grossman identifies, תכלת and ארגמן in particular, is not terribly unusual; the varied contexts of such words do not require a Temple setting; and the lynchpin, בירה, may be historically untenable. However, since Grossman has already determined that Esther is by definition filled with a series of covert inner-biblical allusions, he allows for the general referential quality of the book to prove the deliberateness and directionality of this particular case.[192]

The importance of this procedural objection comes into fuller focus once the exegetical weight Grossman ascribes to these textual associations is appreciated. In Grossman's program of plain and revealed senses, this allusion to the Temple, which has yet to be confirmed as deliberately placed by Esther's authors, becomes decisive for determining the real but hidden meaning of the Scroll.

> Attention to the Temple associations turns the narrative upside down: the atmosphere of gaiety that characterizes the descriptions of the king's feasting turns, in the mind of the "implied reader," into an atmosphere of anguish and destruction. The vivid colors of the feast that, on the level of the plain reading, add majesty to the narrative, suddenly turn

---

192 While versions of cumulative thinking can be seen across the field of biblical intertextuality, a similar approach to the one outlined by Grossman is found in Sommer's study of Second Isaiah (*A Prophet Reads Scripture*). "More important," Sommer writes toward the beginning of his work, "than these case-by-case disquisitions is an implicit cumulative argument that emerges from my work as a whole" (5).

into symbols of destruction for the Jewish people, a commemoration of the Temple, and a condemnation of the Jews of Shushan who luxuriate in the lavish royal feast instead of helping their brothers and sisters who have returned to their land. (24–25)

If Gerleman sees Esther alluding to the Pentateuch in order to deride an earlier story, then Grossman effectively flips the script: echoes to the Temple valorize the land and, in so doing, criticize the Shushan characters' exilic focus and success. However, as crucial components of this novel interpretation rest on references that may not have been deliberate, the present methodological concern notes the exegetical slippage that can accompany arguments for authorial intent that rely too heavily on collective concerns and not enough on the details of the specific textual examples given.[193]

The second methodological issue responds to both Grossman and Gerleman. Though they reach opposed conclusions, the interpretive fundaments on which their works stand admit of broad similarity.[194] In both cases, the plain sense of Esther is assumed deficient, and, as a result, the numerous allusions detected are deemed necessary for understanding the actual meaning of Esther's text. Distinguishing itself from these exegetical points of departure, the present line of argument has sought to demonstrate how the deepest thrust of Esther's connections to Joseph clarifies only after the full internal coherence of the Scroll is appreciated. As Esther's linguistic, thematic, and structural links to Joseph indicate, different layers of the Megillah interact with Joseph to provide the integrated Shushan happenings with an instructive backdrop that suggests a continuation of that which occurred in the past into that which is occurring in the present.

In this vein, Lyons' work on Ezekiel's usage of the Holiness Code once again presents a helpful point of comparison.[195] When analyzing the concepts of repentance and restoration in the two textual corpora, Lyons homes in on a telling detail. Though the prophet's understanding of these concepts diverges from their

---

193 For a more measured and productive implementation of the cumulative approach, consider, for example, Teeter's work on Jeremiah's usage of the Joseph story ("Jeremiah, Joseph"). In contradistinction to Grossman's usage of the principle, which sees it confirming the intent of textual connections that range across the entire canon, Teeter employs it with a more specific purpose – to show how a number of philological and structural links between Jeremiah 37–44 and Genesis 37–50 demonstrate a set of purposeful allusions. By appreciating Teeter's careful work, this critique once again underscores that it is not interested in denying the obvious import of cumulative thinking; rather, it seeks to suggest that such an approach must be balanced against the weight of individual cases and that a specific delineation of the texts in question – something Grossman's work refrains from doing – is in this context often crucial.

194 For other ways in which these two seemingly opposed works dovetail, see the analysis above (§ 3.1.2).

195 Lyons, *From Law to Prophecy*.

expression in the Holiness Code, Ezekiel still invoked Leviticus on the matter but, Lyons notes, in a particular way.

> At first glance, it might appear that the Holiness Code is perfectly suitable for Ezekiel's purpose, since it contains a program for restoration (Lev 26:40–45). Yet as I noted above (section 3.3.1.3), H's program is based on the idea that restoration is contingent upon human repentance – an idea that Ezekiel cannot accept. The Holiness Code does not address the possibility that the people might not repent. Nor does it address the possibility that a repentant people might someday apostatize again. Ezekiel solves these problems in a very radical way. Instead of simply projecting into the future H's covenant, with attendant stipulations, blessings, and punishments, Ezekiel removes the punishments from the covenant and envisions a change that guarantees the covenant stipulations will always be kept. (*From Law to Prophecy*, 123)

The underlying difference between Grossman and Gerleman, on the one hand, and Lyons, on the other, strikes. Instead of viewing allusions upending the sense of the alluding text, as Grossman and Gerleman tend to do, Lyons notes the existence and importance of the opposite possibility – that is, the text that is being referenced can also be molded and selectively quoted to fit the meaning of the text that is doing the alluding. Though the present analysis does not see Esther and Joseph's overarching stances in immediate tension and therefore sidesteps the directness of this theoretical difference, it still aligns itself more with the interpretive approach outlined by Lyons. For as this work has consistently sought to show, Esther interacts with Joseph in a way that does not capsize Esther's plain sense but rather contextualizes that which is already present in and productive throughout the Scroll.

This second consideration leads to a third and final intertextual point. As this analysis explores at length in Part Two, reading Esther as a literary whole must in no way blind historically sensitive readers to the complex compositional history of the book. For the author-oriented intertextual purpose, this recognition brings with it a number of attendant factors that have too often been overlooked. If almost every previous diachronic study of Esther's allusiveness assumes a single purpose behind each and every external reference, the present work follows a different course. By recognizing that an early Esther core likely included some but not all of the connections to Joseph that are found in MT, this analysis, which offers further support for the historical priority of a posited Hebrew *Vorlage* behind AT, demonstrates a gradual development of Esther's intertextual intent. Early versions of Esther, as indicated broadly by AT 1–7:16 without the Additions, sought to invoke aspects of Genesis in a way akin to Ben-Porat and Sommer's second level; the later MT redactors, aware of such present but still somewhat inchoate links, then endeavored to bring the entire Joseph story to bear – Ben-Porat and Sommer's fourth level – by increasing the philological and structural connections to Joseph.

Koller's work illustrates some of the problems that can come when these compositional factors are not adequately considered.[196] Interestingly, his analysis begins in a promising way, as it correctly notes that the MT authors (Marduka, as Koller decides to name them[197]) did not invent the story out of whole cloth but rather took previous versions of an early Esther tale and adapted them (*Esther*, 37). However, despite the foundational importance of such a point, Koller's conclusions fail to account for the decisive implications that this historical notice carries. Though Koller also claims to follow the general diachronic position that the present work forwards,[198] he repeatedly characterizes certain textual aspects that are present in the base AT narrative, and therefore likely part of the Esther tradition that the MT redactors inherited instead of authored, as Marduka's purposeful and deliberate creations. Take, for example, Koller's understanding of Mordecai's introduction. Though Koller argues that "Marduka delighted … in assigning him [Mordecai] a politically resonant gentilic" (45), such a position overlooks that Mordecai's ancestry is introduced in precisely the same way in AT 2:5 – a consideration that suggests such a feature was not Marduka's to assign but rather maintain.

Exactly this problem also extends to Koller's assessment of the initial connections between Mordecai and Saul. "In introducing his first main characters," Koller writes about MT Esth 2:5, "Marduka made two further decisions. First, he made Mordecai and Esther Benjaminites; second, he associated them with the elites who had been exiled in 597 along with Jehoiachin" (49). Once again, attention to AT indicates the shortcoming of Koller's position. Since AT 2:5 also introduces Mordecai and Esther as Benjaminites but does not include the notice of Mordecai's ancestors' exile, Koller's analysis is shown to conflate two textual layers that his own historical conclusion would deem distinct.[199] If those responsible for MT did likely add the exilic notice in MT Esth 2:5, they were not the ones who first made Mordecai and Esther Benjaminites.

Since much of Koller's political read of the Scroll depends on Esther and Mordecai's Benjaminite identity aligning with Marduka's other creative purposes (51), the significance of this critique clarifies. Once Esther's multi-stage compositional

---

196 Koller, *Esther in Ancient Jewish Thought*.
197 Though this catchy name gives the sense of one person being responsible for all of MT, Koller rather suggests that his Marduka only be a stand-in for a larger group of anonymous ancient Jewish authors (30). However, as the present critique outlines, this singular name seems to betray a lingering assumption of unified authorship that comes to jostle Koller's overarching interpretive aims off their historical kilter.
198 For Koller's take on this issue, see *Esther in Ancient Jewish Thought*, 37, n7, in particular.
199 In AT, this verse, 2:5, reads as follows: "Now there was a Judean man in Susa the city, whose name was Mardochaios, son of Iaeiros son of Semeias son of Kisaios, of the tribe of Beniamin."

development is taken seriously, then the comparative evidence is shown to suggest that those responsible for MT created some but not all of the political signposts Koller identifies. While it is possible, if not even likely, that particular compositional layers inside the Scroll reworked previous traditions to emphasize the importance of foreign political power, it remains historically untenable to conclude that all of Esther's varied textual features were initially developed by the same authors to forward this one predetermined aim. Though these details are specific to Scroll scholarship, this larger point speaks to the broader conversation concerning deliberate inner-biblical allusions, which has occasionally struggled to differentiate between final canonical forms and diachronically defensible textual strands.[200]

8.2 The Significance of the Scroll for Discussions of Divine Absence

A final set of remarks centered around Esther's place amidst understandings of divine absence in the entire Hebrew Bible brings this study to a close. Once again, a familiar pattern emerges: much as investigations into Esther's intertextuality have overlooked how the sustained interaction with Joseph sharpens the theological import of God's privation in the Megillah, so has scholarship interested in the intricacies of divine presence and hiddenness failed to consider Esther much at all.[201] In

---

200 For a helpful overview of the history of this tension and the way it has played out in diachronic and synchronic approaches to the study of inner-biblical allusions, see Geoffrey D. Miller, "Intertextuality in Old Testament Research," *CBR* 9:3 (2010): 283–309.

201 While bringing crucial attention to this topic and developing a number of compelling insights about it, Samuel Terrien's classic work, *The Elusive Presence: Toward a New Biblical Theology* (San Francisco: Harper & Row, 1978), fails to mention Esther even once. Such a regrettable trend continues in Joel S. Burnett, *Where is God? Divine Absence in the Hebrew Bible* (Minneapolis: Fortress Press, 2010), which also neglects to deal substantively with the one biblical book that never directly mentions God. Though the Scroll figures somewhat more prominently in Richard Elliot Friedman, *The Disappearance of God: A Divine Mystery* (Boston: Little, Brown, 1995), the larger scheme into which Friedman squeezes Esther has been roundly criticized: since God does not successively retreat across the canon, as Friedman claims, his treatment of the Megillah, which is mainly interested in proving this singular purpose, does not prove particularly helpful. (For fuller critiques of Friedman's proposal and the problematic ways in which his theory overlooks books such as Zechariah, Daniel, and Chronicles, see, for example, Melton, *Where is God*, 15–16, or Frederick E. Greenspahn's review of Friedman's book in *Shofar* 15:4 [1997]: 139–41.) Representing a much more nuanced approach to the topic, *Divine Presence and Absence in Exilic and Post-Exilic Judaism*, ed. Nathan MacDonald and Izaak J. de Hulster (Tübingen: Mohr Siebeck, 2013), brings together scholars of all different areas to explore divine absence from varied quarters; however, even though this book, which explores a number of fresh insights, delimits its focus to the general period in which Esther was written, the Scroll is not addressed. Finally, though the treatment the Megillah receives

this context, Samuel Balentine's 1983 work provides a helpful starting point.[202] If Samuel Terrien's groundbreaking 1978 book seeks to demonstrate how the pivot of divine presence and absence animates so much of the canon, then Balentine endeavors to refine Terrien's ranging discussion by limiting its parameters. While Balentine begins with a study of the Hebrew root ס.ת.ר and develops an important philological tightening of Terrien's broad thematic effort, Balentine's careful exegesis fails to note that the same three consonants at the center of his work form the basis of the protagonist's name in the one biblical book that keeps God entirely off the page.

Though strange in its own right, such an oversight is all the more striking given that Esther's stance helps to draw out the larger point Balentine so effectively makes. If scholarship before Balentine tended to see divine absence as punishment, Balentine explores how the details of the diverse biblical texts paint a far more complicated picture. While the prophets, Balentine notes, frequently explain God's disappearance in terms of human punishment (19), psalms of lament often cry out against the dilemma without perceiving sin as the cause (53). For Balentine, Psalm 44 is a particularly apt illustration of this point: while the opening verses (Ps 44:2–4) "contain a description of the actions of God on behalf of his people in times past" (53), the next section, Ps 44:5–9, is "an expression of confidence in God based upon his faithfulness in the past" (53). For Balentine, then, Ps 44:10 marks a turning point that calls such confidence into question. "The psalmist asserts that God has rejected them (v. 10), and as a result the community has fallen victim to humiliating defeat at the hand of the enemy (vv. 11, 12)" (53). Since the Psalm goes on to insist on the people's continued uprightness (44:18–19), Balentine's point, which sees divine absence reaching beyond simple punishments for sin, comes into focus. "It is against this backdrop," Balentine writes, "that the question 'why dost thou hide they face?' (v. 25) is raised. That the phrase is here expressed in question-form is surely not accidental. The implication is clear: if we have not strayed from our covenantal obligations, and if we have not forsaken God either in our hearts or by our way of life, why then has he hidden his face from us?" (53–54)

After surveying a number of other laments, Balentine concludes. Once it is realized that divine absence is not just downstream to human sin, then a clearer conception of its results can be appreciated.

---

in Kristin De Troyer and Leah Reedier Schulte, "Is God Absent or Present in the Book of Esther? An Old Problem Revisited," in *The Presence and Absence of God: Claremont Studies in the Philosophy of Religion,* ed. Ingolf U. Dalferth (Tübingen: Mohr Siebeck, 2009) is worthwhile, it keeps its focus more on the Greek editions than the Hebrew text.

202 Samuel E. Balentine, *The Hidden God: The Hiding of the Face of God in the Old Testament* (New York: Oxford University Press, 1983).

The principal consequence [of divine absence] is separation from God, effected by a break in communication, by the threat of death and confinement to Sheol, and quite possibly also by the absence of the theophanic presence of God in the temple. Bound up with separation from God is the further consequence of alienation from family and friends. Of particular interest are the expressions of protest which accompany the lament about the hiding of God's face. Through the omission of even general references to sin, protests of innocence, questions to God born out of reproach and complaint, or simply through the general context of the lament as a whole, these psalms seem to indicate that very often God's aloofness did not appear to be justified. At the very least these features serve to raise suspicions of any explanation which would imply a simple and direct connection between the hiding of God's face and divine punishment for sin. (63)

While Balentine does not consider the Scroll, the general frame his work identifies finds intriguing reflection in the Megillah. In Shushan, as a position of calm turns dangerous while the divine remains in retreat, this disconcerting stage is marked by precisely that which Balentine details: alienation from close kin (Esth 2:8, 11), deep mourning (Esth 4:1), and outbursts that question what appears to be unjust circumstances (Esth 4:3, 7–8; 7:3–4; 8:3, 5–6). Moreover, in the aftermath of such intense soul-searching, human events come to align themselves with a previously initiated divine pattern, and, as Balentine makes clear in a later section, the outcome need not be prolonged separation but can also turn into ultimate deliverance.[203]

The resonances between Balentine's insights and the Scroll continue. After shadowboxing with those biblical theologies that orient themselves around decisive moments of direct divine intervention, Balentine forwards his alternate take, which sees the intricacies of God's mystifying comings and goings as a central feature of the ancient Israelite theological mindset.

Israel's struggle with God's hiddenness ought not to be treated as if it were merely a footnote to an otherwise optimistic and unshakeable faith. The evidence of the present study would hardly support such an understanding. It indicates instead that Israel was repeatedly plagued by the experience of God's hiddenness. Time and again the disparity between religious convictions and the realities of actual experience brought the issue into the fore-

---

203 Consider, for example, Balentine's comparison between the function of divine absence in the prophets and psalter. "It is clear that the association of God's hiding with the idea of punishment for sin is most explicitly made by the prophets, not the psalmists. In this sense the prophets may be understood to have provided a different understanding of God's hiding. By linking the hiding of God's face to the idea of punishment for sin, the prophets are able to provide explanation for the most catastrophic dimension of God's hiddenness with which they were confronted: the period of the exile. Furthermore, with the end of the period of captivity, the prophets speak of an end to the period of God's hiding and of the promise of future deliverance. Thus the ultimate consequence of God's hiding is not separation, which is the implication in the psalms of lament (e.g. Ps. 88), but restoration" (76).

front of Israel's thought. When the motif is seen from this perspective, i.e. when it is understood as something more than a secondary accretion, then its significance for Israelite religion can be more readily discerned.

What calls for chief mention here is that fact that the experience of God's hiddenness, just as the experience of his presence, is an integral part of Israelite faith. (171–72)

While Balentine sees this interest as an expression of ancient faith, attention to the one biblical book that keeps God entirely hidden articulates a tension closer to the actual contours of the biblical texts that Balentine otherwise so expertly reads. As human characters become overwhelmed in the maze of earthly events, Esther narrates how even when separation from the divine continues, the providential patterns God previously enacted can extend into the present to bring a chosen nation once again into a deliverance that once seemed so impossible. In this way, the addition to Balentine's work clarifies. Since God can choose to stay shrouded behind that painful cloudiness, a number of the features Balentine associates with God's ultimate return can be applied to moments of sustained retreat, as well.

An examination of one more work that also focuses on divine absence but fails to deal with Esther further establishes the need to consider the Scroll in this context. In his more recent effort to address the textual nuances of God's hiddenness and the historical contexts that might have influenced them, Joel Burnett notes how expressions of divine absence became particularly important in the post-exilic period. For Burnett, so much of the issue revolves around Jerusalem and the Israelite loss of it after 586 BCE.

The narrative framework of Israel's story in these books [Deuteronomy-2 Kings, 1 and 2 Chronicles, and Ezra and Nehemiah] emphasizes Jerusalem as the center of history and as the earthly center of God's relationship to Israel and to humankind more broadly. With the loss of Jerusalem in the Babylonian destruction and exile, this major locus of divine presence becomes the center of divine absence. (*Where is God*, 153)

As a result of this emphasis on Jerusalem, Burnett offers intriguing reads of key biblical texts. The deuteronomic history, in his estimation, is ultimately a story of divine abandonment that ends with an implicit hope for a restored temple (161). Since Chronicles knows of the restoration, the "Jerusalem temple is the institutional bridge between the past ideal and present hopes, and the ongoing center of unique divine presence in human events" (167). Finally, on the prophetic side, Burnett shows how Ezekiel explains much of the exile in terms of God's punitive decision to remove the divine presence from the holy city (157).

Such important insights cause Burnett to conclude in a fashion that deepens Balentine's basic argument. "Divine absence figures in the Hebrew Bible not so much as a problem to be solved but more as an integral part of the biblical portrayal of God" (177–78). While thoroughly underscoring such a position, the present study notes how Burnett's decision to limit his inquiry to Jerusalem prevents him from appreciating the crucial dimensions that Esther's perspective adds to the post-exilic notion of divine absence. For as the Scroll indicates, reflections on the complexities of God's sustained retreat in the wake of exile are not at all limited to Jerusalem but rather become equally – if not potentially even more – acute for those seeking to explore their own identity, heritage, and religion while still living and likely even making a permanent home outside the land.

William Tooman's recent work on Ezekiel demonstrates this very idea.[204] As he effectively shows, precisely this question of divine presence and absence defines key redactional activity throughout this prophetic book. If the earliest textual layer suggested that "Yhwh has disinherited the exiles" (160), while indicating that those who stayed in Jerusalem "will inherit the land" (160), then a later layer "extends the promise of divine presence to all diaspora communities" (162). As these insights suggest and Esther then confirms, questions of divine presence and absence – regardless of how they are ultimately answered – were crucial components of diaspora identity in the wake of the Babylonian exile, and the growing scholarly understanding of this key issue will only be enhanced by extending attention to the perspectives offered by the Scroll, as well.

If Terrien, Balentine, and Burnett steer clear of the Megillah,[205] two more recent efforts helpfully bring Esther into the conversation about divine absence through the introduction of fresher theoretical standpoints. Mixing and matching new interpretive methods with different narrative sections of the Hebrew Bible, Amelia Devin Freedman employs a reader-oriented approach to place Esther next to an ancient Greek novel, *Chaereas and Callirhoe*.[206] As such a creative tack diverges from the diachronic emphasis of this study, it also yields a different conclusion. Since the Jewish queen's activity proves capable of handling the challenges the Megillah brings, no occasion for divine intervention presents itself; as a result, Freedman concludes, Esther's human agency causes God to stay on the sidelines in the Hebrew Megillah (117). In this way, Freedman's interpretation

---

204 William Tooman, "Covenant and Presence in the Composition and Theology of Ezekiel," in *Divine Presence and Absence in Exilic and Post-Exilic Judaism*, 151–82.

205 In an insightful essay, Megan Fullerton Strollo, "Initiative and Agency: Towards a Theology of the Megilloth," in *Megilloth Studies: The Shape of Contemporary Scholarship*, ed. Brad Embry (Sheffield: Sheffield Phoenix Press, 2016): 15–60, explores two deeper reasons for this confusing gap: "the noticeable scarcity or outright exclusion of the name of God in these texts" (151), and "the Megilloth's lack of a strict historical framework and the collection's deficit of attention to specific religious practices – essential to the history-of-religious approach – also contributes to the general exclusion of the Megilloth from works of biblical theology" (152).

206 Amelia Devin Freedman, *God as an Absent Character in Biblical Hebrew Narrative: A Literary-Theoretical Study* (New York: Peter Lang, 2005).

shows its indebtedness to the work she chooses as intertext. Since the Greek novel narrates its protagonist, also a woman, maintaining a passive stance, the deities there are forced to intervene and thus offer the decisive contrast to Esther.

Brittany Melton's equally thought-provoking work takes a different course and advocates reading the five Megilloth together.[207] Following Peter Machinist's influential suggestion that fate is divinely guided in Qohelet,[208] Melton argues that the unusual sequence of events in Esther may similarly reflect God's hidden hand. If Freedman turns to Greek literature for an instructive counterpart, Melton sees Ruth as Esther's most instructive discussion partner. While God in Ruth works through the actions of the characters, the divine in Esther, Melton argues, operates through the situations and, therefore, alongside human initiative.

> The concurrence of divine and human action in Esther stands in contrast to the synergistic dynamic of divine-human action in Ruth, with the effect that it is less clear in Ruth where human agency ends and divine action begins; for in Ruth divine involvement both guides and participates with human agency. In Esther, on the other hand, divine providence and human agency work side-by-side to progress the plot. Due to the separation of divine and human action in Esther God's intervention is perceived more dramatically (*i.e.*, resulting in complete reversals from one moment to the next) than when it is inseparable from human action in everyday life (as in Ruth). The way Ruth reads differently from Esther comes down to seeing God's involvement through, versus alongside, human agents; divine and human action is complementary rather than synergistic in Esther. (*Where is God*, 161)

While the present approach has looked to Joseph to reach a conclusion different from Melton's illuminating inner-Megilloth reading, it concludes by underscoring the significance of precisely the intersection that Freedman and Melton identify – Esther's theological interest in divine absence and its interaction with other related texts. If Melton and Freedman probe the religiosity and intertextuality of the Scroll in mainly synchronic fashions, attention to the deliberately placed allusions to Joseph adds an important dimension to historical Scroll scholarship. For even though diachronic approaches to the Megillah have at times questioned the religious worth of the book, many of the methods developed by historical scholarship are able to accentuate with particular clarity the distinctive combination of God's hiddenness and deliberate textual allusions that so powerfully articulates MT Esther's theological standpoint.

---

207 Melton, *Where is God?*
208 Peter Machinist, "Fate, 'Miqreh,' and Reason: Some reflections on Qohelet and Biblical Thought," in *Solving Riddles and Untying Knots: Biblical, Epigraphic, and Semitic Studies in Honor of Jonas C. Greenfield*, eds. Ziony Zevit, Seymour Gitin, and Michael Sokoloff (Winona Lake, IN: Eisenbrauns, 1995).

Bibliography

Ackerman, James S. "Joseph, Judah and Jacob." In *Literary Interpretations of Biblical Narratives*, vol. 2, edited by Kenneth R. R. Gros Louis, 85–113. Nashville: Abingdon, 1982.

Albertz, Rainer. *Der Gott des Daniel: Untersuchungen zu David 4–6 in der Septuagintafassung sowie zu Komposition und Theologie des Aramäischen Danielbuches*. Stuttgarter Bibelstudien. Stuttgart: Verlag Katholisches Bibelwerk, 1988.

Anderson, Bernhard W. "The Place of the Book of Esther in the Christian Bible." *JBR* 30:1 (1950): 32–43.

Baden, Joel S. *The Composition of the Pentateuch: Renewing the Documentary Hypothesis*. Anchor Yale Bible Reference Library. New Haven: Yale University Press, 2012.

Balentine, Samuel E. *The Hidden God: The Hiding of the Face of God in the Old Testament*. Oxford Theological Monographs. New York: Oxford University Press, 1983.

Bardtke, Hans. *Der Prediger, Das Buch Esther*. KAT. Gütersloh: Gütersloher Verlagshaus Gerd Mohn, 1963.

Beal, Timothy K. *The Book of Hiding: Gender, Ethnicity, Annihilation, and Esther*. Biblical Limits. London: Routledge, 1997.

Ben-Porat, Ziva. "The Poetics of Literary Allusion." *PTL: A Journal of Descriptive Poetics and Theory of Literature* 1 (1976): 105–28.

Ben-Porat, Ziva. "Intertextuality." *Ha-Sifrut* 34 (1985): 170–78 [Hebrew].

Berg, Sandra Beth. *The Book of Esther: Motifs, Themes, and Structure*. Society of Biblical Literature Dissertation Series 44. Missoula, MT: Scholars Press, 1979.

Berger, Yitzhak. "Esther and Benjaminite Royalty: A Study in Inner-Biblical Allusion." *JBL* 129:4 (2010): 625–644.

Bergey, Ronald L. "Late Linguistic Features in Esther." *JQR* 75 (1984): 66–78.

Berlin, Adele. *Esther: The Traditional Hebrew Text with the New JPS Translation*. JPS Bible Commentary. Philadephia: Jewish Publication Society, 2001.

Berquist, Jon L. *Approaching Yehud: New Approaches to the Study of the Persian Period*. Semeia Studies 50. Atlanta: Society of Biblical Literature, 2007.

Berquist, Jon L. *Judaism in Persia's Shadow: A Social and Historical Approach*. Minneapolis: Fortress Press, 1995.

Bezold, Helge. *Ester – eine Gewaltgeschichte*. BZAW 545. Berlin; Boston: De Gruyter, 2023.

Bickerman, Elias J. "The Colophon of the Greek Book of Esther." *JBL* 63:4 (1944): 339–62.

Bickerman, Elias J. *Four Strange Books of the Bible: Jonah, Daniel, Koheleth, Esther*. New York: Schocken Books, 1967.

Bledsoe, Amanda M. Davis. "The Relationship of the Different Editions of Daniel: A History of Scholarship." *CurBR* 13:2 (2015): 175–90.

Blum, Erhard and Weingart, Kristin. "The Joseph Story: Diaspora Novella or North-Israelite Narrative?" *ZAW* 129:4 (2017): 501–21.

Boda, Mark J. and Michael H. Floyd. *Bringing out the Treasure: Inner Biblical Allusion in Zechariah 9–14*. JSOTSup 370. London: Sheffield Academic Press, 2003.

Boyarin, Daniel. *Intertextuality and the Reading of Midrash*. Indiana Studies in Biblical Literature. Bloomington: Indiana University Press, 1990.

Brenner, Athalya, ed. *A Feminist Companion to Esther, Judith and Susanna*. The Feminist Companion to the Bible 7. Sheffield: Sheffield Academic Press, 1995.

Brettler, Marc Zvi. "Identifying Torah Sources in the Historical Psalms." In *Subtle Citation, Allusion, and Translation in the Hebrew Bible*, edited by Ziony Zevit, 73–90. Bristol, CT: Equinox Publishing, 2017.

https://doi.org/10.1515/9783111216119-009

Burnett, Joel S. *Where is God? Divine Absence in the Hebrew Bible*. Minneapolis: Fortress Press, 2010.

Carr, David McLain. "Method in Determination of Direction of Dependence." In *Gottes Volk am Sinai: An Empirical Test of Criteria Applied to Exodus 34,11–26 and its Parallels*, edited by Matthias Köckert and Erhard Blum, 107–40. Veröffentlichungen der Wissenschaftlichen Gesellschaft für Theologie 18. Gütersloh: Kaiser, Gütersloher Verlag, 2001.

Carr, David McLain. *Reading the Fractures of Genesis: Historical and Literary Approaches*. Louisville: Westminster John Knox, 1996.

Cazelles, Henri. "Note sur la composition du rouleau d'Esther." In *Lex Tua Veritas: Festschrift für Hubert Junker zur Vollendung des siebzigsten Lebensjahres am 8. August 1961, dargeboten von Kollegen, Freunden und Schülern*, edited by Heinrich Gross and Franz Mussner, 17–29. Trier: Paulinus-Verlag, 1961.

Clines, David J. A. *The Esther Scroll: The Story of the Story*. JSOTSup 30. Sheffield: JSOT Press, 1984.

Cohen, Avraham. "'Hu Ha-goral': The Religious Significance of Esther." *Judaism* 23 (1974) 87–94.

Collins, John J. *Daniel: A Commentary on the Book of Daniel*. Hermeneia – A Critical and Historical Commentary on the Bible. Minneapolis: Fortress 1993.

Craig, Kenneth M. *Reading Esther: A Case for the Literary Carnivalesque*. Literary Currents in Biblical Interpretation. Louisville: Westminster John Knox, 1995.

Crawford, Silnie White. *The Book of Esther: Introduction, Commentary, and Reflections*. NIB 3. Nashville: Abingdon Press, 1990.

Crenshaw, James L. "Method in Determining Wisdom Influence upon 'Historical' Literature." *JBL* 88 (1969): 129–42.

Dalferth, Ingolf U. *Becoming Present: An Inquire into the Christian Sense of the Presence of God*. Studies in Philosophical Theology 30. Leuven: Peeters, 2006.

Day, Linda. *Esther*. Abingdon Old Testament Commentaries. Nashville: Abingdon Press, 2005.

De Troyer, Kristin, and Leah Reedier Schulte. "Is God Absent or Present in the Book of Esther? An Old Problem Revisited." In *The Presence and Absence of God: Claremont Studies in the Philosophy of Religion, Conference 2008*, edited by Ingolf U. Dalferth, 35–40. Religion in Philosophy and Theology 42. Tübingen: Mohr Siebeck, 2009.

De Troyer, Kristin, and Leah Reedier Schulte. *The End of the Alpha Text of the Book of Esther: Translation and Narrative Technique in MT 8:1–17, LXX 8:1–17, and AT 7:14–41*. Septuagint and Cognate Studies 48. Atlanta: Society of Biblical Literature, 2000.

Dietrich, Walter. *Die Josephserzählung als Novelle und Geschichtsschreibung: zugleich ein Beitrag zur Pentateuchfrage*. Biblisch-theologische Studien 14. Neukirchen-Vluyn: Neukirchener Verlag, 1989.

Dommershausen, Werner. *Die Estherrolle: Stil und Ziel einer Alttestamentlichen Schrift*. Stuttgarter biblische Monographien 6. Stuttgart: Verlag Katholisches Bibelwerk, 1968.

Draisma, Spike, ed. *Intertextuality in Biblical Writings: Essays in Honour of Bas Van Iersel*. Kampen, Holland: Uitgeversmaatschappij J. H. Kok, 1989.

Ego, Beate. *Ester*. Biblisches Kommentar: Altes Testament. Göttingen: Vandenhoeck & Ruprecht, 2017.

Ego, Beate. *Targum Scheni zu Ester: Übersetzung, Kommentar und Theologische Deutung*. Texte und Studien zur antiken Judentum 54. Tübingen: Mohr Siebeck, 1996.

Eslinger, Lyle. "Inner-Biblical Exegesis and Inner-Biblical Allusion: The Question of Category." *VT* 42 (1992): 47–58.

Evans, Craig A and Shemaryahu Talmon, eds. *The Quest for Context and Meaning: Studies in Biblical Intertextuality in Honor of James A. Sanders*. Biblical Interpretation 28. Leiden: Brill, 1997.

Ewald, Heinrich. *The History of Israel*, vol. 1, trans. Russell Martineau. London: Longmans, Green, 1883.

Fewell, Danna Nolan, ed. *Reading between Texts: Intertextuality and the Hebrew Bible*. Literary Currents in Biblical Interpretation. Louisville: Westminster John Knox, 1992.

Firth, David, G. *The Message of Esther: God Present but Unseen*. Bible Speaks Today. Dowers Grove, Ill.: InterVarsity Press, 2010.

Fishbane, Michael A. "Inner Biblical Exegesis: Types and Strategies of Interpretation in Ancient Israel." In *Midrash and Literature*, edited by Geoffrey H. Hartman and Sanford Budick, 19–37. New Haven: Yale University Press, 1986.

Fishbane, Michael A. *Biblical Interpretation in Ancient Israel*. New York: Clarendon, 1985.

Fox, Michael V. "Joseph and Wisdom." In *The Book of Genesis: Composition, Reception, and Interpretation*, edited by Craig A. Evans, Joel N. Lohr, and David L. Peterson, 231–62. Leiden: Brill, 2012.

Fox, Michael V. *Character and Ideology in the Book of Esther*. Studies on Personalities of the Old Testament. Columbia: University of South Carolina Press, 1991.

Fox, Michael V. *The Redaction of the Books of Esther: On Reading Composite Texts*. Monograph Series, Society of Biblical Literature 40. Atlanta: Scholars Press, 1991.

Fox, Michael V. "The Religion of the Book of Esther." *Judaism* 39:2 (1990): 135–47.

Freedman, Amelia Devin. *God as an Absent Character in Biblical Hebrew Narrative: A Literary-theoretical Study*. Studies in Biblical Literature 82. New York: Peter Lang, 2005.

Friedman, Richard Elliot. *The Disappearance of God: A Divine Mystery*. Boston: Little, Brown, 1995.

Gan, Moshe. "Megillat 'Esther Be'aspaqlariyat Qorot Yoseph Be'misrayim." *Tarbiz* 31 (1961–62): 144–49.

Gerleman, Gillis. *Esther*. Biblischer Kommentar Altes Testament 21. Neukirchen-Vluyn: Neukirchener Verlag Des Erziehungsvereins, 1973.

Greenspahn, Frederick E. "Review of *The Disappearance of God: A Divine Mystery*." In *Shofar: An Interdisciplinary Journal of Jewish Studies* 15:4 (1997): 139–141.

Greenspoon, Leonard J., and Sidnie White Crawford, eds. *The Book of Esther in Modern Research*. JSOTSup 380. London: T&T Clark International, 2003.

Greenstein, Edward L. "An Equivocal Reading of the Sale of Joseph." In *Literary Interpretations of Biblical Narratives*, edited by Kenneth R. R. Gros Louis, 114–25. Nashville: Abingdon, 1982.

Grillo, Jennie. "'From a Far Country': Daniel in Isaiah's Babylon." *JBL* 136:2 (2017): 363–80.

Grohmann, Marianne and Hyun Chul Paul Kim, ed. *Second Wave Intertextuality and the Hebrew Bible*. Resources for Biblical Study 93. Atlanta: SBL Press, 2019.

Grossfeld, Bernard. *The Two Targums of Esther: Translated with Apparatus and Notes*. Aramaic Bible 18. Collegeville: Liturgical Press, 1991.

Grossfeld, Bernard. *The Targum Sheni to the Book of Esther: A Critical Edition Based on MS. Sassoon 282 with Critical Apparatus*. Brooklyn: Sepher-Hermon Press, 1994.

Grossman, Jonathan. *Esther: The Outer Narrative and the Hidden Reading*. Siphrut 6. Winona Lake, IN: Eisenbrauns, 2011.

Grossman, Jonathan. "'Dynamic Analogies' in the Book of Esther." *VT* 59:3 (2009): 394–414.

Hartman, Louis F. and Alexander A. Di Lella. *The Book of Daniel*. AB 24. Garden City: Doubleday, 1978.

Hays, Richard B. *Echoes of Scripture in the Letters of Paul*. New Haven: Yale University Press, 1989.

Hazony, Yoram. *The Dawn: Political Teachings of the Book of Esther*. Revised edition. Jerusalem: Shalem Press, 2000.

Humphreys, W. Lee. "Life-style for Diaspora: A Study of the Tales of Esther and Daniel." *JBL* 92:2 (1973): 211–23.

Jarrard, Eric. "'Remember This Day on Which You Came Out of Egypt': The Exodus Motif in Biblical Memory." ThD diss, Harvard University, 2020.

Jobes, Karen. *The Alpha-Text of Esther: Its Character and Relationship to the Masoretic Text.* Dissertation Series, Society of Biblical Literature 153. Atlanta: Scholars Press, 1996.

Kalimi, Isaac. "The Place of the Book of Esther in Judaism and Jewish Theology." *TZ* 59:3 (2003): 193–204.

Kaminsky, Joel S. *Yet I Loved Jacob: Reclaiming the Biblical Concept of Election.* Nashville: Abingdon, 2007.

Kline, Jonathan. *Allusive Soundplay in the Hebrew Bible.* Ancient Israel and its Literature 28. Atlanta: SBL Press, 2016.

Koch, Klaus. "Gibt es ein Vergeltungsdogma im Alten Testament?" *ZTK* 52:1 (1955): 1–42.

Koller, Aaron. *Esther in Ancient Jewish Thought.* New York: Cambridge University Press, 2014.

Kratz, Reinhard Gregor. *Translatio Imperii: Untersuchungen Zu Den Aramäischen Danielerzählungen Und Ihrem Theologiegeschichtlichen Umfeld.* Wissenschaftliche Monographien zum Alten und Neuen Testament. Neukirchen-Vluyn: Neukirchener Verlag, 1991.

Kugel, James L. "The Bible's Earliest Interpreters." *Prooftexts* 7:3 (1987): 269–83.

Kynes, Will. "Job and Isaiah 40–55." In *Reading Job Intertextually*, edited by Katharine J. Dell and William L. Kynes, 94–105. LHBOTS 574. New York: Bloomsbury, 2013.

Lacocque, André. "The Different Versions of Esther." *BibInt* 7:3 (1999): 301–22.

Lacocque, André. *The Feminine Unconventional: Four Subversive Figures in Israel's Tradition.* Overtures to Biblical Theology. Minneapolis: Fortress Press, 1990.

Lacocque, André. *The Book of Daniel.* Atlanta: John Knox, 1979.

Laniak, Timothy S. *Shame and Honor in the Book of Esther.* Dissertation Series Society of Biblical Literature 165. Atlanta: Scholars Press, 1998.

Lebram, Jürgen C. H. "Purimfest und Estherbuch." *VT* 22:2 (1972): 208–22.

Leonard, Jeffery M. "Identifying Inner-Biblical Allusions: Psalm 78 as a Test Case." *JBL* 127:2 (2008): 241–65.

Levenson, Jon Douglas. *Esther: A Commentary.* Old Testament Library. Louisville: Westminster John Knox, 1997.

Levenson, Jon Douglas. *The Death and Resurrection of the Beloved Son: The Transformation of Child Sacrifice in Judaism and Christianity.* New Haven: Yale University Press, 1993.

Levenson, Jon Douglas. *Creation and the Persistence of Evil: The Jewish Drama of Divine Omnipotence.* San Francisco: Harper & Row, 1988.

Levinson, Bernard M. *Deuteronomy and the Hermeneutics of Legal Innovation.* New York: Oxford University Press, 1997.

Loader, James Alfred. *Das Buch Ester.* Das Alte Testament Deutsch 16:2. Göttingen: Vandenhoeck & Ruprecht, 1992.

Loewenstamm, Samuel E. "Esther 9:29–32: The Genesis of a Late Addition." *HUCA* 42 (1971): 117–24.

Lyons, Michael. *From Law to Prophecy: Ezekiel's Use of the Holiness Code.* LHBOTS 507. New York: T&T Clark, 2009.

Macchi, Jean-Daniel. *Esther*, trans. Carmen Palmer. International Exegetical Commentary on the Old Testament. Stuttgart: W. Kohlhammer, 2018.

MacDonald, Nathan and Izaak J. De Hulster, eds. *Divine Presence and Absence in Exilic and Post-Exilic Judaism.* FAT II 61. Tübingen: Mohr Siebeck, 2013.

Machinist, Peter. "Fate, 'Miqreh,' and Reason: Some Reflections on Qohelet and Biblical Thought." In *Solving Riddles and Untying Knots: Biblical, Epigraphic, and Semitic Studies in Honor of Jonas C. Greenfield*, edited by Ziony Zevit, Seymour Gitin, and Michael Sokoloff, 159–75. Winona Lake, IN: Eisenbrauns, 1995.

McLay, Timothy R. "The Old Greek Translation of Daniel iv-vi and the Formation of the Book of Daniel." *VT* 55:3 (2005): 304–23.

Meinhold, Arndt. *Das Buch Esther.* Zürich: Theologischer Verlag, 1983.

Meinhold, Arndt. "Theologische Erwägerungen zum Buch Esther." *TZ* 34:6 (1978): 321–33.

Meinhold, Arndt. "Die Gattung der Josephsgeschichte und des Estherbuches: Diasporanovelle."
Part I, *ZAW* 87:3 (1975): 306–24; Part II, *ZAW* 88:1 (1976): 72–93.

Melton, Brittany N. *Where is God in the Megilloth?: A Dialogue on the Ambiguity of Divine Presence and
Absence.* Oudtestamentische Studiën 73. Leiden: Brill, 2018.

Middlemas, Jill. "Dating Esther: Historicity and the Provenance of Masoretic Esther." In *On Dating
Biblical Texts to the Persian Period,* edited by Richard J. Bautsch and Mark Lackowski, 149–68.
FAT II 101. Tübingen: Mohr Siebeck, 2019.

Miller, Geoffrey D. "Intertextuality in Old Testament Research." *CurBR* 9:3 (2011): 283–309.

Moore, Carey A., ed. *Studies in the Book of Esther.* The Library of Biblical Studies. New York: Ktav
Pub. House, 1982.

Moore, Carey A. "Review of *Esther,* by G. Gerleman." *JBL* 94:2 (1975): 293–296.

Moore, Carey A. *Esther.* Anchor Bible 7B. Garden City: Doubleday, 1971.

Moore, Carey A. "A Greek Witness to a Different Hebrew Text of Esther." *ZAW* 79 (1967): 351–58.

Naveh, Joseph and Greenfield, Jonas C. "Hebrew and Aramaic in the Persian Period." In *The
Cambridge History of Judaism,* vol. 1, edited by W. S. Davies and Louis Finkelstein, 115–29.
Cambridge: Cambridge University Press, 1984.

Newsom, Carol A with Brennan W. Breed. *Daniel: A Commentary.* Old Testament Library. Louisville:
Westminster John Knox, 2014.

Niditch, Susan. *War in the Hebrew Bible: A Study in the Ethics of Violence.* New York: Oxford University
Press, 1993.

Niditch, Susan, and Robert Doran."The Success Story of the Wise Courtier: A Formal Approach."
JBL 96:2 (1977): 179–93.

Nagel, Peter. "LXX Esther: 'More' God 'Less' Theology." *Journal for Semitics* 17:1 (2008): 129–55.

Noble, Paul. "Esau, Tamar, and Joseph: Criteria for Identifying Inner-Biblical Allusions." *VT* 52:2
(2002): 219–52.

Paton, Lewis Bayles. *A Critical and Exegetical Commentary on the Book of Esther.* International Critical
Commentary 13. Edinburgh: T. & T. Clark, 1908.

Porteous, Norman. *Daniel: A Commentary.* Old Testament Library. London: SCM Press, 1965.

Redford, Donald B. *A Study of the Biblical Story of Joseph (Genesis 37–50).* VTSup 20. Leiden: Brill,
1970.

Rindge, Matthew S. "Jewish Identity under Foreign Rule: Daniel 2 as a Reconfiguration of
Genesis 41." *JBL* 129:1 (2010): 85–104.

Römer, Thomas. "The Joseph Story in the Book of Genesis: Pre-P or Post-P?" In *The Post-Priestly
Pentateuch: New Perspectives on its Redactional Development and Theological Profiles,* edited by
Federico Giuntoli and Konrad Schmid, 185–201. FAT 101. Tübingen: Mohr Siebeck, 2015.

Rosenthal, Ludwig A. "Die Josephsgeschichte, mit den Büchern Ester und Daniel verglichen."
ZAW 15:1 (1895): 278–84.

Rosenthal, Ludwig A. "Nochmals Der Vergleich Ester, Joseph-Daniel." *ZAW* 17:1 (1897): 125–28.

Ruiz-Ortiz, Francisco-Javier. *The Dynamics of Violence and Revenge in the Hebrew Book of Esther.*
VTSup 175. Leiden: Brill, 2017.

Schellekens, Jona. "Accession Days and Holidays: The Origins of the Jewish Festival of Purim."
JBL 128:1 (2009): 115–34.

Schipper, Bernd. "The Egyptian Background of the Joseph Story." *HBAI* 8:1 (2019): 6–23.

Schmid, Konrad. "Die Josephsgeschichte im Pentateuch." In *Abschied vom Jahwisten: Die Komposition
des Hexateuch in der jüngsten Diskussion,* edited by Christian Gertz, Konrad Schmid, and
Markus Witte, 83–117. BZAW 315. Berlin: De Gruyter, 2002.

Segal, Michael. "From Joseph to Daniel: The Literary Development of the Narrative in Daniel 2."
  VT 59:1 (2009): 123–49.
Shemesh, Yael. "Measure for Measure in the David Stories." *SJOT* 17:1 (2003): 89–109.
Smith, Mark S. "What Is a Scriptural Text in the Second Temple Period? Texts between Their
  Biblical Past, Their Inner-Biblical Interpretation, Their reception in Second Temple Literature,
  and Their Textual Witnesses." In *The Dead Sea Scrolls at 60: Scholarly Contributions of New York
  University Faculty and Alumni*, edited by Lawrence H. Schiffman and Shani Tzoref, 271–98.
  Studies on the Texts of the Desert of Judah 89. Leiden: Brill, 2010.
Sommer, Benjamin D. *A Prophet Reads Scripture: Allusion in Isaiah 40–66*. Contraversions. Stanford:
  Stanford University Press, 1998.
Sommer, Benjamin D. "Exegesis, Allusion and Intertextuality in the Hebrew Bible: A Response to
  Lyle Eslinger." *VT* 46:4 (1996): 479–89.
Speiser, E. A. *Genesis*. Anchor Bible 1. Garden City: Doubleday, 1964.
Strollo, Megan Fullerton. "Initiative and Agency: Towards a Theology of the Megilloth." In *Megilloth
  Studies: The Shape of Contemporary Scholarship*, edited by Brad Embry, 150–60. Hebrew Bible
  Monographs 78. Sheffield: Sheffield Phoenix Press, 2016.
Talmon, Shemaryahu. "Was the Book of Esther Known at Qumran?" *DSD* 2:3 (1995): 249–67.
Talmon, Shemaryahu. "'Wisdom' in the Book of Esther." *VT* 13:1 (1963): 419–55.
Teeter, David Andrew. "Jeremiah, Joseph, and the Dynamics of Analogy: On the Relationship
  between Jeremiah 37–44 and the Joseph Story." *HBAI* 10:4 (2021): 443–87.
Teeter, David Andrew. *Scribal Laws: Exegetical Variation in the Textual Transmission of Biblical Law in
  the Late Second Temple Period*. FAT 92. Tübingen: Mohr Siebeck, 2014.
Teeter, David Andrew. "The Hebrew Bible and/as Second Temple Literature: Methodological
  Reflections." *DSD* 20:3 (2013): 349–77.
Terrien, Samuel. *The Elusive Presence: Toward a New Biblical Theology*. Religious Perspectives 26. San
  Francisco: Harper & Row, 1978.
Tooman, William A. *Gog of Magog: Reuse of Scripture and Compositional Technique in Ezekiel 38–39*.
  FAT II 52. Tübingen: Mohr Siebeck, 2011.
Tooman, William A. "Transformation of Israel's Hope: The Reuse of Scripture in the Gog Oracles."
  In *Transforming Visions: Transformations of Text, Tradition, and Theology in Ezekiel*, edited by
  William A. Tooman and Michael A. Lyons, 50–110. Princeton Theological Monograph Series
  127. Eugene, OR: Pickwick Publications, 2010
Tov, Emanuel. "The 'Lucianic' Text of the Canonical and Apocryphal Sections of Esther: A Rewritten
  Biblical Book." *Textus* 10 (1982): 1–25.
Tull, Patricia Kathleen. "Intertextuality and the Hebrew Scriptures." *CurBS* 8 (2000): 59–90.
Ulrich, Eugene. "The Parallel Editions of the Old Greek and Masoretic Text of Daniel 5." In *A
  Teacher for All Generations: Essays in Honor of James C. VanderKam*, vol. 1, edited by Eric F.
  Mason, Samuel I. Thomas, Alison Schofield, and Eugene Ulrich, 201–17. Supplements to the
  Journal for the Study of Judaism 153. Leiden: Brill, 2012.
van Wolde, Ellen. "Trendy Intertextuality?" In *Intertextuality in Biblical Writings: Essays in honour of
  Bas van Iersel*, edited by Sipke Draisma, 43–49. Kampen: Uitgeversmaatschappij J. H. Kok, 1989.
Vischer, Wilhelm. *Esther*. Theologische Existenz heute 48. Munich: Chr. Kaiser, 1937.
Wahl, Harald Martin. *Das Buch Esther: Übersetzing und Kommentar*. Berlin: De Gruyter, 2009.
Wahl, Harald Martin. "'Glaube ohne Gott?' Zur Rede vom Gott Israels im hebräischen Buch Esther."
  BZ 45:1 (2001): 37–54.
Wahl, Harald Martin. "'Jahwe, wo bist du?' Gott, Glaube und Gemeinde in Esther." *JSJ* 31:1 (2000):
  1–22.
Westermann, Claus. *Genesis 37–50: A Commentary*, trans. John J. Scullion. Minneapolis: Fortress, 1986.

Wetzel, Thomas. *Violence and Divine Victory in the Book of Esther.* FAT II 136. Tübingen: Mohr Siebeck, 2022.

White, Sidnie Ann. "Esther: A Feminine Model for Jewish Diaspora." In *Gender and Difference in Ancient Israel*, edited by Peggy L. Day, 161–77. Minneapolis: Fortress, 1989.

Wills, Lawrence M. *The Jew in the Court of the Foreign King: Ancient Jewish Court Legends.* Minneapolis: Fortress, 1990.

von Rad, Gerhard. "Joseph Narrative and Ancient Wisdom." In *The Problem of the Hexateuch and Other Essays*, trans. E. W. Trueman Dicken. New York: McGraw Hill, 1966.

von Rad, Gerhard. *Das Erste Buch Mose: Genesis*. Das Alte Testament Deutsch 2–4. Göttingen: Vandenhoeck & Ruprecht, 1949.

Yaakobs, Yehonatan. *Midah ke-neged Midah ba-Sipur ha-Miḳrai*. Alon Shevut: Hotsa'at Tevunot, Mikhlelet Ya'aḳov Hertsog Le-yad Yeshivat Har-'Etsyon [Hebrew], 2005.

Zakovitch, Yair. "Inner-biblical Interpretation." In *A Companion to Biblical Interpretation in Early Judaism*, edited by Matthias Henze, 27–63. Grand Rapids, MI: Eerdmans, 2012.

Zevit, Ziony. "Echoes of Texts Past." In *Subtle Citation, Allusion, and Translation in the Hebrew Bible*, edited by Ziony Zevit, 1–21. Bristol, CT: Equinox Publishing, 2017.

Subject Index

https://doi.org/10.1515/9783111216119-010

Index of Secondary Authors

https://doi.org/10.1515/9783111216119-011

Index of Biblical Passages

https://doi.org/10.1515/9783111216119-012